Transnational Politics

Modern communications make it easier for all types of migrants to stay in touch with their country of origin meaning that migrants' transnational engagement is an increasingly important and relevant topic. *Transnational Politics* shows how the politics of one country, Turkey, plays itself out in another, Germany, through the presence and engagement of migrants and refugees.

This book offers a unique case study of transnational political engagement of Turkish and Kurdish migrants and refugees in Germany and the political impact of these at national and international levels. Turkish and Kurdish organizations in Germany not only mobilize in relation to immigrant political issues of equal rights, discrimination, and citizenship in Germany, but also in relation to the domestic and foreign political situation in Turkey. In this way they become a linkage group between Turkey and Germany.

The case of migrants and refugees from Turkey to Germany is in many ways paradigmatic for how migrants' transnational practices occur and are perceived in a European context. This book will be of value to readers with an interest in the politics of international migration and migrant transnationalism and in the ways in which migrants themselves challenge and contribute to processes of democratization in both their country of origin and settlement.

Eva Østergaard-Nielsen is Marie Curie Research Fellow at the Migration Research Group, Department of Geography, Autonomous University of Barcelona. She has published on the subject of diasporas and the political participation of migrants, notably in *Global Networks: A Journal of Transnational Affairs* and *Sais Review: A Journal of International Affairs*.

Transnationalism
Edited by Steven Vertovec
University of Oxford

'Transnationalism' broadly refers to multiple ties and interactions linking people or institutions across the borders of nation states. Today, myriad systems of relationship, exchange, and mobility function intensively and in real time while being spread across the world. New technologies, especially involving telecommunications, serve to connect such networks. Despite great distances and notwithstanding the presence of international borders (and all the laws, regulations, and national narratives they represent), many forms of association have been globally intensified and how take place paradoxically in a planet-spanning yet common arena of activity. In some instances, transnational forms and processes serve to speed-up or exacerbate historical patterns of activity, in others they represent arguably new forms of human interaction. Transnational practices and their consequent configurations of power are shaping the world of the twenty-first century.

This book forms part of a series of volumes concerned with describing and analysing a range of phenomena surrounding this field. Serving to ground theory and research on 'globalization', the Routledge book series on 'Transnationalism' offers the latest empirical studies and ground-breaking theoretical works on contemporary socio-economic, political, and cultural processes which span international boundaries. Contributions to the series are drawn from Sociology, Economics, Anthropology, Politics, Geography, International Relations, Business Studies, and Cultural Studies.

The series is associated with the Transnational Communities Research Programme of the Economic and Social Research Council (see http://www.transcomm.ox.ac.uk).

The series consists of two strands:
Transnationalism aims to address the needs of students and teachers and these titles will be published in hardback and paperback. Titles include:

Culture and Politics in the Information Age
A new politics?
Edited by Frank Webster

Transnational Democracy
Political spaces and border crossings
Edited by James Anderson

Routledge Research in Transnationalism is a forum for innovative new research intended for a high-level specialist readership, and the titles will be available in hardback only. Titles include:

1 **New Transnational Social Spaces**
   International migration and transnational companies in the early 21st century
   Edited by Ludger Pries

2 **Transnational Muslim Politics**
   Reimagining the Umma
   Peter G. Mandaville

3 **New Approaches to Migration?**
   Transnational communities and the transformation of home
   Edited by Nadje Al-Ali and Khalid Koser

4 **Work and Migration**
   Life and livelihoods in a globalizing world
   Edited by Ninna Nyberg Sorensen and Karen Fog Olwig

5 **Communities across Borders**
   New immigrants and transnational cultures
   Edited by Paul Kennedy and Victor Roudometof

6 **Transnational Spaces**
   Edited by Peter Jackson, Phil Crang and Claire Dwyer

7 **Diaspora and Communication**
   Mapping the globe
   Edited by Karim H. Karim

8 **Transnational Politics**
   Turks and Kurds in Germany
   Eva Østergaard-Nielsen

Transnational Politics
Turks and Kurds in Germany

Eva Østergaard-Nielsen

LONDON AND NEW YORK

First published 2003 by Routledge

2 Park Square, Milton Park, Abingdon, Oxon OX14 4RN
711 Third Avenue, New York, NY 10017, USA

Routledge is an imprint of the Taylor & Francis Group, an informa business

First issued in paperback 2016

Copyright © 2003 Eva Østergaard-Nielsen

Typeset in Times New Roman by
Newgen Imaging Systems (P) Ltd, Chennai, India

All rights reserved. No part of this book may be reprinted or reproduced or utilised in any form or by any electronic, mechanical, or other means, now known or hereafter invented, including photocopying and recording, or in any information storage or retrieval system, without permission in writing from the publishers.

Notice:
Product or corporate names may be trademarks or registered trademarks, and are used only for identification and explanation without intent to infringe.

British Library Cataloguing in Publication Data
A catalogue record for this book is available from the British Library

Library of Congress Cataloging in Publication Data
Østergaard-Nielsen, Eva, 1969–
 Transnational politics: Turks and Kurds in Germany / Eva Østergaard-Nielsen.
  p. cm.
 Includes bibliographical references and index.
  1. Turks – Germany – Social conditions. 2. Kurds – Germany – Social conditions. 3. Germany – Ethnic relations. 4. Marginality, Social – Germany. 5. Transnationalism. 6. Germany – Emigration and immigration. I. Title.
 DD78.T87 O88 2003
 305.89'435043'09049–dc21   2002068197

ISBN 978-1-138-98597-1 (pbk)
ISBN 978-0-415-26586-7 (hbk)

For Andrea and Lukas

Contents

Acknowledgements		x
Abbreviations		xii
1	Introduction	1
2	Migrants' transnational claims-making: rethinking concepts and theories	13
3	Migration, transnational spaces, and German–Turkish relations	33
4	Between homeland political and immigrant political mobilization	46
5	From confrontational to multi-layered strategies: Turkish and Kurdish information campaigns in Germany	70
6	Thresholds of tolerance: Turkish politics within German political institutions	85
7	From 'remittance machines' to 'Euro Turks': Turkey's changing perceptions of Turkish citizens abroad	107
8	Conclusions	123
	Appendix A: Table and figures	135
	Appendix B: Methodology	137
	Appendix C: Migrant associations, political parties, and state agencies with whom interviews were conducted	140
	Notes	148
	References	158
	Index	171

Acknowledgements

My first thank you goes to the people who helped me embark on this research in the first place. I am particularly indebted to my former supervisors William Wallace at the London School of Economics and Philip Robins at St Antony's College, Oxford University, for their continuous support, encouragement, and valuable feedback on earlier drafts of this manuscript. Also, Efhitia Voutira, from the Refugees Studies Programme at Oxford University, served as a great inspiration in my first years of research.

The empirical fieldwork would not have been possible without the generous assistance of members of the Turkish and Kurdish communities there. Leaders and members of migrant organizations in Germany and policy makers in both Germany and Turkey generously took time off to answer my many questions and guide me through meetings and events. Three Turkish and Kurdish families in Germany opened their homes to me, and kindly let me stay with them during my fieldwork. They, and other friends, facilitated contacts for interviews and access to political meetings. I thank the family Demirbilek-Köksal, family Kararhasan, Eren Ünsal, and Arif Şentürk. In Ankara, I want to especially thank Orhan İşık and his family for helping me with accommodation and research and my general introduction to the Turkish way of things.

The research has been financed by first the Danish Research Academy's Scholarship for PhD studies abroad and later by the Economic and Social Research Council's Transnational Communities Programme. In addition, several research institutions assisted me during the fieldwork. In Berlin, the Wissenschaftzentrum Berlin kindly gave me an office and I thank colleagues there for good discussions and research contacts. In particular, Felicitas Hillmann offered assistance and hospitality. In Ankara, the British Institute of Archeology at Ankara provided technical support and accommodation. I must also thank staff at Zentrum für Türkeistudien in Essen, in particular Yasemin Karakaşoğlu, the Friedrich Ebert Stiftung in Bonn, the library at Köln University, and not least the helpful staff at the Library of the Turkish National Assembly in Ankara. Thank you also to Kemal Bozay and Esra Bulut for their efficient research assistance and to Esra for her help with later stages of manuscript preparation.

St Antony's college in Oxford, the International Relations Department at London School of Economics, and the ESRC Transnational Communities

Programme have provided wonderful and very challenging academic environments throughout my research. I feel very fortunate in having met so many friends and colleagues there, many of whom have read and commented on earlier drafts of this work. I would like to thank Anthony Nichols for providing initial contacts into German academia and Celia Kerslake for teaching me Turkish in her spare time. I am grateful to Rebecca Golbert for her meticulous and insightful comments on the entire manuscript in its various stages. Within the Transnational Communities Programme I have benefited from discussions with and comments from Zig Layton-Henry, Alisdair Rogers, and Birgit Brandt. I also thank Steven Vertovec for stimulating discussions and encouraging me to publish this book.

Research in Germany and Turkey and affiliations with British universities have necessitated long spells of absence from family and friends in Copenhagen. My parents Inge Østergaard-Nielsen and Christian Thune have always been wonderfully supportive and helpful. My deepest gratitude goes to my husband Andrea Caggese who has introduced such blissful changes in my life. Without his love and confidence I could never have done this.

AABF	Avrupa Alevi Birlik Federasyonu (The Alevi Unity Federation in Germany)
AADD	Almanya'da Atatürk Düsünce Derneği (The German Association for Kemalist Ideas)
ADÜTDF	Avrupa Demokratik Ülkücü Türk Dernekleri Federasyonu (The Federation of European Democratic Idealist Turkish Associations)
ANAP	Anavatan Partisi (The Motherland Party)
AP	Adalet Partisi (The Justice Party)
ATIAD	Avrupa Türk Işadamları ve Sanayıcıleri Derneği (The Association of Turkish Businessmen and Industrialists in Europe)
ATIB	Avrupa Türk Islam Birliği (The Turkish Islamic Union in Europe)
ATÖF	Almanya Türk Öğrenci Federasyony
ATT	Almanya Türk Toplumu (The Turkish Community in Germany)
CDU	Christlich Demokratische Union (The Christan Democratic Union)
CEM	Cumhürriyet Eğitim Merkezi
CHP	Cumhürriyet Halk Partisi (The Republican Peoples Party)
CSU	Christlich Soziale Union (The Christian Socialist Union)
DEP	Demokrasi Partisi (The Democracy Party)
DGB	Deutsche Gewerkschafts Bund (The Association of German Trade-unions)
DIDF	Demokratik Işçi Dernekleri Federasyonu (The Federation of Democratic Workers Associations)
DITIB	Diyanet Işleri Türk Islam Birliği (The Turkish Islamic Union for Religious Affairs)
DPD	Demokratische Partei Deutschland (The German Democratic Party)
DSP	Demokratik Sol Partisi (The Democratic Left Party)
DTF	Deutsch–Türkische Forum (The German–Turkish Forum)
DTU	Deutsch–Türkische Union (The German–Turkish Union)

DYP	Doğru Yol Partisi (The True Path Party)
EEC	European Economic Community
EMEP	Emeğin Partisi (The Labour Party)
ERNK	Enia Rizgariya Netewa Kurdistan (The National Liberation Front of Kurdistan)
EU	European Union
FDP	Freie Demokratische Partei (The Free Democratic Party)
FP	Fazilet Partisi (The Virtue Party)
GDF	Türkiyeli Göçmen Dernekleri Federasyonu (The Federation of Turkish Migrant Associations)
HADEP	Halk ve Demokrasi Partisi (The People and Democracy Party)
HDF	Sosyaldemokrat Halk Dernekleri Federasyonu (The Social Democratic Peoples' Association)
ICCB	Islam Cemaatleri ve Cemiyetleri Birliği (The Union of Islamic Congregations and Assocations)
IGMG	Islamische Gemeinschaft Milli Görüş (The Islamic Community of National Vision)
IHD	Insan Halklari Derneği (The Human Rights Association)
KOMKAR	Yekitiya Komelên Kurdistan (The Federation of Kurdish Associations in Germany)
LTD	Liberale Türkisch–Deutsche Vereinigung (The Liberal Turkish–German Association)
MHP	Milli Hareket Partisi (The National Movement Party)
MIT	Milli Istihbarat Teşkilatı (The Turkish Secret Service)
NAFTA	North American Free Trade Agreement
NGO	Non-governmental Organization
ÖDP	Özgürlük ve Dayanışma Partisi (The Freedom and Solidarity Party)
OSCE	Organization on Security and Cooperation in Europe
PDS	Partei des Demokratischen Sozialismus (The Party of Democratic Socialism)
PKK	Partiya Karakên Kurdistan (The Kurdistan Workers Party)
PLO	Palestine Liberation Organization
PSK	Partiya Socialist a Kurdistan (The Kurdistan Socialist Party)
RTS	Rat der Türkischen Staatsbürger (The Council for Turkish Citizens)
SPD	Sozial demokratische Partei Deutschland (The Social Democratic Party)
TBMM	Türkiye Büyük Millet Meclisi (The Turkish Grand National Assembly)
TGT	Türkiye Göçmen Topluluğu (The Turkish Migrant Community)
TIDAF	Türk Işadamları Dernekleri Avrupa Federasyonu (European Turkish Entrepreneurs Federation)
TIP	Türkiye Işçi Partisi (The Turkish Workers Party)

xiv *Abbreviations*

TKP	Türkiye Komünist Partisi (The Turkish Communist Party)
TÜSIAD	Türk Sanayicileri ve Işadamları Derneği (Turkish Industrialists' and Businessmen's Association)
VIKZ	Verband der Islamischen Kulturzentren (The Association of Islamic Cultural Centres)
YEK-KOM	Yekitiya Komelên Kurd li Elmanya (The Federation for Kurdish Associations in Germany)

1 Introduction

This book is about how the politics of one country plays itself out in another through the presence and agency of migrants and refugees. It is about transnational mobilization and strategies of migrants and refugees, and the way that such engagement is perceived by political actors in their country of settlement and origin. Diasporas, such as the Jewish and Armenian, are known for their continuous engagement in their homelands. Yet, increasingly all types of migrants and refugees are no longer assumed to make a sharp break with their country of origin. Air travel, electronic communication, satellite television, and the Internet render geographical distances relatively insignificant. Migrants and refugees may, therefore, retain or develop interest in, and engagement with, political developments in their homeland with greater intensity than previously. This can result in anything from the formation of solidarity groups with persecuted movements to the defence of the homeland political regime. In this way, migrants and refugees become a linkage group between their receiving country and their homeland. The distinctive forms of migrant politics introduce the politics of their homeland into their country of settlement and provide an external dimension to the politics of their country of origin by acting as a resource for political allies. Politics and democracy are thus less bounded by state borders.

Migrants' and refugees' transnational political engagement in their homelands raise sensitive issues regarding dual loyalty, the mobilization and manipulation of political power, and the influence of transnationalism on national and international systems. Indeed, the presence in one country of 'transnational communities' or 'diasporas', that is, immigrants or exiles whose social, economic and political universe reaches beyond state borders to their homeland, has been proclaimed to constitute an increasingly important feature of not only contemporary domestic politics but also transnational and international relations (Sheffer 1986; Huntington 1997; Adamson 2002).[1] Certainly, the phenomenon of migrants' transnational political networks and practices goes to the core of one of the central issues within political science: the fading dichotomy between the domestic and the international. Migrants' transnational political networks and practices challenge state-bound assumptions about political communities and societies underlying so much of the social science literature.

However, migrants' transnational practices are not only interesting in the relatively few instances where they challenge state policies and authority. They are interesting because they not only transgress boundaries of political systems and societies, but also at the same time uncover boundaries of political participation. When migrants engage in the political affairs of their country of origin they do so in a particular political and institutional context. Their mobilization and agency is facilitated or constrained by their local surroundings (Guarnizo and Smith 1998). In other words, an integral part of their agency is the perception and reaction of political actors, in both the countries of settlement and origin, to their activities.

Most studies of migrants' political activity focus on North America, where the political activities among well-established groups such as Jews, Greeks, and Armenians, as well as more recently arrived groups such as Mexicans, have been recognized as a significant part of North American domestic and international politics. However, in Europe as well, immigrants and refugees retain and develop an interest in, and political ties with, their country of origin. European policymakers are increasingly faced by demands from migrants or refugees, who urge them to pursue a particular policy towards their homeland. While at the same time, governments in Europe are met with demands from the homeland governments of transnational communities to restrain the political dissidence of such communities.

The case of immigrants and refugees from Turkey in Germany is in many ways paradigmatic for how migrants' transnational practices occur, and are perceived, in a European context. Turks in Germany are hardly under-researched within studies of migration and migrant incorporation, but their transnational relations have only recently (re)emerged in research on this group (Freeman and Ögelman 1998; Faist 2000b). More recently, Kurds from Turkey have been studied as a diaspora or a transnational community (Wahlbeck 1999; Mertens 2000). Migrants and refugees from Turkey are interesting because they are the largest immigrant ethnic minority in Europe. Moreover, they constitute the largest single group of immigrants in Germany, with more than 2.4 million Turkish citizens and former Turkish citizens at the end of 2000. Size apart, there are a number of reasons why this is an interesting case for studies of transnational political mobilization and its impact.

First, domestic political developments in Turkey over the last two decades have provided plenty of occasions for Turks and Kurds to make common cause with their political, ethnic, or religious counterparts in their country of origin. These include the military coup in 1980 and the continued influence of the Turkish military in Turkish politics, the development of the Kurdish issue into an armed conflict between the Turkish military and Kurdish *Partiya Karakèn Kurdistan* (PKK), human rights deficiencies, the persecution of the religious minority Alevis, and the rise, and banning, of the Sunni *Refah Partisi*. Beyond concrete events are the ongoing debates, such as that between secularists and islamists in Turkey about what constitutes Turkish national identity and which course Turkey's domestic and foreign policy should take. The extent to which these events and developments unfold among Turks and Kurds abroad highlights the role of the country of origin in the durability and construction of migrants' transnational political networks.

Second, the international relations between Turkey and the European Union (EU), most notably the issue of Turkey's EU candidacy and the importance of Turkey as a security political ally, has been a source of mobilization among Turks in Germany. This international context has added to both the German and Turkish governments' interest in, not to mention political sensitiveness towards, the transnational relations between Turkey and the immigrant communities from Turkey residing in Germany. The Turkish state and recent governments have realized that Turkish citizens in Germany will not return and have shown an increased interest in maintaining good long-distance relations with these citizens.

Third, the German migrant incorporation regime is among the most exclusive in Europe. Issues not only of citizenship rights and dual nationality, but also of discrimination and social exclusion of Turkish citizens, mother-tongue teaching, and religious education have become the subjects of transnational dialogue between Turkish citizens, and German and Turkish authorities. Until very recently, children of Turkish citizens did not qualify for German citizenship even if they were born in Germany. As a result, less than a fifth of Turkish citizens had naturalized by the end of 1999 [Zentrum für Türkeistudien (ZFT) 2001], although 37 per cent were born in Germany (Federal Commissioner for Foreigners 2001). This trend is now reversing, but the demand of many Turks in Germany (and the Turkish government) for dual citizenship has not been met.

Fourth, Turkish citizens – and former citizens – constitute a very heterogeneous group, and this heterogeneity is in, and of, itself a continuous source for political mobilization. Most importantly, they include the two main types of transnational communities: economic migrants (former guest workers and their families) and political refugees and asylum seekers. The vast majority are a result of labour migration, but an increasing number of Turkish citizens, mainly of Kurdish origin, arrive in Germany as asylum seekers and, therefore, already have a decidedly negative relationship with the Turkish state and government. However, it must be noted that these two categories overlap in practice. The dynamics of part of the emigration from Turkey, especially from the southeast of Turkey, to some extent defy the traditional categorization of immigrants as either economic migrants or political refugees. Although the so-called economic migrants may not have faced direct political persecution, their economic situation may have been heavily influenced by the political sentiment towards them. Being an economic migrant does not mean that one automatically has a more loyal stance towards the homeland's political authorities, although, not surprisingly, large groups among migrants and their descendants defend the Turkish state and government, while refugees and asylum seekers criticize them. Moreover, cross-cutting these categories are several minorities. Most importantly, there are the Kurds, an ethnic minority, who struggle for equal rights in Turkey and abroad, but not all of whom are refugees or asylum seekers. There is also a religious minority, the Alevis, whose particular brand of Islam has been discriminated against by the Sunni majority in Turkey and abroad. This means that besides groups opposing and defending the Turkish regime from afar, there is a whole host of other homeland political agendas relating to the sub-groups within the communities.

4 Introduction

A cornerstone of the analysis of transnational political practices in this book is constituted by these different attitudes to the political regime in the homeland, that is, the political agendas and activities of the various ethnic, religious, and political movements of migrants from Turkey. Much work on migrants' transnational political movements tends to focus on either dissident movements or pro-state movements (Shain 1991; Constas and Platias 1993). Covering the simultaneous presence of various movements, with differing relations to the homeland, enhances our understanding of transnational political mobilization. Rather than presenting a systematic comparison between 'Turkish migrants' and 'Kurdish refugees' this study include the host of different groups in order to highlight their changing relations with their country of origin. Indeed, a comparison among different movements from the same country of origin, Turkey, residing and operating in the same receiving country, Germany, complements comparative studies both of one migrant group in several countries and of several different migrant groups in one country. Studies of one group in several countries highlight the significance of *receiving country's* political institutional context (see Koopmans and Statham 2001; Østergaard-Nielsen 2001b). Studies of several groups in one country demonstrate the significance of the *country of origin* of the different groups (Smith 1998; Shain 1999). The analysis in this book adds to both sets of approaches because it shows the different dynamics of transnational political mobilization among migrants from the same country living in the same country. These differences are not related to differences in receiving countries or countries of origin but to different characteristics of transnationalness among the various movements, including differing relationships with political agents in the homeland and receiving country. In short, the dynamics of transnational political mobilization depend on the compatibility between migrants' homeland political agendas, and the interest of political actors in their homeland and receiving country.

Migration studies and transnationalism

Migrants' transnational engagement in their homeland, in particular in the form of more elitist exile networks, is by no means a new phenomenon (see Shain 1989, 1991). Yet, migrant's transnational links with their country of origin have only recently re-appeared in migration studies, in particular in US-based research (Rogers 2000; Portes 2001). While previous studies of diaspora politics focused on the policy impact of these groups (see Sheffer 1986; Constas and Platias 1993), more recent studies of migrants from Central and Latin America demonstrate how migrants challenge or bridge politics in their country of origin and settlement (Smith and Guarnizo 1998; Portes *et al.* 1999; Vertovec and Cohen 1999).

In particular, the case of Mexican migrant transnationalism has a number of interesting parallels and contrasts to the Turkish case. A large population of Mexicans (20.6 million Hispanics are of Mexican origin with 8 million born in Mexico) has settled in the US through migration flows (Rivera-Salgado 2000), and the flow of Mexican migrants has had significant socio-economic and political impact on both sides of the border as well as on US–Mexican relations.

Migrant remittances represent Mexico's third largest source of foreign exchange after oil and tourism. Turkey receives a smaller sum of remittances than Mexico, but still ranks among the top three receivers of migrant remittances in the world [International Monetary Fund (IMF) 2001]. Migration management has been tied to regional integration and trade agreements such as North American Free Trade Agreement (NAFTA), as in the case of Turkey and the EU.

Lately, Mexicans in the US have become an important political factor in both their country of origin and their country of settlement. Mexican migrants have begun to naturalize at increasing speed, making them an important political voting block in American elections (Rivera-Salgado 2000). Parallel to this development, Mexico has sought to 'intensify, broaden, and institutionalize' its relationship with Mexican communities abroad (Smith 2001; see also Roberts et al. 1999). This includes setting up special programmes for Mexican communities abroad, extending voting rights in presidential elections, and in general reversing the perception of them as 'pochos' (derogatory term for Mexican–Americans who speak Spanish with an accent) (Rivera-Salgado 2000; Smith 2001). Meanwhile, Mexican migrants have formed transnational grassroot organizations ranging from hometown associations and cross-border indigenous rights movements to new advocacy networks for Mexican absentee voting rights. These organizations participate in politics on both sides of the border, challenge both US and Mexican policies and thus have the potential to bridge Mexican and US political arenas (Rivera-Salgado 2000).

As the following chapters will show, the case of migrant transnationalism in the context of Mexico and the US provides an interesting perspective on the Turkish case. Clearly, the two cases are embedded in very different historical, international, and domestic political contexts. Moreover, the case of Mexican transnational electoral politics is more extensive than that of Kurds and Turks in Germany. Mexican examples of transnational election campaigns and migrants' cross-border voting in the country of origin, or block voting in the country of settlement, have only recently become noticeable in this case study. Still, both the perceptions and policies of Mexico, and the multi-level mobilization of Mexican migrants, have interesting parallels with the case of Turkey and Turkish (and to some extent Kurdish) migrants. In addition, this case study provides a detailed and differentiated analysis of the interface between receiving country's political actors and migrant transnationalism in a European context, where migrants' transnational politics in and of itself is more scrutinized than is the case with Mexican origin migrants in the US.

Between migrant politics and homeland politics

The political mobilization and participation of migrants is an important subject in our understanding of migrant incorporation. In the past decade, there have been substantial contributions from comparative analyses of migrants' political participation in different European countries (see among others, Hammar 1985 and 1990; Layton-Henry 1990; Ireland 1994; Soysal 1994; Doomernik 1995; Garbaye

2000; Koopmans and Statham 2000). These studies, including detailed work on immigrants from Turkey, show that immigrants have indeed engaged themselves in the politics of their country of settlement with increasing frequency, claiming their political and social rights as members of society. However, with few exceptions, such studies have largely maintained the distinction between national and international politics, and migrants' transnational engagement in their country of origin is rarely dealt with in a systematic way. The absence of research on Turkish migrant political transnationalism has less to do with the actual occurrence of the phenomena and more to do with the extent to which it is observed and the political context in which it is observed. When looking at the political activities of migrants, European-based research has tended to focus on immigrant political participation – migrant efforts to better their situation in the receiving country, such as obtaining more political, social, and economic rights, fighting discrimination, and the like. The significance of transnational ties is mainly included as a factor in the analysis of political integration rather than as a phenomenon in its own right. There are, for instance, few studies of the transnational activities of the few successful 'diaspora political' lobby groups in Europe: the Armenians in France (in English publications at least) or the Cypriots in London (see Demetriou, forthcoming). This is not unrelated to the fact that they are not an 'immigrant group' on par with those groups who arrived as guestworkers or refugees during the last five decades.

Thus, when the political activities of immigrant groups in Europe are taken into account, the focus is generally on their level of participation in the politics of their receiving country. This political engagement is predominantly seen as related to the degree of inclusion in the political system of the receiving country, and the extent to which the immigrant communities are integrated in their receiving country (see also Shain 1989: 14). Similarly, regarding the general level of integration, scholarship seems to assume that the more integrated these immigrant communities are, the more they participate in the politics of their country of settlement and the less they participate in the political affairs of their homeland (see among others, Miller 1981; Weiner 1986; Layton-Henry 1990; Esman 1992 and 1994). This assumption contradicts studies of North American diaspora political phenomena, in which the wealth and high rank of the Jewish and Greek diasporas are seen as conducive to their political influence on US policies towards their respective homelands (see among others, Sheffer 1986; Constas and Platias 1993; Shain 1999).

This book challenges the above-mentioned static 'zero-sum' assumption of the political activities of ethnic minorities. The overall hypothesis is that the political organization and participation of immigrants and refugees from Turkey in Germany cannot be fully understood outside a transnational perspective which includes their relationship with Turkey. Recent events in German–Turkish relations underline the relevance of a transnational approach in the analysis of migrants' and refugees' political mobilization. Consider the three following examples of how migrants' transnational ties and linkages play into and bind together receiving country and homeland politics on issues such as the scope and effectiveness of transnational political networks, German debates on dual citizenship, and the way in which cross-border party membership impacts on the role of migrant organizations in local politics in Germany.

One of the more high-profile examples of the scope and effectiveness of migrants' transnational networks is Kurdish political mobilization in Europe in general and Germany in particular. A recent example of such transnational organization came when the PKK leader Abdullah Öcalan was captured in Kenya in February 1999. Within hours of the capture, a worldwide embassy protest action took place. Protests were well coordinated via phones, faxes, and the Kurdish TV station MEDYA TV. Kurds lay siege to or occupied Greek, Kenyan, Israeli, and Turkish embassies and consulates throughout Europe, Canada, Russia, and Australia. Germany, which hosts the largest Kurdish minority from Turkey, bore the brunt of the protest action. There were protests in every major German city, firebombing of Turkish businesses and property, and a tragic incident in Berlin where three Kurdish activists were shot by security guards as they tried to storm the Israeli Embassy (Rogers 1999). This incident is but one of many examples of how the Kurdish issue in Turkey also plays itself out on German soil. Not only asylum seekers and refugees from Turkey, but also migrants and their descendants, who have discovered their Kurdish identity from afar, mobilize in support of the Kurdish struggle for equal rights in Turkey. With their restricted access to democratic participation in Turkey, Kurdish organizations and movements, most of which are peaceful, use Germany as a site for information campaigns and claims-making. They urge German authorities to put pressure on the Turkish government to find a solution. In turn, Turkish authorities demand that German authorities curb Kurdish dissidence. As will be described further in Chapters 5 and 6, Germany has taken a long series of domestic and foreign policy measures in this direction.

Although only a fraction of Kurds in Germany engage in more radical Kurdish activism, this issue has been frequently mentioned in relation to the next example: the German debate on dual citizenship during 1998–9. In this debate, those opposing dual citizenship juxtaposed migrants' transnational political engagement with political integration in Germany. The debate was brought about by the electoral promises of the *Sozialdemokratische Partei Deutschland* (SPD) and *Bündnis90/Die Grüne* to reform German citizenship law. This reform was meant to reverse the trend of low naturalization among migrants. Notably Turkish citizens are reluctant to part with their Turkish citizenship in the process of applying for German citizenship. Thus, when dual citizenship gained a prominent place in reform plans, it was met with unanimous approval by both the Turkish organizations in Germany and the Turkish government.

By contrast, dual citizenship was strongly opposed by the *Christlich Demokratische Union* (CDU) and, in particular, its sister party the *Christlich Soziale Union* (CSU). In general, these parties refuse to accept that migrants' transnational links could modify the state-centric model of loyalty to a single political community. They branded dual citizenship as the institutionalization of dual loyalties, a pathway to parallel societies and thus a threat to German national identity. CSU led a succesful signature campaign, which gained a high profile in both the German and Turkish media. Moreover, statements from the CDU and CSU emphasized that transnational political loyalties and practices have no place in German society. The issue of Kurdish dissidence was a frequently cited example, and more radical statements from the CSU even envisaged how dual citizenship would allow Turkish or Islamic parties to have a say in the German Bundestag (*Süddeutsche Zeitung*, 9 January 1999). Turkish organizational leaders in Germany strongly opposed this campaign, which they felt 'branded them as terrorists' and generally whipped up sentiment against immigrants (*Frankfurter Rundschau*, 6 January 1999). But the SPD – Die Grüne government was unable to withstand the pressure after the issue of dual citizenship decided a local election in Hesse in favour of the CDU. The heated German political debate on facilitating naturalization in general, and dual citizenship in particular, showed that issues of transnational political practices and 'dual loyalties' sit uncomfortably within German integration policies.

A final example pertains to the way in which migrant organizations in Germany are scrutinized for their transnational ties to political actors in their homeland. For years, Sunni Islamic organizations have campaigned for Koran lessons within the German educational system. German authorities see the logic in welcoming Koran lessons into the classroom, where the lessons' content and form can be closely monitored. The main point of disagreement is the question of who should be responsible for the lessons. Not surprisingly, migrant organizations claim that they should be delegated the task of these courses since they are already running such courses within their own realm. Thus, in Berlin, the Islamic Federation was given the task of running Koran courses, but only after their right to do so was disputed at several levels of authority and finally confirmed at the Supreme Administrative Court (*Frankfurter Allgemeine Zeitung*, 11 April 2000).

The local authorities sought to keep the Imams out of the classroom for a variety of reasons. More generally, they see the role of Islam in the integration of Muslim youth as ambiguous. In the context of this book, most relevant is how the issue of Islamic transnational ties to political parties in Turkey played a key role. 'Who is really behind this?' was an often repeated question in the German press when dealing with this issue (see *Die Zeit*, 4 February 1999). This referred to the links between the Islamic Federation Berlin and the Turkish Sunni *Milli Görüş* movement. *Milli Görüş*, as will be described in Chapter 4, is scrutinized for its ties to the Turkish *Fazilet Partisi*, which has been closed down by Turkish authorities several times for challenging Turkish principles of secularism. Thus, homeland political ties become a focal point in educational political discussions of Islamic lessons in German schools.

These very different examples of the interface between the host state and migrants' transnational loyalties and politics show how transnational political practices may make the migrants the object of public and state scrutiny, in particular if such practices are seen as a threat to national security. For the homeland government, dissident political activities from abroad constitute a potential threat, and it may seek to induce the host state to restrain such activities. In less extreme cases, the phenomenon of transnational politics raises the sensitive issues of dual state authority and dual loyalty among migrants, that is, the issue of the compatibility between transnational political ties with the homeland, and political integration in the receiving country.

Research strategy and organization

There are at least two conceptual paths leading to the study of Turkish and Kurdish transnational political practices. On the one hand, there is the search for a more holistic understanding of migrant political participation that goes beyond the dyadic relationship between migrants and host state authorities. On the other hand, there is the relevance of exploring an in-depth case study of migrants' transnational political practices in the context of Europe, since much of the conceptual literature comes out of studies in the US.

Starting points such as these translate into a three-level analysis of: (a) transnational political mobilization; (b) transnational political participation; and (c) the way that such participation is perceived and acted upon by relevant actors in Germany and Turkey. The scope of these levels is dictated by the aim to uncover some of the feedback mechanisms between migrants' transnational political practices and their political institutional environment. In this book, I explore not only how migrants' political practices trickle up through the political systems of the countries of origin and settlement, but also how host state and homeland political actors' perceptions of, and reactions to, such activities are part and parcel of migrants' mobilization and participation.

At the first level of analysis, the study aims to look at forms of migrants' transnational political mobilization among groups and movements. The analysis will raise questions about ideologies and agendas of different movements. It will probe how 'transnational' or tied in with homeland politics Kurdish or Turkish organizations are, and which national and transnational networks they are part of. Are they, for instance, established by local initiatives or have they been set up through the encouragement of, or with support from, organizations, political parties, or governments in other countries? To what extent does this affect their work and agenda setting, and their relationship with other migrant organizations?

The second level of analysis has many overlaps with the first and third, as it deals with how migrants' transnational political practices are articulated within the political institutional context in both the countries of origin and receiving countries. There has been curiously little systematic study of the homeland political *strategies and activities* of Turkish and Kurdish migrants in Europe. Descriptions of the organizations usually stop at their ideological distinctiveness. Admittedly, it is a complex and vast field of activities, but even a rough investigation into these matters may shed some light on how migrants' transnational political practices are anchored in their local context. Migrants' organizational patterns are central components in research on these issues. How do they form their networks? How do they attract members? How do such networks go about *trying to* influence politics? Which strategies and means do they use? And, importantly, why do different migrant groups choose different strategies to promote their agendas?

The third level of analysis brings in the perception and policy of the state. To the extent that the communities of immigrants from Turkey are engaged in the politics of their homeland, this raises questions regarding the interests of the receiving country state and the homeland state in these matters. The argument is that the presence of a large community of citizens of one country in another can lead to a spatial diffusion of domestic politics.[2] That is, the presence, and political activities, of Turkish citizens in Germany introduce domestic Turkish politics into Germany. The main questions addressed in this respect are: How do German political actors perceive and act upon the homeland political activities of the immigrated Turkish communities? Which groups and activities are deemed desirable/undesirable? To what extent do the Turkish state and other Turkish political agents regard the communities from Turkey abroad as a resource base or a threat? And to what extent is this reflected in political activities within the immigrant communities?

As these paths of inquiry indicate, this book is concerned with how migrants go about their transnational engagement rather than why they may embark on such a course in the first place. The findings are based on a detailed empirical analysis of the scope and forms of Turkish and Kurdish migrants' political engagement and the reactions to such engagement by German and Turkish authorities. The empirical research for the case study in the book was undertaken during fieldwork in several rounds between 1996 and 2000. During this period, I undertook more than 50 interviews with migrant organizations and 67 interviews with representatives from German and Turkish political parties, organizations, and state agencies (see Appendix C for a selected list of these interviews). I participated in board meetings, seminars, festivals, and demonstrations organized by the migrant organizations, collected their publications, and went through parliamentary archives and newspaper data bases in both Turkey and Germany (see Appendix B, for a more thorough presentation of methodology).[3] In between the more formal parts of the research, I enjoyed the hospitality of Turkish and Kurdish friends, watched Turkish TV, and participated in picnics, dinner parties, and even a couple of amazing Turkish weddings.

Finally, a couple of notes on the terminological challenge that migrants and refugees from Turkey pose. First, not all Turkish migrants are Turks; some are Kurds. By no means all of these Kurds emphasize their Kurdishness or, indeed, support the (more or less) separatist agenda of the main nationalist Kurdish organizations. In general, it is often close to impossible and a reductionist exercise to draw a sharp dividing line between Turkish citizens according to ethnic affiliation (see also Gitmez and Wilpert 1987). Furthermore, other distinctions, such as the religious division between Alevi and Sunni Muslims, or the political distance between left- and right-wing movements, overlap with the ethnic distinction between Turks and Kurds. At times, this book will use the term 'Turkish citizens' to refer to both Kurds and Turks, but mostly it will simply use the latter terms alongside each other to acknowledge that not everyone in Turkey sees himself or herself as a Turk. It must be noted, however, that all groups included in this book relate to, although they do not necessarily identify with, the same political regime in their homeland.

Second, in this analysis migrant organizations are viewed as the institutionalized representation of the interests of the various groups within the community. The main problem with such an approach is that the organizations are not necessarily representative of the communities as a whole. For instance, far from all Kurds or Alevis are members of the organizations who claim to represent the Kurdish or Alevi communities in Germany. Even those who are members may not agree with all of the political agenda of the organization or party. This 'problem of representation' is to be found in most studies of political movements and mobilization and will be discussed further in Chapter 4.

Structure of chapters

The complexity of migrant transnationalism and political practices has led to a rapidly growing range of concepts and theory building. Chapter 2 provides a critical discussion of a selection of categories, concepts, and theories. First, it deals with concepts such as 'diasporas' and transnational communities and prevailing understandings of determinants of migrant transnationalism. Second, it examines the relevance of 'political opportunity structure', a concept central to theories of how receiving states shape migrants' political participation. The continuous use of different sites by transnational political networks points to the fundamental tension between states and transnational political practices, and I argue for the concept of 'multi-level institutional channeling' as more appropriate for the particular dynamics of migrants' transnational political practices. Finally, the chapter deals with a range of more normative understandings of how migrants' transnational engagement may affect processes of democratization in both their countries of settlement and origin.

The extensive migration from Turkey to Germany has had widespread implications for both countries and their relations with each other. Chapter 3 describes how migration has tied Germany and Turkey together, not least, through the intricate web of transnational spaces brought about by Turkish and Kurdish migrants' ongoing relations with their localities of origin. Migration is, however, only one of many important economic and political issues of cooperation or dispute between Turkey and Germany. Turkish and Kurdish transnational political engagement can only be fully appreciated in the context of this overall political relationship, which serves as a backdrop to the agendas and leverage of the homeland political movements and the reactions of the receiving country and homeland. Thus, this chapter also seeks to describe this wider backdrop and place transnational political engagement within this context

Chapter 4 provides a detailed analysis of the main trends and developments in homeland political mobilization among Turks and Kurds in Germany over the last two decades. The description of homeland political or immigrant political agendas of a selection of migrant organizations paints a picture of the transnational landscape, addressing the question of how significant Turkish politics is in the political organization of Turkish citizens in Germany. The chapter finally describes how the homeland political identities and agendas of the various movements and their organizations make it difficult for them to work together. It is precisely the ethnic, religious, and party-political plurality of the communities that constitutes a cornerstone of the analysis in the following chapters.

While Chapter 4 deals with the ideological, ethnic, and religious plurality among migrants from Turkey, Chapter 5 deals with another important dimension setting the various organizations and movements apart: the means and strategies by which they pursue their political agendas. More specifically, it addresses the ways in which, within the same political system between Turkey and Germany, different organizations work 'inside' or 'outside' the system, and it assesses the significance of the transnational dimension herein. The chapter demonstrates how some organizations employ 'confrontational', sometimes even illegal, strategies while others are more engaged in 'institutional participation'. Moreover, it describes how migrant organizations move beyond these categories as they draw on their transnational networks or formulate their demands within discourses more appropriate for negotiations with host state political actors. The findings of this chapter challenge the applicability of the bounded understanding of the significance of political structures of the receiving country for migrants' transnational political practices.

This analysis continues in Chapter 6, which deals with the ways in which transnational political practices unfold within German political institutions such as trade unions and political parties. Another main issue addressed in Chapter 6 is how the various political agents in Germany perceive and tolerate the homeland political activities of Turkish citizens in Germany. The analysis demonstrates how distinct patterns of dialogue have come about between specific German political institutions and particular Turkish and Kurdish movements and organizations.

The final empirical chapter turns to the reactions of the Turkish Government and other relevant political actors in Turkey, to the political activities of Turkish and Kurdish communities in Germany. The chapter on the perception of the homeland comes after, and not before, the analysis of homeland political mobilization. This reflects the overall conclusion that, in this case, the role of the homeland is to control rather than mobilize citizens abroad. The main efforts of the Turkish authorities are reactive rather than pro-active. Accordingly, the chapter addresses the question of how the Turks and Kurds living in Germany and their political organizations are perceived by the Turkish political authorities (state, government, main political parties, groups, and movements). The chapter demonstrates how transnational communities constitute an ambiguous asset for their homeland. On the one hand, political dissidence abroad is seen as a threat and is the target of strategies of constraint directly and via the political institutions of the receiving country. On the other hand, current political debates reflect a change in the political relationship with citizens abroad and recognition of their potential to represent Turkish interests abroad. From being 'our workers abroad' they are now 'our citizens abroad' – a re-definition of the Turkish state to include the emigrants in the polity of the homeland.

2 Migrants' transnational claims-making
Rethinking concepts and theories

From guest workers to diasporas or transnational communities?

People who move across borders have many names. Some of these, such as 'guest worker', 'refugee', or 'ethnic minority', refer to the conditions on which they have been accepted in their new country of residence. Recently, concepts such as 'diaspora' or 'transnational community' have become more prominent in research on migration and migrant incorporation. However, what is the added value in applying these terms? And what is the difference between a diaspora and a transnational community?

The concept of migrant transnationalism reintroduces the ties, which migrants may have back to their country of origin. Migration is viewed as an ongoing process whereby migrants 'forge and sustain simultaneous multi-stranded social relations that link together their societies of origin and settlement' (Glick Schiller *et al.* 1995: 48). Such a transnational approach to immigration acknowledges that migrants identify with more than one state at a time. Migrants may at the same time be incorporated in the economy, political system, and daily life of the society of their country of settlement, and maintain or develop connections with their homeland.

The 'trans-migrant' or 'transnational communities' approach has caught up with the already booming literature on 'diasporas'. Traditionally, the concept of diaspora referred to victimized exile groups unable to return to their homeland for political reasons. This is because the concept has developed in the context of a historical classic precedent: the exile of the Jews from their historic homeland after the destruction of the second Temple in AD 70, and their dispersion throughout many nations. Recently, however, the concept of diaspora has come to describe both exiles and economic migrants. Indeed, almost any group whose awareness of their identity is defined by a territorially discontinuous relationship with a group settled "elsewhere" is a diaspora' (Marienstras 1989: 120). In his editorial preface to the first issue of the journal *Diaspora, a Journal of Transnational Studies*, which is dedicated to the studies of these phenomena, Tölöyan writes that:

> Diasporas […] the term that once described Jewish, Greek and Armenian dispersion now shares meanings with a larger semantic domain that includes

words like immigrant, expatriate, refugee, guestworker, exile community, overseas community, and ethnic community.

(Tölöyan 1991: 4–5)

In other words, the so-called modern diasporas are as diverse as the phenomena of international migration are complex. Such inclusiveness, however, makes the concept of diaspora less useful analytically. Consequently, the conceptual literature on 'who' is a diaspora is growing in leaps and bounds resulting in lists of criteria trying to establish which immigrated groups merit the label diaspora, and the division of diasporas into different categories (see among others, Safran 1991; Clifford 1994; Cohen 1997).

In an analysis of migrants' political practices, this very inclusive definition of a diaspora leaves much to be desired in terms of understanding the differences between different types of migrant groups in general and their *political relationship* with the homeland in particular. Designating both Kurdish refugees and Turkish guest workers as a diaspora does not account for the very different relationship these groups have with their homeland – Turkey. In other words, it does not consider the difference between a diaspora in exile possessing no state with which to identify and a diaspora consisting of voluntary migrants identifying with the state they left. To some extent, such a distinction is made by Cohen, who introduces the categories of 'victim-diasporas' as well as 'trade' or 'labour' diasporas. These categories are, however, based on the reason for departing from the homeland and the position of the diaspora in the receiving country, but not on the relationship with the political regime of the homeland.

This is related to the paradoxical fact that the very notion of the homeland, a crucial part of the definition of a diaspora, remains vague and, hence, ambiguous in literature on diasporas. Is the homeland the territory, the nation, or the political regime in the homeland?[1] The omission of whether or not the diaspora has a state as a defining characteristic is unfortunate since the interaction between diasporas and their home government plays a significant part in their transnational activities. Where a diaspora has no home government or state, it is the agenda devoted to obtaining one that may mobilize the diaspora. For exiled groups, the so-called 'victim-diasporas', the homeland is a territory with fundamental symbolic value. For other immigrant groups, the homeland is also the political regime, which they seek to support or criticize but not to overturn.

The numerous attempts to assess which ethnic groups constitute diasporas, and which do not, stem from the fact that the concept and definition of a diaspora is largely descriptive and static and applied to the phenomenon once the phenomenon is manifest. It is, however, important to note that the specific and ongoing political relationship between a diaspora and its homeland is not necessarily a function of whether members of the diaspora fled or left their homeland voluntarily or to what extent they want to return or resettle.

One way of distinguishing the concept of diasporas from the wider concept of 'transnational communities' is to view it as a special type of consciousness among migrants. As formulated by Levitt (2001):

> Transnational communities are building blocks of potential diasporas that may or may not take shape. Diasporas form out of the transnational communities spanning sending and receiving countries and out of the real or imagined connections between migrants from a particular homeland who are scattered throughout the world. If a fiction of congregation takes hold, then a diaspora emerges.
>
> (Levitt 2001: 203)

Still, critical voices argue that when the concept of diaspora is narrowed down it usually becomes too closely linked with the project of the nation-state. The concept of diaspora has a legacy of dispersal and search for nationhood, which means that researchers too often equate this 'fiction of congregation' with national and ethnic projects only. For instance, Anderson's concept of 'long distance nationalism' refers to migrants engaging in nation-building processes from afar. This negates the wider experiences and practices of contemporary migrants who, as argued by Soysal (2000), 'display new forms of making claims, mobilizing identity and practicing citizenship which lie beyond the limiting dominion of ethnically informed diaspora arrangement transactions and belongings' (Soysal 2000: 1). That is, migrants' transnational political practices also include engagement in wider universalistic and democratic projects.

Transnational communities are arguably a broader term than diaspora and have less historical baggage making the term more applicable to the new way of looking at migrants. The term 'community' must, however, be applied with caution, since it implies a sense of cohesiveness that cannot be assumed and indeed is rarely identified within larger groups of migrants abroad. This book does not try to analyse to what extent Turks and Kurds abroad are a diaspora or a community. Instead, it looks at the politics of their political practices – in particular, those practices that relate to what is going on in their country of origin, Turkey. It uses the term transnational political networks to designate the links and organizations that engage in democratic processes in Turkey – and in Germany.

Analyses of transnational political practices range from liberal uses of the term to the attempts to lay down more strict criteria for what it designates. In order to make sense of a very dispersed field of inquiry, recent studies seek to map transnational political practices by looking at the intensity of the field (see Portes et al. 1999). One such attempt is to distinguish between 'broad' and 'narrow' transnational practices as opposite ends of a continuum of different practices. The more a transnational political practice is institutionalized and has migrants involved, and the more migrants move around to carry it out, the narrower it is understood to be (Itzigsohn et al. 1999). Thus, in terms of political practices 'narrow' refers to actual membership of parties or hometown associations while 'broad' refers to the (occasional) participation in meetings or events. In a similar vein, the concept of 'core' transnationalism defines activities that are a regular, patterned, and an integral part of an individual's life. By contrast, 'expanded' transnationalism refers to more occasional practices (Guarnizo 2000; see also Levitt 2001). Such distinction helps identify the more durable patterns of transnational political participation, and as such this mapping exercise is a necessary first step to delimit where the field of inquiry begins. Migrants engaged in 'narrow' or 'core' political transnationalism are few and far between compared to the wider, more sporadic engagements among those who stay in touch with and are occasionally mobilized by political events and actors in the country of origin (Guarnizo and Portes 2001; Østergaard-Nielsen 2001b).

Determinants of transnational political mobilization

When and why do some migrants engage in transnational political activities while others do not? More specifically, the central issue, as formulated by Smith, M.P. (1999), is to understand why 'principles of trust and solidarity are constructed across national territories as compared to those which are entirely locally based and maintained' (Smith, M.P. 1999). Some researchers discuss the extent to which a given migrant group has or develops such orientation in the first place (Guarnizo and Portes 2001). Others speculate on the reasons for the particular directions such orientation may take, such as ethno-nationalism, strict versions of the homeland religion, cosmopolitanism, hybrid third space identification (Schiffauer 1999). Common for all is the understanding that migrants may continuously (re)construct their relationship with their country of origin.

According to orthodox assimilation theory, engagement of migrants and refugees in their homeland's politics would, sooner or later, disappear as their connections to the country of origin paled in comparison to their life in the new country. The focal point of their social network, consumption, and investments would move to the place of settlement. Membership of hometown associations or political parties in the country of origin would be replaced by engagement in immigrant political issues on equality of social and legal rights. In the case of refugees, solidarity work would cease when the conflict in the homeland was solved, or they simply wanted to put possibly traumatizing events behind them and start anew. Although this does describe the experience of some migrant and refugee groups it was never the rule and is even less so today when electronic communication and media render geographical distances relatively insignificant. Via satellite-tv, radio, fax, telephone, e-mail, and Internet migrants can follow and, to some extent, participate in political processes in their country of origin.

Political identity and membership of immigrants and refugees are not a function of integration into the receiving country, but a result of the complex interplay between the events and policies of the country of origin, and the process of migration and settlement in the receiving country. Moreover, when there are different ethnic, religious, or party-political sub-groups among migrants and refugees, the processes of mobilization are also influenced by the intra-communal relations among these different groups and movements.

Yet, any homeland government and other authorities will similarly seek to avoid political opposition from citizens abroad. The less opposition is tolerated at home, the less it is tolerated abroad. Reactive measures to diaspora political dissidence include control of the secret service (sometimes via the diplomatic missions abroad), withdrawal of passports, and harassment of relatives remaining in the homeland. These measures may also entail pressuring the 'host' state to ban a specific political movement or to demand extradition of political activists. Among homelands known for such activities are Italy under Mussolini, Yugoslavia under Tito, and the USSR under Stalin (see Shain 1989: 156–62). The extent to which the case of Turkey may be added to this list will be discussed further in Chapter 7.

One factor, which is rarely subject to systematic analysis, is the way in which the mobilization of ethnic communities can also be provoked, or furthered, by their relationship with other ethnic, religious, or party-political sub-groups from their homeland in their receiving country. The relationship among the different political agendas relating to the different ethnic and religious communities in the homeland may arouse hostility among the communities leading to the continuation of a conflict in the receiving country. Such dynamic has been termed 'conflict-import' (Brieden 1996), and have been noted in as diverse cases as conflict between 'Arabs' and 'Jews' in the US (Shain 1999) and Muslim versus Hindu violence within South Asian communities in the UK following the destruction of the Babri Masjid in Ayodhya in India (see Kundu 1994). It is, however, important to note when and how conflicts among migrant groups abroad can take a different course than in the homeland because of the different context. Ethnic or religious groups, which are a majority at home, may have their experience of the majority–minority relationship transformed as they become a minority themselves in the receiving country.

The context in the receiving country

Homeland political orientation among migrants cannot be ascribed to the mobilizing efforts of the sending country only. Not only are such practices often re-active rather than pro-active, but the extent to which such efforts fall on deaf ears or fertile ground relates to the societal and political–institutional context in the receiving country also. Drawing on ethnographic or more quantitative sociological research methods and data, it has been argued that transnational political orientation is related to: (a) mode of migration; (b) length of stay; (c) migrant/refugees' structural position in the receiving countries; as well as (d) political opportunity structures for migrants' political participation. Yet, transnational connections of migrants and refugees serve partly to de-couple or at least to question some of these understandings.

Mode of migration US-based studies have concluded that political refugees who left on a collective basis take a more active political stance towards their homeland than economic migrants, who left on an individualized basis (see Landolt *et al.* 1999; Portes 1999: 465). This observation can surely be recognized throughout Europe as well, although it should be noted that the political refugee/economic migrant categories are blurred because of the inseparability of economic and political reasons for departure and because of shifts in immigration rules of the political regimes. Since the mid-1980s, restricted immigration controls make the asylum application one of the few 'open' doors to Europe. Furthermore, refugees may wish to leave political activism behind while the so-called economic migrants become politicized from afar. Similarly, a comparative study of Bosnian and Eritrean refugees shows that the study of political refugees requires a more sceptical conceptualization of transnationalism than that found in recent studies of migrants' transnational identification. In particular, Bosnians are sometimes reluctant to engage in their homelands' politics (Al-Ali *et al.* 2001).

Length of stay There is also the argument that the longer the migrant/refugee group stays abroad, the less they are interested in their homeland. For instance, Miller states that 'as a general rule most students of foreign labour would agree that the degree of homeland identification is inversely related to the migrants' length of stay' (Miller 1981: 44; see also Weiner 1986; Esman 1992, 1994). Younger generations have a stronger interest in involvement in the politics of the receiving country, and transnational political engagement is, therefore, largely a one-generation phenomenon (Portes 2001: 190). It is questionable whether one can correlate length of stay with a greater/lesser understanding of transnational political identification. Rather, there can be qualitative differences among the so-called first, second, and third generations. Second- and third-generation immigrants tend to participate more in the politics of their receiving country. They often have different agendas, such as discrimination and rights issues, stemming from their wish to be regarded as equal members of society. However, more political participation does not exclude the possibility of transnational political activities. Indeed, it contradicts the findings of North-American studies of established migrant groups, which note that the influence of well-established ethnic lobbies is seen precisely to be related to their far from marginal position in society (Sheffer 1986; Constas and Platias 1993). The apparent discrepancy between research on diasporas in North America and immigrant politics in Europe indicates the need for empirical studies of diaspora, transnational, or homeland political activities of immigrants in Europe.

Structural position in the receiving country A related discussion is that of how the socio-economic position in the receiving country impacts transnational political orientation. It has been noted that contexts that are less receptive of immigrants tend to encourage a stronger identification with the homeland. Such a process of identification is also referred to as 'reactive identity' (Portes 1999: 465) and has been found among several migrant or refugee groups in the US such as Salvadorans (Landolt *et al.* 1999: 291), Mexicans (Smith, R. 1998: 212), and Guatemalans (Popkin 1999). Similarly, it has been argued that 'diaspora consciousness' is constituted both negatively and positively. It is constituted negatively by an experience of discrimination and exploitation of the immigrants in their receiving country, and constituted positively through identification with a homeland, or even with global historical cultural/political forces such as 'Africa' or 'Islam'. In this way, Clifford argues, 'diaspora consciousness makes the best of a bad situation'. That is, diasporas mediate the experiences of separation and entanglement, of living here and remembering/desiring another place (Clifford 1994: 311–12). Studies in Europe, including several of Turks, have argued that a sense of social exclusion and marginalization makes Turkish youth, in particular, turn to more radical forms of Turkish nationalism or Islam (see, among others, Heitmeyer *et al.* 1997; Schiffauer 1999).

Clearly, it makes sense for migrants to orient themselves towards transnational social spaces if this enables upward mobility in their locality of origin (Goldring 1997). However, again there are many exceptions to this rule. I have met Turks and Kurds qualifying for the label of socially marginalized who could not care less about Turkish politics as well as university students, hardly among the excluded in society, who are very much into rallying around political issues in Turkey. Only very careful anti-essentialist ethnographic accounts (see Armruster 2002) can move beyond homogenous constructions of the link between social base and political identification, between the personal and the political in transnational political spaces (see also Glick Schiller and Fouron 1999; Skrbis 1999).

Political opportunity structures Moreover, while social exclusion and marginalization may contribute to certain identification processes, such dynamics do not take place in a vacuum. How does the receiving country's particular political institutional context impact the scope of transnational political practices? One dimension of this question is whether or not migrants' transnational engagement depends on the extent to which they have obtained political rights in their country of settlement. It could be expected that when migrants acquire citizenship and political rights they would concentrate on using those and leave their homeland's politics behind. Yet, new research among migrants in the US finds that migrants' transnational political engagement does not depend on whether or not they have American citizenship (Guarnizo and Portes 2001). Another dimension of the relationship between migrants' transnational engagement and the receiving country is how the particular system of migrant incorporation, in particular the notion of political opportunity structures, may impact the scope of transnational political practices. On the one hand, it has been argued that 'exclusive' political systems can strengthen transnational orientation among migrants (Abadan-Unat 1997; Portes 1999). The example of such a system is usually Germany where migrants are categorized as foreigners and not given political rights unless they naturalize – and in that process give up their original citizenship. On the other hand, it has been argued that a multicultural incorporation regime, as in Holland, can contribute to transnational political orientation because of the resources and space given to institutionalization of ethnic and religious organizations (Faist 2000a: 214; see also Vertovec 1996; Kaya 1998).[3]

Migrant politics or homeland politics?

The earlier sections highlight how migrants' transnational political mobilization is uneasily reduced to any one set of factors in the homeland or receiving country. Migrant organizations take their cue from actors, events, and their own position in both settings. Accordingly, they also enter into dialogue on a range of issues rather than only one. The following is a listing of the main issues:

Immigrant politics are the political activities that migrants or refugees undertake to better their situation in the receiving country, such as obtaining more political, social, and economic rights, fighting discrimination, and the like. It is this dimension of migrant's political participation that has been the overriding focus for research in particularly Europe in the last decades. In most countries, migrant organizations are considered important spokes-partners for dialogue on such issues. Immigrant politics can also be transnational when the country of origin becomes involved in helping its nationals abroad to improve their legal and socio-economic status.

Homeland politics denotes migrants' and refugees' political activities pertaining to the domestic or foreign policy of the homeland. That is, it means opposition to or support for the current homeland political regime and its foreign policy goals. Yet, one of the main issues in the dialogue between migrants and their countries of origin is about their own legal, economic, and political status in the homeland. With this type of claims-making, which I will refer to as *emigrant politics*, migrants work towards the institutionalization of their transnational status as residents abroad but also economically, socially, and politically engaged in their country of origin. They ask for favourable investment schemes, tax, and toll exemptions, and regulation of pension schemes and child benefits in their country of origin. And interestingly in this context, they ask for extended channels for influence on politics at home such as advisory councils, external voting rights, and the right to run for office.

As mentioned earlier, *diaspora politics* can be seen as a subset of homeland politics confined to those groups that are barred from direct participation in the political system of their homeland – or who do not even have a homeland political regime to support/oppose – like the not so often used concept of émigré politics (Cohen 1997). For others, diaspora politics, as mentioned earlier, has a much wider connotation in line with the recent more inclusive definitions of the term diaspora and thus overlaps with the term homeland politics. Yet, analysis that uses the phrase 'diaspora politics' is usually about the politics of sensitive issues such as national sovereignty and security political disputes (see Constas and Platias 1993). Finally, another (again, somewhat overlapping) subset of homeland politics is the *trans-local politics*; that is, initiatives from abroad to better the situation in the local community where one originates. Engagement in development in the home community, it is argued, may have wider political ramifications as the empowerment of local communities serves as a catalyst for wider political change (Itzigsohn 2000; Levitt 2001).

Clearly, these dimensions of migrants' transnational political practices overlap and blend into each other relating to the particular constellation of diverging/converging interests of the main actors involved. Notably, migrant politics and homeland/diaspora politics are inseparable categories when the immigrant political claims for ethnic or religious distinctiveness send strong homeland political signals to the political regime of the country of origin, which may try to suppress such proliferation at home. Alternatively, supporting immigrant political claims can be one way that the sending country incorporates citizens abroad in its foreign policy agenda towards the country of settlement.

Ways of advocacy: dynamics of multi-level channeling

The motivation to establish and maintain group solidarity is a cornerstone in the analysis of migrants' transnational mobilization and the scope of their organization. However, migrants do not operate in a vacuum. Understanding migrants' motivation is only the first step towards analysing their political activities. How is political connectedness organized across borders to guarantee commitments and motivate social action? How are migrants' transnational political practices articulated and received within the political institutional context in both the sending country and the receiving country? Migrants' organizational patterns are central components in research on these issues. How do they form their networks? How do they attract members? How do such networks go about trying to influence politics? Which strategies and means do they use? And, importantly, why do different migrant groups choose different strategies to promote their agendas? In answering these questions the migrant associations, organizations, and federations stand central, because they often represent the institutionalization of ethnic, religious, and party-political currents and movements from the homeland *and* the receiving country.

Migrants' transnational practices unfold within a political institutional environment, which span at least their country of origin and settlement. A basic typology divides migrants' transnational practices into direct and indirect participation: *direct participation* is when migrants or refugees attempt to influence events in the homeland through voting, or other political and economic support to political actors in the homeland. *Indirect participation* is when migrants or refugees draw upon their resources in order to influence the government of the receiving country to pursue a particular policy towards their homeland. In both cases, transnational political practices are anchored in their local context. How do such transnational networks interact with or accommodate to local power structures? Which institutions shape the transnational field and which institutional channels are used to put transnational linkages into practice? A systematic appraisal of such dynamics calls for comparative empirical data as mentioned by several scholars based in the US (see Mahler 1998; Guarnizo and Smith 1998).

Transnational political networks' continuous use of different sites points to the fundamental tension between states and transnational political practices. Herein, both the receiving and sending states play a central role by setting the boundaries of inclusion, exclusion, and citizenship, allowing or prohibiting various forms of political mobilization within their boundaries. As mentioned, political institutions in the sending state have been heralded as central actors in shaping the field of transnational political practices. Scholars in the US observe how sending countries, including both government and political parties, extend their notion of membership to appeal to citizens abroad (Smith 1998; Itzigsohn 2000; Levitt 2001). There are, however, only few comparative studies of how receiving states shape transnational political networks' choice of sites and venues for their practices.

Comparative studies of immigrant political participation in Europe, dealing with the dyadic relationship between immigrants and their receiving country, consider the significance of receiving countries' 'political opportunity structure' for migrants' collective patterns of organization and the strategies of participation. Political structures of opportunity include the significance of the political rights granted to these immigrants and the attitude of society and governments towards their political organization and participation (see, among others, Miller 1981; Hammar 1985, 1990; Layton-Henry 1990; Ireland 1994; Soysal 1994; Doormenik 1995; Abadan-Unat 1997). Such studies hold that receiving societies shape the collective organization of migrants by providing certain resources for, and models of, organizing (Soysal 1994: 84, 235; Doomernik 1995). Similarly, the more the rights and access to relevant political gatekeepers in the receiving country (trade unions, political parties, or NGOs), the more the immigrants' political activities are channeled into the political system of the receiving country and adapted to the political discourse and ways of negotiating various demands (see Ireland 1994; Soysal 1994). Hence, a study of mainly Turkish immigrants' political participation in different European countries concludes that Turkish migrants display different organizational patterns, responding to the particular institutional environment of the host country and using the resources available (Soysal 1994: 235; see also Doomernik 1995).

Similarly, the concept of 'institutional channeling' was launched to describe how immigrants' forms of political participation in Europe are shaped by the specific political opportunity structures available to them (Ireland 1994). Ireland focuses on the ways in which 'the institutional framework and the "linking processes" embedded in them structure the participation of immigrant groups in Western Europe' (Ireland 1994: 10). The institutional context includes: (a) political opportunity structures such as the citizenship laws and legal status of the immigrants; (b) gatekeepers such as trade unions, political parties, and humanitarian 'solidarity groups', which act as 'midwives' for the immigrants' political participation, as they control access to the channels of political participation (Ireland 1994: 10, 252). The more inclusive the political system, the more activities take the form of *institutional participation*, which is explicitly and directly aimed at the host society and takes place through the channels available in a positive fashion. Alternatively, migrant activities take place 'outside the system' in the form of *confrontational participation*, which is political activity taking place outside legally available channels, such as unannounced demonstrations or more serious illegal actions.[4] A typology of political practices certainly aids the analysis of often very complex and multi-level data, although I suggest not working with a clear-cut distinction between the 'inside' and 'outside' of a political system, but rather with a continuum spanning from illegal migrant activities to working within receiving country political institutions.[5]

Still, such typology is not exhaustive when it comes to migrants' transnational political participation in general, and to this case study in particular. Indeed, while the slightly functionalist understanding of the significance of political opportunity structures may account for how immigrants or refugees participate in immigrant political issues, it does not capture significant parts of the complexity of how transnational migrant organizations advocate homeland political issues. Importantly, it does not answer the question of why some of these organizations choose one set of strategies while other organizations choose another within the same political system. In order to catch the attention of policy makers in their receiving country or homeland, various strategies are employed spanning from demonstrations, informal meetings with politicians, economic support to political compatriots back home, to the distribution of press releases and information leaflets, and, alas, terrorist activities. That is, within one political system different migrant organizations and movements may be working 'inside' or 'outside' the system, how, then, may we understand the circumstances leading to the very different strategies and forms of participation of migrant organizations? I suggest that when it comes to homeland political claims-making, the following points should be considered in applying the notion of political opportunity structures and institutional channeling:

First, it is questionable whether or not the local political context matters for homeland political activities in the same way as it does for immigrant politics. As is the case with immigrant politics, homeland political strategies depend on the extent to which the members of the community have access to the formal policy making in the receiving country. But receiving country political institutions can seek to constrain the political space given to certain forms of homeland political advocacy when they are seen as counterproductive to political integration. Thus, it is necessary to consider a broader notion of political structure, which not only encompasses the formal access to political systems, but also addresses the fuzzier dimension of which issues are considered legitimate for dialogue along these channels. More specifically, different groups of migrants may employ different means and strategies because their access to receiving country policy makers depends on how controversial their agenda is in the homeland, their degree of opposition to or support for the homeland regime, and the extent to which they are linked to a political party in the homeland.

Second, homeland political organizations and movements may draw on a different range of resources than immigrant political counterparts, including those outside the local political institutional context. Indeed, the concepts of political opportunity structures and institutional channeling presume a boundedness of the political sphere, the lack of which is the very definition of transnational practices. Homeland political organizations may pool financial resources and draw on expertise and manpower in sister organizations elsewhere. They may reinforce their campaigns by coordinating them with political counterparts in other countries, such as producing joint informational material or organizing and coordinating confrontational activities (demonstrations/mass meetings) to happen simultaneously. Cross-border networks mean that supporters from other countries travel to add to the numbers demonstrating at a particular venue. Importantly, the use of the media and the Internet are both becoming an increasingly important vehicle for dissemination of information by transnational political organizations. The Internet has joined TV as a source of transnational communication. In the last couple of years, a wide range of newspapers, newsletters, virtual libraries, and other sources of information are available on the net.

Third, where local institutional structures may serve to constrain, global institutional structures may facilitate transnational political practices. Transnational political activists may also direct their activities at international institutions and networks. In particular, transnational political networks that oppose a state, which has strong allies in their 'host' states or simply is too powerful for other states to meddle with, may turn to international organizations such as the UN, Organization on Security and Cooperation in Europe (OSCE), European Council, and the like. The continuous lobbying by the Palestine Liberation Organization (PLO) for recognition of Palestine as a member of the UN is one of the more classic examples. Another example is the Tibetans, who have advocated their story of persecution and discrimination by the Chinese in international fora rather than their 'host' state, India. However, only more resourceful groups manage to lobby international organizations at a more professional level on their own. Rather, the so-called trans-state advocacy networks of NGOs are very valuable (see Keck and Sikkink 1998). Coopting of NGOs at both the national and international levels is a much sought after strategy for migrants' transnational political networks since such organizations facilitate contact with levels of policy making that are otherwise difficult to gain access to for a migrant organization (see Ellis and Khan 2002).[6]

Another, probably more important, role of international organizations is to provide a normative frame of reference for those groups advocating democratization and human rights agendas. In particular, discourses of human rights provide the language for negotiation between migrants' transnational political networks and states, and international organizations provide the site where such negotiation may take place. This trend is also noted in the case of migrant political claims-making. Soysal (1994) argues that a 'post-national' citizenship is emerging as migrants' rights are increasingly legitimized at an international level mainly through international conventions guided by human rights concerns (Soysal 1994; see also Bauböck, 1994). Studies of 'transnationalism' within the discipline of International Relations have established the significance of the institutionalization of international cooperation; that is, international (non-governmental, inter-governmental, and supranational) organizations for the work of non-state actors lobbying for democratization and human rights (Risse-Kappen 1995). Also, research on diaspora political groups in the US has argued that cold war bi-polarity between Western and Soviet foreign policy interests meant that migrant groups based in the West (in particular the US) would position themselves accordingly. Migrants opposing political regimes supported by the Soviet Union were welcomed, and those supporting such regimes spoke to deaf ears (Shain 1999). Today, there seems to be more ample leverage for foreign policy lobbying of migrants as ideals of democracy, pluralism, self-determination, and human rights are, at in least in principle, heralded as central to foreign policy making of Western states in the post-cold war era. Moreover, the treatment of minorities has increasingly become a trans-state issue, with the introduction of new and broader regional security structures, implementation of norms of humanitarian intervention, and calls for the implementation of universal principles of human rights. Accordingly, in some cases states, usually at the weaker end of international power hierarchy, have become more open to the idea of subordinating their domestic politics to the scrutiny of foreign states and international organizations (Smith, G. 1999).

Considering this complex institutional environment, I would argue that a process of 'multi-level institutional channeling' is taking place. Transnational political networks' strategies and activities may not only adapt to their local institutional environment but also be shaped as they appropriate global (Western liberal) norms of democracy and human rights via their interaction with national and international institutions.

Thoughts on the consequences of transnational political practices

Transnational political networks enter political processes at local, national, and international levels as actors in their own right. However, observations like these raise as many questions as they answer. What makes some transnational political networks more influential than others? And how do we go about measuring this influence? When, if at all, do migrants' transnational political activities bring about change? Who benefits from migrants' transnational political practices? And what are the consequences for the role of state in domestic and international politics?

One of the key parameters for discussing change, which at the same time offers a normative evaluation of migrants' transnational practices, is the way in which transnational political practices contribute to democratic political processes. 'Democratic political processes' mainly refers to both democratization in the country of origin and the evolvement of multicultural democracy in the receiving country (see notably Shain 1999; Faist 2000a: 328).

The effect on the receiving country

Prevalent research does not agree on the impact that migrants' transnational political networks may have on the receiving country. Host states have to balance a range of interests when considering the limits of tolerance *vis-à-vis* migrants' political movements on their territory. Studies of 'host'-state reactions to homeland political movements illustrate that 'host'-state responses may veer from enthusiastic support to prohibiting any kind of operations (see Bell 1981: 165ff; Sheffer 1986; Shain 1989). But, transnational political practices are not only about diaspora-political instances where refugees are against the political regime of their homeland forcing the receiving country to consider relations with the homelands' political regime in its dealing with refugee groups. Most of the transnational political practices in which migrants engage are not controversial in the homeland.

Still, far from everyone welcomes this development. In the US, Huntington (1997) is among the shriller opponents. He argues that while immigrants wanted to become American in the past, the 'disintegrative cult of multiculturalism' legitimates homeland political claims for US intervention in the affairs of their homelands. As a further consequence of this 'domestication' of foreign policy, foreign capital, and interests increasingly influence American elections turning senatorial elections into contests between Indians and Pakistanis or Arabs and Jews throughout the country (Huntington: 1997: 46–7). This is a development, which, in Huntington's opinion, erodes the democratic relationship between policy makers and their electorates. By contrast, Shain (1999) has put forward the more constructive argument that the foreign policy lobbying of ethnic groups in the US keeps foreign policy makers true to the principles of human rights and self-determination in their dealings with countries abroad (see also Ruggie 1997). The consequences for the domestic scene are also positive: as migrant organization leaders are advocating principles of human rights, they feel compelled to adhere to these principles in their dealings with other groups of migrants within the US (Shain 1999).

More of such normative discussions of the 'good and bad' of transnational political practices can also be found in the more migrant-oriented literature. Within European-based scholarship it is stressed that transnational political loyalty and political incorporation in the receiving country are not mutually exclusive (Faist 2000a; Østergaard-Nielsen 2000; Fennema and Tillie 2001). Similarly, Portes (1999) argues against such practices having disintegrative consequences for the host society and culture. Migrants' transnational political orientation gives them a voice that they would otherwise not have. This serves to empower them, invest them with a sense of purpose and self-worth, and thus 'act as an effective antidote to the tendency towards downward assimilation...' (Portes 1999: 471; see also Goldring 1997). Indeed, for some researchers transnational practices can contribute to the development of multicultural democracy. Participation in campaigns for democratization in the homeland can give otherwise marginal groups of refugees and migrants a broader interface with the political system of the receiving country (Shain 1999; Østergaard-Nielsen 2002b).

Again, there are also research findings that indicate a slight caution to such arguments. First, transnational political practices can also serve to dis-empower. Glick Schiller and Fouron (1999) note how transnationalism among Haitians in the US reduces their participation in US-based grass-root struggles for social justice. Similarly, in Europe, migrants and refugees may use their free time to mobilize around homeland political agendas, which are untenable in even the most optimistic international relations analysis, instead of rallying for better social and legal conditions. That is, although political loyalty in general is by no means a zero-sum game between the receiving country and the homeland, processes of political mobilization related to the homeland may serve to 'de-politicize' migrants *vis-à-vis* the host state in particular instances.

Second, transnational political practices might serve to exclude in cases with migrant populations fractured by majority/minority issues. Certain organizations may find it hard to cooperate because of their homeland party political, ethnic, or religious differences. This may skewer their representation in immigrant political fora if minority groups are marginalized by majority groups. It may hinder their attempts to build broader and more cogent immigrant platforms. Finally, mutual slandering because of homeland politics may serve to exclude groups because other groups depict them as radical or uncooperative. These organizations could otherwise have served as bridge builders between receiving country politicians and marginalized factions of the migrant community.

The effect on the sending country

In terms of the country of origin, recent research has argued how outside political participation benefits democratic processes at home. The very term 'grass-root transnationalism' implies bottom-up participation in what may be otherwise top-down democracies. For instance, translocal initiatives may not only benefit the home village or region but also challenge political rule at the national level (Portes 1999). Similarly, the formation of 'transnational civil society', with the communicative power to question, criticize, and publicize may strengthen democratic control at home. And in cases where migrants can participate directly in the politics of their country of origin from afar, they are understood to have a platform from which they can obtain less biased information and thus exert an influence in the politics of their homeland that would be unobtainable if they had not left.

While such findings are a valuable contribution to the constructive dimension of the relationship between sending countries and their citizens abroad, some caution should be included. First, it is very difficult to find empirical evidence to substantiate the claim that migrants influence democratization and social change in their country of origin. Part of the difficulty with assessing the transnational political networks' contribution to democratization in homelands relates to the lack of accountability of transnational political networks. It is, for instance, difficult to determine 'who represents who' in terms of political organization of migrants if these organizations are vague about their rootedness among migrants and their political ties to the country of origin.

On the one hand, it is questionable how representative the transnational political networks are of the wider immigrant and refugee groups abroad. That is, to what extent are those organizations that often advocate democratization at home actually based on democratic principles; to what extent are they anchored within the population of migrants/refugees abroad. Not all 'grassroots' transnational practices are very rooted, as the organizations may not have much input from their members or anything that remotely looks like democratic election processes. They may be run by small elites abroad or, indeed, by the party executive in the homeland. Such more elitist networks may be influential in homeland politics. However, their claims for representation by organizations is usually difficult to evaluate since organizations rarely underestimate their membership and support.

On the other hand, it is not always clear to what extent transnational political institutions represent the groups in the country of origin. Exile may provide a platform for voicing discontent with totalitarian regimes, but sometimes such intervention may hamper rather than bridge disputes in homeland politics. Leaders of legal parties in the homeland may not always be delighted with the efforts of the more radical transnational political movements abroad, and most certainly do not want to be identified as closely linked to them (Østergaard-Nielsen 2002a). And what about all those transnational political practices that enter into homelands with democratically elected regimes? Clearly, all governments want supportive lobby groups abroad – in particular, when they reside in countries that are influential in global politics. Yet, some sending countries such as Armenia (Panossean, forthcoming) and Cyprus (Demetreou, forthcoming) are ambivalent about the wish for political influence from afar since those who left have lost touch with the everyday reality of their homelands and focus on more emotive issues – mirroring Anderson's description of the long-distance nationalist (Anderson 1992). In the case of countries in conflict, it has even been argued that 'transnational mobilization and international involvement can exacerbate problems encountered by domestic coalitions, and introduce additional obstacles to the effective pursuit of social change' (Maney 2000). While opposing groups who would not otherwise cooperate in the country of origin can be brought together abroad, this can also lead to formation of rival blocks that are exported back to the domestic policy area.

Defining effectiveness

As already hinted earlier, it is in any case very difficult to 'measure' the influence from abroad in terms of democratization and social change. Some of the difficulty stems from methodological issues. Data on the channeling of economic and political support through cross-border networks are hard to come by. Even more accessible processes are difficult to assess since actual electoral participation by migrants is usually marginal, and the few migrant candidates are not very controversial in terms of the general party-political agenda.

Similarly, it is difficult to pinpoint exactly how much influence transnational political networks can exercise by putting pressure on their 'host' governments. An analysis of US policies towards the Middle East, Haiti, Cuba, or Northern

Ireland would be deficient without considering the efforts of Jews, Arabs, Haitians, Cubans, or Irish diasporas, respectively. However, usually homeland political lobbying does not redirect foreign policy away from governments' already defined national interests such as economic or security political relations with the homeland/or other countries in the region. Indeed, it is important to emphasize that far from all homeland political groups are very successful. Many a homeland political campaign is ignored or even forbidden if the political movement uses too radical means to get noticed.

Policy makers may balance national interests with the human rights dimension when considering the claim of a homeland political movement (Østergaard-Nielsen 2001a). As mentioned earlier, migrants may turn to international conventions when trying to reach the attention of relevant policy makers. Studies of other transnational actors such as human rights advocates, environmental organizations have found that a high degree of 'international institutionalization' tends to legitimize transnational activities and to increase access to national politics and the ability to influence policy-making (Risse-Kappen 1995: 6). International institutionalization means the extent to which a specific issue-area, such as human rights, is regulated by international norms of cooperation, that is, bilateral agreements, multilateral regimes, and/or international organizations. Similarly, a study of diasporas in the US concludes that those diasporas that speak for furthering democracy and human rights issues in their homeland are the most successful, since they comply with international agreements and norms (see Shain 1999).

However, to measure transnational networks' effectiveness in terms of their ability to influence changes in government behaviour only, is too ambitious and narrow a yardstick for success. It is difficult to research the extent to which one single factor influences a policy decision where a seamless web of interests is balanced by the policy makers. Therefore, in order to assess the effectiveness of diaspora politics it is necessary to establish other success criteria – which should be considered achievements in their own right.[7] I suggest that the establishment of channels of dialogue between diaspora political groups and political representatives and institutions of the receiving country or homeland is in itself a measure of the effectiveness of homeland political activities.

Challenging the state?

Whatever their actual impact on democratization in sending or receiving countries, the phenomena of transnational political practices in and of themselves further erode the (quite dated) distinction between foreign and domestic policy. They contribute to what has been referred to as a 'diffusion of domestic politics' (Miller 1981) or a 'globalization of domestic politics' in both the sending and receiving countries.

In the light of such observations, it has been argued that the scope and impact of transnational political practices challenge the role of the state in contemporary world politics. Admittedly, the very notion of diaspora politics cuts to the heart of the realist–pluralist debate, since it challenges the dichotomy of internal and external affairs. Debates on the role of the state have been fluctuating between Realists and Liberalists within the discipline of international relations for the past four decades. Realist resistance to legitimization of other actors to be considered alongside the state is opposed by liberal approaches that stress the impact of non-state actors such as NGOs and multinational companies or the impact of transnational diffusion of people, goods, and ideas. Among the main arguments are that non-state actors [especially (international) NGOs and multinational corporations] are growing in number, and that interdependence and modern means of communication are facilitating the ability of these actors (including revolutionary groups, religious movements, and political parties) to influence the ideas, values, and political persuasions of people around the world. Most Realists agree with Liberalists that the significance of non-state actors, such as NGOs and multinational companies, should be taken into account in any interpretation of international relations and global politics. It is on the degree to which non-state actors matter that they differ (Keohane and Nye 1971; Rosenau 1993; Risse-Kappen 1995; Josselin and Wallace 2001).

Migrants' transnational political practices may challenge state institutions, and contribute to changed domestic and foreign policy decisions. Indeed, they are the sort of actors who may seek to influence events in their homeland without direct interaction with the state of either their receiving country or homeland, but through inter-societal penetration in order to bring about a change in another society. Such phenomena are mentioned in the works of early as well as later advocates of transnationalism (see among others, Kaiser 1971, Keohane and Nye 1971; Wapner, 1995).[8] Similar transnational activism by global social movements does not simply become politically relevant when it intersects with state behaviour (see Wapner 1995: 39–40, 312).

Also, within migration studies there is a debate on who influences whom. Recent literature on migrant transnational practices has questioned the post-national discourse on 'de-territorialization' that characterized the earlier analysis of, in particular, sending countries' policies towards nationals abroad (see notably Glick Schiller *et al.* 1995). They point to the processes of 're-territorialization', to the very degree to which state institutions co-opt or are at least involved in channeling migrants' transnational practices. As importantly, they question whether migrants' transnational practices challenge state institutions or serve their interests (see, among others, Mahler 1998, 2000; Smith, M.P. 1999; Faist 2000a: 327). In the following analysis, state institutions certainly figure as important actors, which form and reconstitute transnational political ties and networks. Indeed, one of the major challenges is to assess the balance between state authority and non-state autonomy in the analysis of migrant homeland political practices. Such ambiguity is probably more prevalent in research on homeland political networks, which are more directly plugged into party politics in the homeland, than with the more local – local oriented networks. Still, it points to careful application of two central concepts in the more recent literature on migrant transnational political practices: 'bottom up/grassroots transnationalism' and 'transnational civil society'.

Research on migrants' transnational networks does not have to assess the exact impact of transnational political practices in order to be meaningful. Such analysis rests more comfortably with data on more established diaspora political lobbying in countries such as the US. Rather, the networks and their practices are interesting in and of themselves because of the way they interact with state institutions in both the receiving countries and the homeland. It is the very way that transnational political practices are anchored in their local context, the way that they shape, and are shaped by their political interlocutors in both the homeland and their receiving countries.

The following analysis will focus on how the global and local politics of migrants' transnational networks and practices are part and parcel of the understanding of migrants' agency. It will illustrate how there is a multi-level process of institutional channeling at work. While the institutional and normative local context of transnational political practices, including the way that such practices are embedded in local discourses on immigrant incorporation, shape (constrain) their institutional space for action, the global context of human rights norms facilitate such agency.

To sum up, the political structures of opportunity are an important variable for the analysis of migrants' political activities. However, ascribing the political mobilization and activities as a function of their structural position within this transnational setting would be a reductionist exercise. In order to understand the more specific instances of mobilization of the various groups of Turkish citizens residing in Germany, it is necessary to include the motivation and agency of the various actors involved. That is, it is necessary to include the way in which the conflicting or concurrent goals and strategies of the migrants, as well as the relevant political actors in their 'host' state and their homeland, combine to determine the agendas, strategies, and the effectiveness of the politics of immigrant communities.

3 Migration, transnational spaces, and German–Turkish relations

Migration and transnational spaces

Why did so many Turks end up in Germany? Contrary to other classic examples of mass migration from one country to another, there are no colonial ties between Germany and Turkey, as in the case of France and the Mahgreb countries, nor are the two countries geographically close, as is the case with Mexico and the US.

The approximately 2.4 million Turkish citizens and former Turkish citizens in Germany originate in post-war labour recruitment. The match in expectations between labour market policies in Germany (import of labour) and Turkey (export of labour) meant that almost 650,000 Turkish workers participated in the official labour exchange agreements between these two countries from 1961 to 1973 (Irbec 1993: 1). When labour recruitment was halted in 1973, an unexpectedly large proportion of the guest workers did not, despite the intentions of most, return to Turkey (Martin 1991; ZfT 1997a: 8–9). Instead, workers chose to bring their families to Germany. Between 1974 and 1980, the number of Turkish children living in West Germany increased by 129 per cent, and after 1980 more than 40 per cent of the Turks in Germany were less than 18 years old (Abadan-Unat 1995: 280; Meier-Braun 1995: 17).

Alongside labour migration and family re-unification, more than 370,000 Turkish citizens have applied for asylum in Germany in the period 1979–2001, first, in connection with the 1980 military coup in Turkey, and, in particular since the late 1980s, in connection with the Kurdish conflict in Southeast Turkey (see Appendix A). It is, however, not the case that Kurdish migration is solely politically motivated while Turkish migration is solely economically driven. Many Kurds (estimated to constitute one-third of those originating in Turkey) arrived as guest workers, while a number of Turks arrived as asylum seekers.

The term 'Turkish migrant' initially brought to mind the image of a factory worker catapulted from an Anatolian village to a big European city on a temporary basis. Today, it is increasingly recognized that Turkish migrants have come to stay and that they have become a very heterogeneous group in terms of socio-economic status as well as ethnic, religious, and political orientation. Social statistics paint a picture of slow general improvement in levels of education, particularly with regard to Turkish youth, in Europe. General aggregates are, however, somewhat deceptive compared to the very differentiated development among Turkish migrants. Alongside the fast growing business community (see below) there are staggering high youth unemployment rates (22 per cent in 1998), which is not only more than double the national German average, but also supersedes that of other labour migrant descendants (ZfT 2001: 395). Alongside the increase in Turkish youth in higher education are the still high numbers of young people leaving school with no qualifications.

The period of guest worker recruitment on a rotational basis and the practices of the contemporary settled communities of Turkish citizens in Germany represent two different kinds of transnational relations between Turkish migrants and Turkey. Guest workers have engaged in transnational activities, such as travelling back and forth, sending home remittances, purchasing property in Turkey, and sending children to attend schools in Turkey because they assumed that they would eventually return home. Gradually, as they realized that they were staying in Germany, these types of direct transnational practices were complemented by another set of indirect transnational practices which aimed to establish various Turkish institutions abroad.[1]

Today, no one visiting a large German city can ignore the Turkish presence, be it the taxi-driver, the *döner kebabçı*, or the newspaper salesman. There are the coffee houses, the Turkish discos – during my fieldwork there were five in Cologne alone, pop-events, theatres, and restaurants. There are the travel agencies, driving schools, banks, import/export firms run by Turks for Turks and advertised in Turkish newspapers and the special 'yellow pages' for Turkish citizens found in *Länder* such as Berlin and Nordrhein-Westfalen.[2] Not least, there is a growing number of mosques and Cemevis (Alevi Muslims' places of worship) run by Turkish Sunni and Alevi Muslims, respectively. As one elderly Turkish migrant once commented during an interview: 'We used to say that we are in "Gurbet" [place away from home], but we are no longer in "Gurbet" – Turkey is here.' (Interview with former trade unionist, 16 October 1996.)

Present-day Turkish or Kurdish transnational practices are clearly not a reproduction of how things are in Turkey (see Faist 2000a). Still, they are, particularly in Germany, regarded as signs of 'parallel worlds'. Surveys commissioned by public authorities record how Turks socialize with other Turks rather than members of the wider society (Seifert 1996: 427). However, another survey shows how an increasing number of Turks (up from 30 to 40 per cent between 1999 and 2000) feel equally attached to Germany and Turkey (ZfT 2000a). And importantly, the naturalization rates are rapidly increasing. In 1990, less than 1 per cent of Turkish citizens had obtained German citizenship. In 1999, this figure had grown to 17.5 per cent (see Appendix A).[3]

In particular, the increasingly available Turkish electronic and printed media means that Turks and Kurds can follow the news and debates in the homeland. More than a decade ago Turkish state-television channels, TRT, became available on cable throughout Europe and it was soon followed by private channels on satellite TV. One study found that 74 per cent of Turks in Germany watched the Turkish News, and that 40 per cent watched only Turkish TV. In addition, 95 per cent of Turks read Turkish newspapers and 55 per cent only Turkish newspapers.

This explains why more than 200,000 copies hit the streets in Germany every day (ZfT 1997b).

Other developments indicate that Turks in Germany stay in touch with their homeland. Indeed, this staying in touch has become a lucrative market for telephone companies and airlines. There are direct flights from most major German cities to not only Istanbul and Ankara, but also other cities in regions with a large out-migration. The yearly number of planes taking off for a Turkish airport from Germany is close to 30,000 (that is approximately 80 planes a day), and the number of persons travelling to Turkey by plane every year has risen from less than half a million in 1980 to 4.3 million in 2000 (Federal Department of Statistics 1980, 1997, 2001).

Economic transnational relations between Germany and Turkey seem unique in a European context. One dimension of these relations is the remittances. In 1964, Turkish citizens abroad sent home a total of US$ 45 million. This rose to US$ 1.2 billion in 1973, equalling 90 per cent of the commodity exports and approximately 60 per cent of the commodity imports of Turkey in the same year. Throughout the 1990s, Turkish remittances rose steadily from US$ 3.2 to 4.5 billion, making Turkey the third largest receiver of remittances in the world – with Germany as the third largest payer (IMF 2001). Compared to Italians and Greeks in Germany, Turks send more money home on a regular basis. Only citizens from former Yugoslavia in Germany send higher remittances to their homeland (Federal Ministry of Labour and Social Security 1996: 190–1). Added to this, money is invested, collected, or transferred to Turkey for more specific purposes such as to aid the victims of the August 1999 earthquake, to participate in Islamic banking, or to support political and ethnic movements or village associations in the home region. Thus, not surprisingly both state-run and private economic agencies in Turkey woo the Turkish citizens abroad for their spare funds. Here, they are in competition with commercial banks and companies in the West.

Business networks are another type of transnational economic relation where Turkish migrants play an important role. There are currently 800 German companies working in Turkey (*Frankfurter Allgemeine Zeitung*, 21 May 1999). Yet, there are an estimated 55,200 Turkish companies in Germany (ZfT 2001: 113). This is not least related to the transformation of a significant proportion of Turkish guest workers into Turkish shop owners. An estimated 293,000 people are employed by Turks in Germany alone, with a yearly turnover of DM 50.3 billion in 1999. One of the most common enterprises is the *Döner* industry, but there are also large well-to-do industrialists and one of their main organizations, *Avrupa Türk İşadamları ve Sanayıcıleri Derneği* (ATIAD), likes to identify with other entrepreneurial immigrant groups which have experienced rapid social mobility outside of their homeland such as the Chinese and Indians (ATIAD 1997).[4]

This brief presentation of Turkish migration to Germany and migrants' links back to Turkey serves to illustrate how migration and migrants have woven a web of informal relations between the two countries. These relations also have to be understood in the context of government to government relations.

German–Turkish relations

German and Turkish governments usually refer to German–Turkish relations as long standing, close, and important.[5] The two countries were 'brothers in arms' from the rapprochement between Friederich the Great and Mustafa III ensuing in close diplomatic relations and extensive military cooperation, which made the Ottoman Empire an important ally for German imperialist expansion. While Turkey hosted refugees from the Nazi regime, the special status of Germany was the main (if not the only) reason for Turkey not joining the allied forces until the last minute during Second World War (Steinbach 1996: 412–16).

German and Turkish statesmen especially stress that Germany and Turkey have no colonial past, but a more equal cooperative one, centred around military aid and trade, resulting in an intricate web of political, economic, and social relations tying the two countries together.[6] Germany was Turkey's biggest trading partner during Second World War and has been again since the 1960s (Kramer 1998: 3). Germany is the most important donor of aid to Turkey and Turkey the second largest recipient of German aid after India (Steinbach 1996: 418). But behind this glossy rhetoric lies a more complex historical and contemporary relationship. First, German–Turkish relations have always been characterized by asymmetrical inter-dependence with Turkey at the weaker end. Furthermore, in particular since the 1980s, the actual relationship between Germany and Turkey did not always match the positive rhetoric surrounding it. Indeed, at times the legacy of the 'special friendship' has been tested to the full, as tension between the two countries intensified over issues such as German migration control and migrant incorporation, acceptance or deportation of asylum seekers from Turkey, Germany's position and role in Turkey's EU candidacy, and Germany's position on Turkey's human rights record and the armed conflict with the Kurdish minority in southeastern Turkey. An outline of these four main issues is particularly relevant, since they are key themes in the mobilization of both pro-Turkish and dissident groups from Turkey in Germany, and provide a necessary backdrop to the reaction to such mobilization of the Turkish and German governments.

German–Turkish relations and migration

Initially, as stated by the advisor to the Federal Institute for Labour, Helmuth Wicken, the guest worker experience was expected to contribute to a 'strengthening and consolidation of the traditional German–Turkish relationship' (Meier-Braun 1995: 15). However, at the same time, it is the issues related to the immigration and settlement of Turkish citizens in Germany which have played into the reluctant German attitude to the membership of Turkey in the EU and the periodic halt to military and economic aid from Germany to Turkey.[7] Among these immigration related issues are: German reluctance to grant the right to free movement of Turkish citizens, German integration policies, in particular their citizenship policies, the relationship between Germans and Turks in Germany, and the intra-communal strife among various segments of the diasporas from Turkey in Germany.

'They asked for labour and people came.' This often repeated left-wing parole neatly sums up the main dilemmas facing German governments after the guest worker recruitment during the 1960s and the 1970s: how to control further immigration and how to integrate those who had chosen to stay? In contrast to the cooperation between Germany and Turkey on labour recruitment, halting immigration was largely a result of unilateral measures employed by the German authorities. This reflected the usual asymmetrical power relationship between receiving and sending country at the time. Turkey accepted all these measures, but tried, alongside international organizations such as the International Labour Organization, to protect and improve the position of already emigrated guest workers (see Chapter 7).

One outstanding issue was the right to free movement for Turkish guest workers. The Ankara Association Agreement signed in 1963 had set out a step-by-step schedule for lifting restriction on freedom of movement for these workers.[8] In particular, the regulations on workers' freedom of movement played a significant role in the negotiations of the treaty, and a three-step plan was envisaged whereby this should happen by the twelfth and the twenty-second year of the Agreement. It never did (Steinbach 1996: 419). By 1980, all official visitors from Germany raised the question of how to persuade the Turkish guest workers to return to Turkey. The Turkish government was pressurizing the German government for Turkish workers to have unrestricted access to the German labour market. The German government was already struggling to persuade Turkish workers to return home and most certainly did not wish to open the borders further. Thus, when Chancellor Kohl visited Turkey in 1985, as the first western head of government since the 1980 coup, his visit was overshadowed by these issues. Ankara was particularly angered by Germany's opposition to the implementation of the second stage of the Association Agreement, whereby workers were to be allowed free movement on 1 January 1986. The German government offered Ankara a deal whereby the claim to free movement of workers would be bought off with a package of economic aid (Steinbach 1996). This deal was eventually accepted by the Turkish government, but President Evren summed up the Turkish disappointment with German attitudes as: 'Our German friends used our workers very cheaply. They squeezed the orange and now want to get rid of the skin. They are being selfish.' (Pope and Pope 1997: 183).

Free movement remains a thorny issue in German–Turkish relations. Many voices in Turkey have regarded the restrictions on free movement as a violation of the Association Agreement (Ismet 1990: 189–90).[9] Yet, the German government has been unwavering in its opposition to the free movement of Turkish workers. For instance, when Prime Minister Yilmaz visited Germany in November 1997, Germany's Chancellor Kohl praised the friendly, loyal, and supportive attitude of Turkey towards Germany, which Germany would repay by supporting Turkey's integration in the EU. He did, however, admit to having one reservation: if Turkey were to become a full member of the EU, he considered it likely that 7–8 million people would come from Turkey to Germany to look for work. In his reply to this, Prime Minister Yilmaz urged the Chancellor to have faith in the dynamics of

Turkey's economic development which would confound such predictions, and suggested that a means of regulations would be found which would solve the problem of free movement (*Sabah*, 1 October 1997).

Issues of Turkish migrants and their descendants' role and place – or rather lack thereof – in German society have posed another major challenge for German policy makers and has been the object of much scrutiny by Turkish governments. Several points illustrate this. One of the most important issues is that of the exclusiveness of German citizenship.[10] German citizenship was difficult to obtain for Turkish citizens in Germany until the SPD/*Die Grüne* Government changed German citizenship laws in January 2000. Until then, the principle of *jus sanguinis* meant that children of Turkish citizens born in Germany did not automatically qualify for German citizenship and when they did, they had to go through arduous application procedures to get it.[11] More importantly, Germany does not allow for dual citizenship.[12] When applying for German citizenship, Turks and Kurds had, and still have, to give up their Turkish citizenship – something which holds value for a large number of Turkish citizens (but not necessarily Kurds) born outside of Turkey. Needless to say, the German changes to citizenship rules were welcomed by both the Turkish migrant organizations in Germany and policy makers and the press in Turkey, but both sets of actors would have preferred changes which allowed for dual nationality.

Turkey has allowed dual citizenship after constitutional changes in 1995. Earlier, consulates in Germany were known to harass Turkish citizens wishing to part with their Turkish passport (Özdemir 1997: 53–4).[13] In 1998, acknowledging that many Turkish citizens were forced to give up their Turkish citizenship since their receiving country did not permit dual allegiance, the Turkish government decided that Turkish citizens who give up their Turkish citizenship with the permission of the state should have similar rights as if they had kept their Turkish citizenship (see Chapter 7).

Furthermore, during the 1980s Ankara became more and more focused on the situation of Turkish citizens in Germany. A rapidly increasing number of Turks are studying at German universities, and Turkish entrepreneurs have become significant contributors to the German economy. Yet, at the same time Turks are generally less educated and more frequently unemployed than both the German average and the average among other migrant groups originating in labour recruitment. These facts, as well as widespread discrimination and xenophobia aimed at Turks, are repeatedly criticized by Turkish politicians. Indeed, Germany's treatment of Turkish citizens is perceived as a violation of human rights. With the tragic incidents in Mölln and Solingen in 1992 and 1993, respectively, this criticism intensified to the extent that an equation was made between Turkey's problems with its Kurdish minority and the treatment of Turkish citizens in Germany.[14] For instance, Turkish Prime Minister Tansu Çiller was quoted during a debate in the *Bundestag* as wishing that 'the Turks in Germany had just 10 per cent of the rights that Kurds in Turkey have.' (*Deutscher Bundestag* 1993b).

Alongside the issue of direct discrimination is the more complex question of German integration policies. Assimilationist policies are criticized for not leaving room for Turkish distinctiveness abroad, yet multicultural policies are seen as supportive of ethnic and religious subversive movements abroad. In other words, the Turkish state wants German tolerance of Turkishness but only the national version. This means, as will be clear in the following chapters, that German local integration policies becomes a matter of bilateral attention between Turkey and Germany.

Last, but not the least, is the issue of German tolerance of organizations and movements that Turkey sees as a security political threat. A number of movements, organizations, and parties which are banned in Turkey find space to voice their agendas more freely in Germany and the rest of western Europe. The German *Verfassungsschutz* (the Federal office for the protection of the constitution) watches all of these organizations closely, and German authorities have banned several organizations (such as the extreme left-wing *Devrimci Sol* and more notably, the PKK) and sentenced the leader of one extreme Islamic organization to several years of jail time.[15] However, the Turkish state and government has repeatedly accused Germany of tolerating such dissident groups and has called for further restrictions on their activities (see Chapter 7).

Asylum seekers

The issue of acceptance and deportation of asylum seekers has been a contested issue in German politics and German–Turkish relations. The number of asylum seekers from Turkey arriving in Germany increased threefold between 1979 and 1980, the year of the Turkish military coup. However, months before the coup, Germany introduced visa requirements for all Turkish citizens in order to curb immigration and what was perceived as misuse of the asylum system. This meant that less than half the amount of Turkish citizens entered Germany in the months after the coup compared to the months before. And less than 5,000 applied for asylum in the months after the coup compared to the more than 16,000 in the months before. (*Deutscher Bundestag* 1981a; see also Appendix A). The visa restrictions and changed asylum law led to a campaign by Turkish newspapers to make Germany revoke its decision. The campaign was taken so seriously by the German authorities that they deployed the diplomatic representation in Turkey to explain the reasoning behind the law to Turkish politicians and journalists in Turkey and they also conducted talks with Turkish journalists in Germany (*Deutscher Bundestag* 1981a).

Since 1983, the annual number of asylum seekers has been rising steadily, peaking at 28,327 in 1992. The asylum seekers associated with the 1980 coup were mainly individuals affiliated with banned political organizations or implicated in unlawful activities prior to 1980 (Kirisci 1991: 8).[16] Since 1985, the refugee flows are thought to have been dominated by Kurds fleeing the military campaign in southeastern Anatolia or the continuing social and economic hardship which the Kurdish minority faces.

The very fact that Turkish citizens apply for asylum in Germany is a thorn in German–Turkish relations. Turkey finds it awkward that Turkish citizens arriving in Germany claim to be politically persecuted and in need of asylum. Indeed, given that asylum can be considered as a pre-condition for diaspora political dissidence, Turkey criticizes Germany for accepting and hosting anti-state forces. The German government argues that granting asylum does not imply support for the asylum seekers' particular political agenda or activities.

Only a limited number of those who have fled to Germany have been granted asylum due to the tighter asylum procedures. Since 1995, the practice of protection from deportation has meant that between 650 and 800 Turkish citizens a year have been granted leave to remain when their return to Turkey was considered unsafe. This means that a much larger number of unsuccessful applicants are deported back to their country of origin. The debate in Germany on the deportation of rejected asylum seekers has been intensifying since the 1990s.[17] This deportation dilemma has been further complicated by the fact that deportation of asylum seekers is at the discretion of the *Länder*. Hence, not least at *Länder* level, a long range of proposals to impose or lift bans on deporting asylum seekers back to Turkey has occupied the local administration and governments and mobilized lobbying from Kurdish organizations (for) and some Turkish organizations (against). In particular the CDU/CSU asserted that unsuccessful Kurdish asylum seekers should be deported to Turkey, whereas the several SPD controlled *Länder* governments, maintained that Turkey could not be considered a 'safe third state' for Kurds, and that Kurds could not be sent back to Turkey under Germany's new asylum legislation (in force since 1 July 1993). Since 1991 deportation bans of more than six months have to be decided unanimously by all the *Länder* Interior Ministers (see Marshall 2000: 106). Such a ban was imposed at federal level at the end of 1993, on the grounds that the safety of Kurdish asylum seekers upon their return to Turkey could not be guaranteed. The ban lasted for 10 months.

Germany and Turkey's EU candidacy

Turkey's quest for full membership of the EU has been, and is, one of the most difficult problems for EU enlargement.[18] This difficulty stems from a complete mismatch in the expectations of Turkey and the EU member states, worsened by the muddling of the economic, political, and even socio-cultural factors involved.

Turkey and the European Economic Community (EEC) signed an Association Agreement in Ankara in September 1963, which envisaged a three-step integration leading to full membership in 1987. Turkey felt that further economic and political integration into Europe was a well-deserved extension of their faithful security political partnership in NATO. However, the EU and its member states were against Turkey's full membership for the following main reasons: Turkey is a large country with political instability overshadowing economic growth. It poses a threat to the structural funds of the EU. Turkey has a population growth 10 times that of the average for EU member states (European Commission 1989: 4). Moreover, Turkey borders difficult neighbours such as Syria, Iraq, and Iran, not to mention the republics of the former Soviet Union. With the military coup in 1980, Turkey excluded itself from a round of enlargements whereby Greece joined the EU. The difficult relationship with Greece and the Cyprus issue added to the continued stalling of EU–Turkish negotiations.

In 1987, Turkey put in an ill-timed application for full EU membership. In the Commission's reply in 1989, Turkey was found 'not ready' for full integration into the EU. Soon after, the end of the Cold War added to the sensitivity of these issues. A range of central and eastern European countries began lining up for a comprehensive enlargement process. Despite its strategic geographic position as both a link to, and bulwark against, countries of Central Asia, Caucasia, and the Middle East, Turkey found itself at the back of the queue. The ensuing disappointment of the Turkish elite with EU countries in general, and Germany in particular, worsened (Balkir and Williams 1993: 40). The sensitive issue of Turkey's Europeanness began to dominate discussions in both policy making and academic circles. Articles on Turkey as 'the other' for European identification (Neumann and Welsh 1991), followed by the notion of 'clashes of civilizations' (Huntington 1993) linked contemporary Turkey–European relations with Europe's past fear of the conquering Ottoman Empire at worst, and its fear of Islam at best.[19] In Germany, the notion of the compatibility between Turkey's religious identity and EU membership has been questioned by the CDU and, in particular, the CSU.

However, although such notions still play a dominant role in discussions within both European and Turkish academic and political circles, more pragmatic reasons must be given prominence in any analysis. During the 1990s, Germany has been regarded as a key factor in the rejection of Turkey (Balkir and Williams 1993: 243). Among the reasons for this is that Germany is a major contributor to the structural funds of the EU. Another important critical issue in German–Turkish relations has been German criticism of the situation of human rights and democracy, in Turkey in general, and surrounding the Kurdish issue in particular. These issues have worried all Turkey's western partners and constitute a significant obstacle to Turkey's further integration into European cooperation (Robins 1996: 129; Müftüler-Bac 1997: 21–2; Barkey and Fuller 1998: 165–6). When Turkey was rejected as an EU candidate at the EU summit in Luxembourg in 1997, Turkey–German relations hit an all-time low as Turkey was particularly disappointed with the lack of support from Germany. Turkish Prime Minister Yilmaz went so far as to compare the German government's EU-enlargement policies with '*Lebensraum Politik*', the expansionist ideology of the Hitler period (*Frankfurter Rundschau*, 5 October 1998). During the German federal election in 1998, Yilmaz publicly reminded Turkish descent German voters not to forget the Luxembourg Summit (see Chapter 7 for further description).

Only with the SPD/*Die Grüne* coalition government in September 1998 did the 'ice-age' in German–Turkish relations begin to thaw. At the Helsinki Summit in 1999, the German government did not oppose, but instead supported Turkey's EU candidature. Initially, the Turkish government greeted this development positively. Yet, it is also acknowledged that because of the Copenhagen criteria, real membership negotiations are not immediate. Quite typical of the sentiment in Ankara, one national assembly deputy commented: 'EU candidacy includes so much that it takes away the happiness', and then he continued to outline the parallels, rather than differences, between the SPD/*Die Grüne* government and it's predecessor [interview with National Assembly deputy for *Anavatan Partisi* (ANAP), 25 October 2000].

Germany and human rights problems in Turkey

The German government did not cut off relations with Turkey during the Turkish state crises and coups in 1960, 1971, and 1980 (Steinbach 1996: 418). However, since 1980, the human rights violations in Turkey, not least the insurgency in southeastern Anatolia and the systematic abuse of human rights by the Turkish state in dealing with the Kurdish opposition, have captured the attention of German politicians. All German political parties have employed a critical view of domestic political developments in Turkey, although the sharpness of such criticism declines steadily from left to right on the party political spectrum.

In particular, while they were in government (1983–98), the CDU and CSU as well as the *Freie Demokratische Partei* (FDP) continued to stress that they did not want to alienate and isolate Turkey, which was seen as an important economic and security political partner. By contrast, the SDP, *Die Grüne*, and lately, the *Partei des Demokratischen Sozialismus* (PDS) have called for further pressure on the Turkish government to better the human rights and democracy situation, in order to find a political solution to the Kurdish problem. They have also called for the government to stop the export of weapons to Turkey, and to accept and not deport asylum seekers from Turkey. Only a minority of the entries on Turkey in the *Bundestag* up through the 1980s and the 1990s do not relate to the issue of human rights and democracy in Turkey. A pattern emerges in which the German governments' policies toward Turkey were particularly challenged by the SPD in the1980s, *Die Grüne* from the mid-1980s, and PDS in the 1990s. The SPD, however, has become less and less dominant in this respect, compared to the early 1980s, with a now more open-armed and constructive take on Turkey's place in Europe. Indeed, German–Turkish relations have improved since the SPD/*Die Grüne* coalition government came into power in 1998. The presence of *Die Grüne* in the SPD-led government coalition (1998–) has helped to quiet some of the critical voices linking Turkish human rights violations and the Kurdish issue to EU candidacy. Still, the feeling of being unjustly slighted by the West has been an often-repeated refrain in Ankara. The main argument is that Germany criticizes Turkey without considering the particular security political and economic dimensions of the Kurdish issue, and without acknowledging the progress made by Turkey in the area of human rights and democracy.

Military cooperation

German concern with human rights deficiencies in Turkey and the Kurdish conflict has also contested the continuity of a major dimension in German–Turkish relations, namely weapon deliveries. German and Turkish military cooperation dates back to when Mahmut II asked Friedrich Wilhelm II for German instruction officers to help modernize the Ottoman Army. After the Second World War, security political relations between Turkey and Germany were institutionalized through common membership in NATO. There was a convergence of German and Turkish security political interests based on perceptions of the USSR as a threat. With the Truman Doctrine, both countries gained significance by being designated as guardian blocks in the western security system against Soviet expansion. Partly under the auspices of NATO, military cooperation between Germany and Turkey increased. The most important components were arms aid worth several hundred million US dollars yearly, free delivery of used military equipment, and cooperation on arms production (Steinbach 1996: 418).

Today, Turkey has the largest army in NATO, and since 1980 its military expenditure has increased considerably. From 1982 to 1991 military expenditure among European NATO countries grew by 0.6 per cent per year on average, except for in Turkey where annual growth averaged 4 per cent. Similarly, arms procurement expenditures shrank by 0.1 per cent per year for European NATO countries during this period, but in Turkey they grew by 10 per cent per year [Stockholm International Peace Research Institute (SIPRI) 1993]. The same growth is observed in the late 1990s (SIPRI 2001). Thus, Turkey is among the ten main recipients of major conventional weapons in the world and it spent 4.3–5.4 per cent of its GDP on military expenditure in 1997–99. Germany and the US are the main suppliers of weapons to Turkey. From 1960 to1992 Germany supplied arms worth GBP 1.92 billion, some of which were supplied under the NATO Cascade programme (*Financial Times*, 31 March 1992; SIPRI 1998, 2001).[20]

Throughout the 1980s, the German opposition in the *Bundestag*, notably the *Bundnis90/Die Grüne* and later the PDS, repeatedly requested a halt to the delivery of weapons to 'a country at war with one of its ethnic minorities' (see among others, *Deutscher Bundestag* 1993b). However, not until March 1992 did the government briefly take measures in this direction, due to evidence that German tanks were being used in the Turkish military's armed struggle against Kurdish separatist movements.[21] Foreign Minister Hans-Dietrich Genscher told a news conference that 'the persecution of the Turkish civilian population by military units was unacceptable', and that all German arms supplies to Turkey would be suspended (SIPRI 1995: 775–6).[22] The Turkish government responded with indignation to the German move. In an interview with the *Cumhurryiet* newspaper on 29 March, Turkey's President Özal said that since unification Germany had sought 'to intervene everywhere in order to prove that it was a major power' and that 'in the past Hitler's Germany did the same thing, although in other ways' (Keesing 1992: 38822).

In April and May 1994, there was also a short-lived halt to arms sales to Turkey. Foreign Minister Kinkel lifted the ban on the grounds that there was insufficient evidence that German military equipment was being used in actions against the Kurds (Keesing 1994: 39978 and 0026–7). Finally, in March 1995 the German government, protesting against yet another offensive of the Turkish army in northern Iraq, blocked payment of a DM 150 million subsidy for the construction of two frigates for the Turkish navy (Keesing 1995: 40469). Since 1995 German military aid to Turkey has been stopped and German weapons only end up in Turkey by way of normal purchase (Kramer 1998: 4). Even such sales still cause rifts and cracks. Turkish demand for Leopard-II tanks posed a major internal problem for the SPD/*Die Grüne* government as the latter opposed the sale (*Süddeutsche Zeitung*, 21 October 1999). Still, arms exports to Turkey have increased under the SPD/*Die Grüne* government (*Tageszeitung*, 2 November 2000).

Migration, migrant transnationalism, and international relations

Post-war immigration plays a significant role in the development of Turkish–German (and Turkish–European) relations. Generally, migration may in and of itself affect relations between the host country and homeland. Deutsch *et al.* (1957), in their theoretical contribution to understanding regional integration, argued that increased social and economic interaction between the populations of two countries leads to greater mutual understanding and eventually the formal political institutionalization of the bilateral or multilateral relationship. However, the experience of post-war migration to Europe has proved this theory wrong. When migration control and migrant incorporation become issues for resolution in bilateral negotiation, they do not always serve to improve relations between the sending and the receiving countries. For instance, a study of migration between Algeria and France found that issues arising from Algerian immigration reinforced a situation of dependency (Adler 1977). Similar conclusions are reiterated in recent research on the politics of migration in Euro–Mahgreb relations (Collinson 1996; see also Mahler 2000).

Turkey and Germany are inextricably linked through trade and economic support, security-political cooperation, and the multilateral ties in the realm of the EU and other international organizations. The extensive post-war migration has served to further link the domestic and foreign politics of the two countries. German domestic policies towards migrants play into foreign relations with Turkey. Turkish domestic policies affect flows of migration which are the concern of German authorities. In addition, issues which are not directly linked to migration, such as military cooperation or Turkey's EU candidacy are, as will be further described in Chapters 6 and 7, 'scaled up' because of the presence of such large number of Turkish citizens in Germany. Thus, sometimes migration has also played a significant role in curtailing closer political cooperation between Turkey and Germany.

Indeed, at times the issue of migration of Turks and Kurds, and their integration in Germany, has been a source of tension between German and Turkish governments. In those cases, the style and content of the mutual criticism of Germany and Turkey have been characterized as 'psychologically damaging' for both countries (Steinbach 1996: 420). It may be argued that the discrimination of Turkish citizens in Germany proved a welcome counter argument for Turkish political authorities at a time when Turkey's human rights abuse contributed to western European reluctance to include Turkey further in Europe. However, it must also be considered that the discrimination of citizens living abroad is a sensitive issue for any homeland. Problems of discrimination and integration are particularly sensitive when the sending country is as proud of its heritage as Turkey is, and when it parallels a process of political exclusion from European integration in which the 'Europeanness' of Turkey is challenged. In extreme cases, Turkey is scrutinized as non-European in terms of culture and religion. More commonly it is perceived as lacking in terms of standards of democracy, human rights, economic re-distribution, and standards of living.

Yet, importantly migration has also linked Turkey and Germany through the intense transnational relations in which migrants themselves engage. Family reunification and chain migration, high levels of remittances, intense business networks, and extensive use of Turkish media are all indicators that Turkish migrants and their descendants keep in touch with Turkey. Added to this are the transnational links among ethnic, religious, and party-political organizations which will be described in detail in the next two chapters. Through these organizations, migrants themselves engage in diplomatic relations between their country of origin and settlement.

4 Between homeland political and immigrant political mobilization

Patterns of homeland political mobilization among Turks and Kurds in Germany are as complex as the multi-level processes and actors involved. Since the 1970s, homeland political trends and movements have come and gone and come back yet again. This chapter presents the political mobilization within the main groups of Turks and Kurds in Germany in order to highlight the political plurality of the various parts of the community: How 'political' or 'transnational' are these main groups? Of which national and transnational networks are they a part? Who do they represent? Are they established through local initiatives or have they been set up with encouragement or support from organizations, political parties, or governments in Turkey? What are their goals? How would one characterize their relationship with German, Turkish, and European authorities? Once the homeland political engagement within the main groups is established, the chapter addresses the dynamics among the main groups. It explores, in particular, how Turkish politics divides the federal organizations to the extent that it becomes difficult for a common platform to be formed both among the main groups and within them.

Four decades of homeland political mobilization

Migrants and refugees from Turkey have a higher degree of organization in political organizations and parties of the homeland than do citizens of former Yugoslavia, Italy, and Greece (Federal Ministry for Labour and Social Security 1996: 410–11). Many of these organizations go back several decades although their aims, strategies, and membership bases have fluctuated over the years.

In the 1960s, there was little in the way of political mobilization among the Turkish citizens in Germany, because a majority of these were guestworkers, believing themselves to be temporary residents in Germany.[1] The earliest form of organization were the Turkish workers associations, which aimed to provide a 'home away from home' where the Turkish workers – at that time mostly living away from their families – could meet and drink Turkish tea, play backgammon, and discuss current events in Turkey. As one migrant who arrived in 1958 recalls:

> In the beginning of the 1960s the Turks were organized in workers associations. Right or Left or religious or Kurds or Laz – that did not matter. Only that you were Turkish and a worker.
>
> (Interview with IGMetall, 13 October 2000)

Among students from Turkey several organizations were founded, and their first federation, the *Almanya Türk Öğrenci Federasyonu* (ATÖF), was founded by nine Turkish student organizations in 1962.

Already from the mid-1960s both the ATÖF and the Turkish workers associations had become increasingly linked with Turkish politics. In the following decade and a half, they supported a wide range of parties and movements in Turkey in a more or less institutionalized way. At this stage, the homeland-political mobilization was mainly party-political and the main groups were divided between left-wing and right-wing parties. Indeed, the polarization between the extreme left and the extreme right in Turkey was replicated among the Turkish communities in Germany throughout the 1970s, sometimes culminating in violent clashes on German soil. This development was reinforced with the military coup in Turkey in September 1980. In relation to the coup, all political parties in Turkey were banned, politicians were exiled, and supporters of left- and right-wing parties and organizations, as well as trade unions, were imprisoned. Many went underground and left for western Europe. It is likely that a substantial number ended up in Germany because they had relatives and contacts in the rapidly growing community there.

Already by the beginning of the 1980s, and notably from the mid-1980s, two developments may be identified that added to the complexity of homeland-political organization in Germany. First, during the 1980s there was an increasing emphasis on *immigrant political agendas*, which were to supplement or, in some cases, meant to replace the *homeland political agenda* of the organizations. That is, it was increasingly recognized by the communities themselves that they had come to stay, and hence they started voicing their demands for more inclusive German policies of integration. Thus, in order to represent the interests of their members as immigrants, and not as Turks or Kurds, there was an increasing effort by organizations to redefine themselves as immigrant organizations. There were also a number of attempts by various political organizations to merge, in order to strengthen their positions as representatives advocating more immigrant rights, as will be discussed further at the end of this chapter. These developments were, and still are, heralded as the end of homeland political orientation among Turks in Germany, both by the communities themselves and in academic literature on the subject (see among others, Özcan 1992).

Today, most of the associations and federations do voice demands on behalf of their members as immigrants. In addition, many of them lobby the Turkish government for the right to vote in Turkish elections from abroad. Yet, as will be discussed further later, the present landscape of organizations indicates the continuing significance of homeland politics alongside immigrant politics. Many organizations, for example, represent only Turks rather than various groups of immigrants from other countries. Accordingly, the homeland political heritage and current agendas of these organizations have made it difficult to form a common platform for Turkish citizens *vis-à-vis* German political authorities and policy makers.

In a second development, the complexity of homeland political engagement was reinforced by the mobilization around ethnic and religious agendas. Here,

48 *Between homeland and immigrant political mobilization*

ethnic mobilization is understood as the mobilization around common origin, language, and the like. As will be described at greater length later, these developments are related to a particular Turkish understanding of national identity on the one hand, and the Turkish version of laicism on the other. Turkey hosts a vast plurality of different cultural traditions and languages, but in this book mainly the mobilization around Kurdish identity will be addressed. The Kurdish organizations constitute an integral part of the political work of their counterparts in Turkey, because the freedom of expression and political organization granted to Kurds in Germany has allowed for discussions and for the formulation of demands not possible in Turkey. Also, religious groups have become increasingly active in Germany. Through the 1980s there has been a rapid institutionalization of Sunni Muslim movements among Turkish citizens in Germany. Partly as a counter reaction to this, but mostly in response to political developments and persecution in Turkey, the Alevi community has also started organizing itself very rapidly.

This means that the following sections will concentrate on three main, often overlapping, categories: first, those groups mobilized around Turkish party-political ideologies and parties; second, those groups mobilized around freedom for religious expression; and third, the ethnic mobilization around Kurdish identity. Intersecting these categories are the organizations based on occupation, such as the students' organizations at German universities or employers' associations (see also Appendix B).[2]

Who represents whom?

Before turning to the different groups and movements in greater detail, it is worth commenting on one of most difficult issues in any analysis of transnational political mobilization: the issue of how representative migrant and refugee associations are with respect to the constituency they claim to represent.

The main movements have undergone a remarkably similar process of institutionalization in the last two decades. The vast majority of Kurdish and Turkish associations are very local, foremost serving as meeting points for parts of the communities. However, during the last two decades they have established federations to coordinate their work and represent them at federal – even European – level. It is in the work of the federations that the political, and especially homeland political, identity of the organizations is identifiable. Thus, the description of these federations constitutes a cornerstone in the analysis of the changing patterns of homeland political mobilization of Turkish citizens in Germany. These organizations serve as representatives of the different homeland political interests *vis-à-vis* Turkish, German, and wider European authorities. They reflect, and, it may be argued, serve to reinforce the divisions among party-political, ethnic, and religious groups among migrants and refugees.

Organizational developments, in terms of members and followers, are significant for understanding the overall patterns of mobilization in the various political movements and groups. However, the issue of how representative these federations are is a grey area both in terms of factual data (members x of organization y) and the conclusions that may be derived from these numbers. This means that the organizations cannot be assessed on their claimed membership alone; such figures should be treated with great caution because data can be hard to obtain and is often not verifiable from sources other than the associations and federations themselves.[3] Not surprisingly, the organizations themselves will tend to give estimates of members which include 'followers and supporters', that is, non-paying members. Often, an organization will compensate a low number of actual paying members with the high attendance at their political events, such as big meetings in stadiums, demonstrations, and the like. However, these figures should be treated with caution as well. Large-scale political events are also social events, and the cheering crowd may not be devoted to the cause of the organization for the rest of the year.[4] Also, there seems to be some 'mass-meeting-tourism' going on, where notably younger people turn up due to a mixture of curiosity and boredom (NRW 1997). Thus, in the following description the size of the various federations is indicated by their number of membership organizations.

Transnational party-political mobilization

The whole spectrum of Turkish party-politics is represented in Germany in one way or another. The left-wing spans from the 'orthodox' communists and more extreme Maoist groups, to the much more middle-of-the-road organizations related to the social democratic parties in Turkey, many of which defend the basic principles of Kemalism. Similarly, the right-wing organizations also include very different groups such as the radical right-wing and nationalist organizations and the more moderate organizations that are closer to the conservative liberal parties in Turkey [such as *Dogru Yol Partisi* (DYP) and ANAP].

The leftist movements

In Turkey, the more radical leftist movements have experienced a major decline since the 1970s, when leftist factions in Turkey included 60,000 armed militants (Pope and Pope 1997: 132). In the period until the coup in 1980, Turkey's major cities were divided into civil-war-like zones of extreme right and extreme left. However, during the 1980s the movements in Turkey experienced an extended period of rivalry and splits. The ideological confusion of these communist groups after 1989, as well as the increased mobilization around ethnic issues such as the Alevi and the Kurdish questions, has drained these movements of members and sources of funding. Still, both in Turkey and Germany a multitude of groups and material may be found among Turks and Kurds, which use language and rhetoric very similar to that of the 1970s.

Thus, the more revolutionary factions of Turkish politics are by no means mass-movements, and their circles of followers while devoted, are few in number. Such left-wing movements have, as mentioned, been active in Germany since the mid-1960s, and most notably in the 1970s. They can be divided into the groups of 'orthodox communists', which originate in Moscow-oriented communism and related to Turkish parties such as the *Türkiye Komünist Partisi* (TKP) and the *Türkiye Işçi Partisi* (TIP), and 'the New Left', which originated in revolutionary, mainly Maoist, but also Albanian communism (for more detail, see Özcan 1992; Østergaard-Nielsen 1998). The New Left differs from the more orthodox communists in terms of ideology and, seemingly more importantly, in terms of aims and activities. The New Left uses far more extreme and revolutionary strategies than the orthodox communists. Their mainly historical aim of organizing a revolution in Turkey from Europe means that they are watched closely by the German *Verfassungschutz*; and thus work underground and generally are difficult to track down.

While the orthodox communists have tried to follow a strategy of fusion, the New Left has, in Turkey as well as in Germany, been characterized by an extensive process of fission. Accordingly, today the orthodox communists in Turkey are mainly represented by the *Özgürlük ve Dayanişma Partisi* (ÖDP), which also organizes panel discussions and other events throughout Germany (*Sabah*, 4 June 1997). The New Left, on the other hand, is represented by a range of smaller parties, of which the main groups are: the *Devrimci Sol*, the DKHP-C, the MLKP, and the TKP-ML. One informant once noted that 'By now every letter of the alphabet has been used up, and they have started using hyphens and backlashes to set themselves apart'. Admittedly, to find ones way through the jungle of leaflets and banners and posters is not easy. There is more polarization and division within the radical New Left than in any of the other groups within the Turkish and Turkish–Kurdish communities. In part, this follows the changes and divisions within radical left-wing movements in Turkey (and on a larger international scale).

Since 1980, groups related to both the orthodox communists and the New Left have founded immigrant political organizations in Germany with a different name and (somewhat) different outlook than their political counterparts in Turkey. In particular, two of these organizations illustrate how revolutionary ideology has been exchanged for a critical stance towards Turkish politics, how migrant politics is inseparable from homeland politics, and how specific party political links may be cut or re-introduced. The main immigrant politically oriented organization of the New Left, the *Demokratik Işçi Dernekleri Federasyonu* (DIDF), was founded in 1980 in order to counter 'discrimination on the basis of race, language, gender or religion' (interview with DIDF, 14 July 1997). Similarly, former orthodox communists formed the *Türkiyeli Göçmen Dernekleri Federasyonu* (GDF) in 1988 'due to demands from the migrants to promote equal rights for immigrants in Germany' (GDF 1994). Both organizations are among the smallest of the Turkish federations in Germany, with approximately 25 membership organizations each.

The GDF and the DIDF organize a host of migrant political activities emphasizing their role as migrant, rather than Turkish, political representatives.[5] However, they also engage themselves in Turkish politics, albeit in quite different ways. Both organizations voice their opinion on developments in Turkish politics, and in doing so they are usually the most critical opponents of Turkish state and government policies or of the inability of the opposition to bring about change. Moreover, in particular, the GDF repeatedly calls for voting rights in Turkish elections for Turks living outside Turkey. With a more critical tone, DIDF publishes information on the Kurdish issue and human rights abuse in Turkey (DIDF 1995, 2000). While the GDF stress their lack of particular party political ties to Turkey, the DIDF emphasize their close contacts to 'democratic parties, organizations and human rights movements in Turkey, Turkish Kurdistan, and Europe' (DIDF 1993). Most notably, the DIDF conveys the speeches and opinions of the marginal left-wing Turkish political party, the *Emeğin Partisi* (EMEP) in their membership journal, and host meetings with party leaders in Germany (DIDF 1998; own observations).

Both organizations also engage themselves in the Turkish politics that takes place in Germany. Indeed, the GDF stresses that the democratization of Turkey is an important part of their immigrant political agenda since nationalist propaganda from Turkey or 'islamization... by fundamental political Islamic groups' divides the communities abroad (GDF 1998). The organization, therefore, combines its call for a solution to the problems of democracy in Turkey and the Kurdish conflict, with its aim to further more positive dialogue between Kurdish and Turkish immigrants in Germany. In this way, the homeland politically oriented work is legitimized in the name of harmonious coexistence and cooperation among Turks and Kurds in Germany.

The 'Grey Wolves'

The main 'other' for the above-mentioned left-wing groups is the nationalist movement popularly referred to as the 'Grey Wolves' (*bozkurtlar*). In Turkey, this movement is headed by the *Milli Hareket Partisi* (MHP). The ideology of the MHP includes both pan-Turkism and pre-Islamic Turkish mythology, with strong religious elements.[6] MHP is anti-communist and anti-separatist (anti-Kurdish). In Germany, the main Turkish nationalist organization is the *Avrupa Demokratik Ülkücü Türk Dernekleri Federasyonu* (ADÜTDF), also called the *Türk Federasyon*, which was founded in 1978 in Frankfurt by 64 nationalist organizations from not only Germany, but also Austria, Holland, France, and Belgium.[7] Throughout the 1980s, the *Türk Federasyon* gradually lost support, but this trend has been reversed in the 1990s. Presently, the federation claims to have around 200 membership organizations. The *Türk Federasyon* itself interprets this increase as being a result of Turkish citizens' experience of discrimination in Germany. This experience has made them turn to an organization that celebrates Turkish identity. Indeed, in the aftermath of the fire attacks on Turks in Solingen and Mölln the organization claims to have nearly doubled its number of members (*Verfassungsschutz* 1997: 167).

The *Türk Federasyon* likes to present itself as an immigrant political organization without explicit links to the MHP. However, their monthly journal, *The Türk Federasyon Bülteni*, published since 1996, indicates very strong links with

Turkish politics. In the journal, one finds information about the various membership organizations and their activities, and also articles praising the ideology of MHP and not least stating the evils of the ideologies of left-wing and Kurdish organizations in Turkey and Germany.[8] Perhaps more tellingly, at the organizations twentieth annual meeting in 1998 in Germany, the new board was 'elected' by a mere announcement to a 15,000 strong crowd, in the presence of the leader of MHP, Devlet Bahçeli, who later gave a rallying speech (own observations 23 May 1998). Indeed, the *Türk Federasyon* is one of the migrant organizations most closely associated with a Turkish political party.

Federative activities, however, also include immigrant politics, such as a campaign against drug abuse and guidelines to parents finding it hard to control their children in German society. Many of the membership organizations of the *Türk Federasyon* are sports organizations, mainly football and 'fighting sports'. The most important activity of *Türk Federasyon*, however, seems to be its function as an ideological and political focal point for its members. Their meetings (local as well as federative) play very heavily on symbols of Turkish nationalism with flags, songs, the chanting of slogans on Turkey's greatness, and large crowds making the hand sign of the Grey Wolves (a fist with the little finger and index finger raised). These meetings are rarely attended by outsiders, as the *Türk Federasyon* restricts access in response to their very negative image in the German press. In an attempt to change this image, the *Türk Federasyon* seems to have made a conscious effort to rid itself of its violent image stemming from the role of the Grey Wolves in Turkish politics in the 1970s and the clashes between left and right in Germany in the 1970s and 1980s. If an organization wants to become a member of the federation, they must first be approved by the board and 'demonstrate that they are able to keep their heads cool despite provocations from the radical left' (interview with *Türk Federasyon*, 13 February 1998).

The Kemalists

The vast majority of Turkish migrant organizations belong to the moderate right- or left-wing spectrum of Turkish politics. These organizations are first and foremost important immigrant political spokes-partners *vis-à-vis* both German and Turkish officials. Even so, these groups usually do have an opinion on Turkish politics, and more or less institutionalized ties with various Turkish social democratic or conservative liberal parties. Thus, although these groups often present themselves as representatives of *all* Turkish citizens in Germany, they are clearly not viewed as such by the other groups in the community.

One of the main migrant organizations to display explicit relations with the Social democratic parties in Turkey is the *Sosyaldemokrat Halk Dernekleri Federasyonu* (HDF). The HDF, which today represents around 40 organizations in Germany, was founded in Berlin in 1977, in the presence of parliamentarians from the Turkish social democratic *Cumhürriyet Halk Partisi* (CHP). Indeed, one of the leaders of the HDF, Ercan Karakaş, later represented the CHP in the Turkish Grand National Assembly. Today, the HDF formulates its relationship with social democrats in Turkey as being that they '[We] have a relationship of solidarity with the social democratic movement in Turkey, but at the same time view them with critical eyes' (*Tageszeitung*, 17 September 1994). Still, prominent members of the Turkish, as well as German, social democratic parties turn up for general assemblies and other events (see *Milliyet*, 24 October 1993; *Milliyet*, 24 October 1995).

The HDF's priority has clearly shifted from being mainly focused on Turkish politics to emphasizing the issues pertaining to immigrants in Germany. However, the legacy of Turkish social democratic ideology [both the CHP and the other main social democratic party, the *Democrat Sol Partisi* (DSP)] is still to be found in the activities and material of the HDF. As is the case in Turkey, Turkish social democrats in Germany consider themselves guards of Turkish laicism and Kemalism outside of Turkey. The Kemalist legacy makes for less cooperation with Kurdish organizations than is the case among the more left-wing organizations. The laicist principle means that there is little cooperation with the Sunni Muslim organizations.

A more clear-cut example of this trend are the organizations called the *Almanya'da Atatürk Düsünce Derneği* (AADD), which were set up to promote the ideas of Kemalism and protect the name of Atatürk in Germany.[9] The leader of the AADD in Cologne was previously a member of the HDF but set up the AADD to counter the resurgence of Islam and Kurdish nationalism among Turks in Germany, by informing Germans and Turkish youth about Atatürk. As their leader formulates it:

> We inform the youth with seminars. We tell them which dangers there unfortunately are for Turkish people in Germany. For example, it is dangerous to mix with fundamentalists, separatists and racists. We inform them why Atatürk said "Peace at home is peace in the world" and on the significance of the nation. The nation is like the body. When the finger hurts the whole body hurts. So one must be sensitive to separatism.
> (Interview with AADD, 10 October 2000)

Accordingly, the AADD publishes material on Turkish history, and issues such as the ideas of Atatürk or 'Armenian terrorism'. Their leader writes letters of complaint to German newspapers and policy makers whenever they, in his opinion, misunderstand Turkey's domestic or foreign policy.[10]

The Conservative Liberals

A large group of Turkish citizens in Germany is said to belong to the moderate right. This group is growing in Germany with the emergence of the 'business-class' of Turkish employers and lawyers among others. Besides the Turkish employer associations, one of the most significant organizations representing this group in terms of membership and political influence, is the *Hürriyetçi Türk Alman Dostluk Cemiyeti* (Hür-Türk). The Hür-Türk was founded in 1979 in Bonn on the initiative of the then leader of the Turkish *Adalet Partisi* (AP), Suleyman Demirel, as well as politicians from the German CDU. According to the Hür-Türk's written material, the organization was founded because: 'Turkish fellow citizens in Germany who belong to the political centre also had the wish to form associations and seek friendly relations between Germans and Turks.' (Hür-Türk 1990). Today, almost 20 years later, the organization represents approximately 55 organizations in Germany and nine in Ankara. The Hür-Türk presents itself simultaneously as conservative-liberal in its political ideological orientation, while stressing that it 'does not belong to any political party' (interview with Hür-Türk, 22 May 1998). Admittedly, from the reports in the membership journal of the Hür-Türk, many of the member organizations do not seem very political, but serve as cafes or sports clubs. However, at the federal level, the Hür-Türk is far from apolitical as it attracts support from politicians in the CDU in Germany, and the ANAP and the DYP in Turkey. The organizations' leaflets usually contain a list of 'honorary members' dominated by prominent politicians from these three parties. Indeed, the leader of the Hür-Türk is a member of *Bundestag* for the CDU.

The Hür-Türk seeks to present itself as having foremost an immigrant political agenda, in particular, to bring German and Turkish citizens together. A wide range of activities is carried out to meet that aim. Clearly, the Hür-Türk is also eager to promote the image of Turks as successful employers who contribute significantly to German society (interview with Hür-Türk, 18 February 1998). There are close organic and institutional links to Turkish employers' associations.[11] However, from the publications and interviews with Hür-Türk leaders it is clear that not only the relations between Germans and Turks in Germany, but also the relationship between Germany and Turkey is a priority. While social democratic (and of course leftist) organizations always stress their critical dialogue with Turkish policy makers, the Hür-Türk itself claims that 'work behind the scenes', that is, informal diplomacy between Turkey and Germany, is an integral part of the work of the executive committee of the Hür-Türk. Especially during periods of mismatches in expectations between the German and Turkish government, the leader and general secretary utilize their personal networks to facilitate informal talks between German and Turkish politicians. Leaders of the Hür-Türk are almost always present when politicians and officials of the highest rank visit Turkey (interview with Hür-Türk, 22 May 1998). In turn, the homeland political dimension also serves to mobilize members and membership organizations. For instance, when an organization in Wolfsburg joined the federation of the Hür-Türk, the reason quoted in the membership journal was that:

> […] our federal leader, Dr. Hans Stercken, has provided very useful services during his long service for both communities. Furthermore, due to his political concerns he has prevented the extension of the arms embargo against Turkey. Those are the decisive reasons for our decision to join the Hür-Türk.
> (*Hür-Türk Journal* 1998/2: 14)

To represent the opinion of both the right-wing political parties in Turkey and be affiliated with the CDU involves a continuing diplomatic effort, given the way in which German–Turkish relations have developed in the 1990s. Hence, thorny issues in the relationship between German and Turkey are cautiously treated in the membership journals. The Hür-Türk supports close security-political and economic cooperation between Turkey and the EU, is very much against Kurdish separatism, and treats the issue of Islam with a very sensitive approach, indicating that Turkish right-wing organizations are much closer to Turkish Sunni Muslim organizations in Germany than are the leftist and social democratic organizations.

Religious mobilization: Sunnis and Alevis

Islam in Turkey and among the Turks and Kurds in Germany is a complex affair. Most importantly, of the Turkish citizens in Germany approximately two-thirds are Sunni Muslims and one-third are Alevis. Socially, as well as politically, these groups are separate. There is a high degree of endogamy within Alevi and Sunni communities (see Mandel 1996: 157), and Alevis and Sunni movements abroad support different Turkish political parties and principles. Because of the discrimination they have experienced at the hands of the Sunni majority, Alevis have been strong supporters of the principle of laicism since the founding of the Republic of Turkey. Since there is nothing in the way of cooperation between the organizations representing the two groups, they will be treated separately. In addition, the Sunnis and Alevis are by no means homogenous groups. The subsequent sections will briefly present the main developments of the various movements and federations in Germany.

The Sunnis

Almost all Turkish citizens are Muslims, and their religious organizations have attracted a great deal of attention from both Turkish and German authorities. Indeed, the increase in Sunni Muslim organizations in Germany since the 1980s has been interpreted as a 're-islamization' of the Turkish communities there. Admittedly, the number of religious organizations in Germany have risen as Turkish migrants decided to stay, and these organizations are voicing demands for the freedom and support necessary to practice their religion in Germany. In addition, developments in Turkey have served to draw attention to the religious identity of Turks and Kurds in Germany. Notably, the rise of the Sunni Muslim *Refah Partisi* (during the 1990s), its participation in the coalition government with the DYP in 1996/97, and its subsequent bans have reinforced German perceptions of Turks as coming from a Muslim country.[12]

The landscape of Sunni Muslim organizations in Germany is heterogeneous, reflecting the plurality of Sunni Muslim movements and ideologies in Turkey.[13] The first Turkish Sunni movements to set up organizations in Germany were Sufi-tariquats such as Süleymancilar and Nurcular, the special religious orders in Turkey that emphasize religious education. Thus, in the early 1970s the first Sunni organization, called the *Verband der Islamischen Kulturzentren* (VIKZ), was set up by the Süleymancilar because 'no one else seemed to be meeting the religious needs of the workers'. This initiative was soon followed by other Sufi movements such as the Nurcus, as well as groups more explicitly associated with a Turkish political party such as the *Islamische Gemeinschaft Milli Görüş* (IGMG). In part, as a reaction to these developments, the Turkish State's Directorate of Religious Affairs, Diyanet, set up their own federation, the *Diyanet Işleri Türk Islam Birliği* (DITIB), in 1982. Between them the VIKZ, *Milli Görüş*, and DITIB represent an estimated 1,300 mosques and praying places in Germany, with the DITIB in charge of more than 775, and the VIKZ and the *Milli Görüş* with 300 and 275, respectively (*Deutscher Bundestag* 2000).

Sunni organizations between homeland politics and immigrant politics

Because of their different historical trajectory, the Sunni organizations in Germany have very different relations with Turkey and Turkish politics. They range from being a part of the Turkish administration (DITIB) to being closely linked to a particular political party (*Milli Görüş*), to trying their best to avoid being linked to Turkish politics and instead emphasizing their membership of more global Sunni networks (Süleymancilar and Nurcus). Indeed, these latter movements' networks are truly world-wide. Their offices include the same material translated into dozens of different languages and scripts. The Süleymancilar and the Nurcular are eager to emphasize that they differ from other Sunni Muslim organizations by 'not being the tool of Ankara – or any Turkish party' (interview with VIKZ, 15 July 1997). Also, both Süleymancilar and Nurcular stress that they are not 'fundamentalists', meaning that they are not in favour of introducing the Şariat in Turkey. However, in the material of both organizations the principle of laicism as it is practiced in Turkey (or France) is the object of much scrutiny.[14] It is, for instance, argued that: 'In many states, laicism is misused for political reasons. It has become a tool in the hand of politicians with which they can suppress and discriminate against religious communities.' (Jama'at Un-Nur 1995).

In stark contrast to these organizations, the *Milli Görüş* has explicit political links to the homeland. Although the issue of economic support is not something that the organization wishes to make public, the *Milli Görüş* does not (any longer) hide its close relationship with the Turkish Islamic oriented *Fazilet Partisi*. The General Secretary of the *Milli Görüş*, Mehmet Sabri Erbakan, is the nephew of Necmettin Erbakan, who founded and headed the predecessor party to the *Fazilet Partisi*, and at the last two national elections in Turkey several leaders of the *Milli Görüş* stood as candidates, of which two were elected in 1995 and one in 1999. These politicians, as well as others from Turkey, come to speak when the *Milli Görüş* organizes their annual large-scale festivals in Germany, with up to 50,000 participants (see *Türkiye*, 15 June 1997). Still, the *Milli Görüş* does not like to represent itself as a party-political branch of *Fazilet*. A leading member of the *Milli Görüş* formulates it like this:

> The role we play in Europe is different from Turkey. Here we are dealing with a different reality and here we are a religious organization. We are building mosques, not party centres or offices. We are educating imams... but

obviously it is clear that up to 90 per cent of our members, because they are religious oriented people, automatically prefer Refah, now Fazilet.

(Interview with *Milli Görüş*, 11 October 2000)

The *Verfassungsschutz* watches over the *Milli Görüş* because it does not support the Kemalist notion of secularism. Although the *Milli Görüş* does not explicitly wish for the introduction of Sunni Muslim rule, it makes general calls for increased tolerance of the Sunni Muslim way of life in Turkey as well as in Germany. The *Verfassungschutz* also monitors the other more explicitly homeland political Sunni organizations in Germany: the *Islam Cemaatleri ve Cemiyetleri Birliği* (ICCB). With only around 1,000 members and an estimated 3,000–4,000 participants in its large-scale meetings, the ICCB is small and marginal compared to the *Milli Görüş* (*Verfassungsschutz* 2000: 203). The organization is, however, the most radical of all Sunni organizations. In the publications of the ICCB the former leader, Kaplan, presents himself as 'The Emir of the Believers and the Kalif of the Muslims'. In German press, however, Kaplan is regarded as the 'Khomeni from Köln' (see among others, *Tageszeitung*, 20 January 1987), because he continuously advocated the introduction of Islamic rule in Turkey – sometimes with revolutionary means modeled on the Iranian revolution.

The immigrant-oriented work of the Sunni Muslim organizations follows two inter-related strands: an *inward* part of their work consists of catering to the religious needs of Muslims by providing praying places/mosques, Imams, and Koran schools, and organizing hac, that is, pilgrimage to Mecca. Usually, the Sunni organizations have a fund for burial costs, which is relatively ample. They also provide social services for youths such as sports clubs, and for women, including training courses in computers or needlework. The organizations (apart from ICCB) argue that Islam has much to offer Turkish youth who find it difficult to gain a foothold in German society. Within this argument the DITIB is criticized by the other organizations for not having any knowledge of the situation in Germany. The DITIB representatives rarely have a good command of German as they are sent from Ankara on a five year basis only.

In addition, the last two decades have witnessed Sunni organizations lobbying for general recognition of the Muslim communities in Germany. This more *outward* part of their activities is centred around the problems faced by Muslims living in a Christian country. Sunni Muslim organizations are increasingly aware of their often very negative image in German society, policy-making circles, and the press. In recent years, they have been 'opening the doors to visitors', including publishing material on their understanding of Islam, and on their activities and role in the community. In this respect, all organizations stress that they are very much concerned with constructive dialogue with Christians and other religious communities. Indeed, most organizations, bar the ICCB, have moved away from the 'backyard mosques' and towards dialogue with German local and national authorities on the role and place of Islam in German society.

The list of demands for recognition of Islam is long: the organizations lobby for religious teaching in German schools, for better representation of the Sunni

Muslim faith in German school books, and for clear marking of foodstuff that contain ingredients Muslims should not eat. High on the agenda is, of course, the recognition of Islam as an official religion in Germany on par with Judaism. In some ways these immigrant political agendas relate to the homeland political agenda. The quest for practice of religion in public space in Germany reiterates the political agenda of Sunni Muslim movements in Turkey. Successful lobbying in Germany on the issue of head-scarves or Koran schools would send a strong message to the political authorities in Turkey.

The Sunni Muslim organizations have tried to form common platforms to represent the federations *vis-à-vis* the German authorities. The first such platform was the Islamrat, formed by the VIKZ and the Jama'at Un-Nur, among others, in 1986, and now including 23 Muslim federations including *Milli Görüş* (NRW 1997: 175). However, the Süleymancilar have left, allegedly because they did not want to be in the same organization as the large, influential, and explicitly party-political *Milli Görüş* (interview with VIKZ, 15 July 1997). Instead, the VIKZ has, along with 17 other organizations including the Avrupa Türk Islam Birliği (ATIB), founded the Zentralrat der Muslime in 1994. The Islamrat and the Zentralrat have largely the same goals. Only the DITIB is not a part of any such efforts but works on its own because of its official representative status.

The Alevis

As opposed to the Sunni Muslim groups or the Kurdish movements, the Alevis became mobilized relatively late even though they have been discriminated against at various levels since the birth of the Turkish Republic. The Alevi issue represents an important political and social phenomenon in Turkey.[15] The exact number of Alevis is unknown, but estimates centre around 20 per cent of the population in Turkey and considerably higher among citizens living in Germany (Poulton 1997: 256). One moderate estimate states that there are approximately 13 million Alevis in Turkey and approximately 600,000–700,000 Alevis in Germany (ZfT 1998a: 157). Both Kurds and Turks are Alevis, with Kurdish Alevis as the 'minority within the minority'; an estimated 10–30 per cent of Turkey's Alevis are Kurds (Barkey and Fuller 1998: 67).

Alevism has its roots in the folk-Islam of Anatolia, and is usually traced back to the thirteenth century. Alevis distance themselves from the Iranian Shia, the Syrian Alawites, or, for that matter, any other Shia group. It is, however, an easily made assumption that Alevis are the Shiites of Turkey, as they, as opposed to Sunnis, believe in Ali as the rightful successor to Muhammed. The Alevis themselves explain that 'Alivi' means 'supporter of Ali' in Turkish [*Avrupa Alevi Birlik Federasyony* (AABF) 1997: 5]. Academic interpretations link Alevism with pre-Islamic traditions of fireworship in Iran (Barkey and Fuller 1998: 66), and, indeed, Alevism also differs markedly from the other branches of Islam in both content and form. Regarding form, the rituals are centred around a Cem (the Alevi place of worship) and not a mosque. There is no ramadan nor *hac*. Men and women carry out the religious rituals together in which music and dance play a central role, and women do not wear head-scarves.

Especially in the 1990s, there has been increasing attention to the political alignment of Alevis in Turkey. There seems to be a consensus on the fact that Alevis are left-wing in general and social democrats in particular. This political alignment is sometimes explained rather dryly as 'the enemy (Kemalism) of our enemies (Sunnis) is our friend' (interview with AABF, 3 December 1997). Thus, given their interest in curbing the powers of the Sunni majority, Alevis were strong supporters of the founding of the secular Republic (Vorhoff 1995: 17). Alevis are also associated with Marxist–Leninist influenced parties and movements (see Feindt-Riggers and Steinbach 1997: 28–9; Poulton 1997: 254), most likely a result of their history of discrimination by Turkish authorities (for this argument see Vorhoff 1995: 18). Left- and right-wing clashes in the 1970s were often also Alevi and Sunni feuds, such as the violent incident in the Turkish town Kahramanmaraş in 1978 where 107 people were killed and more than a thousand wounded (Pope and Pope 1997: 135). The association between Alevis and communist ideology explains why Alevis were particularly hard-hit by the military coup in 1980 and its aftermath with the rise of the Sunni Turco-Islamic synthesis and the *Refah Partisi* (later *Fazilet Partisi*).

This discrimination became intolerable in the beginning of the 1990s with two central tragic events. In July 1993, 37 young artists were killed and more than 80 people wounded when radical Islamists set fire to a hotel in the Turkish town of Sivas in which Alevi artists were staying while participating in a festival in honour of Pir Sultan Abdal. Less than two years later, in March 1995, two people were killed in Istanbul when alleged Islamist fundamentalists shot at two coffee houses known to be used by Alevis in the neighbourhood of Gaziosmanpaşa. This led to large-scale, violent demonstrations in which 27 people were killed and more than 100 wounded (AABF 1997: 20). In the aftermath of these events, Alevis have been increasingly dissatisfied with their traditional political party, CHP, leading to much speculation about the direction of the 'Alevi vote' in Turkish politics (see Poulton 1997: 257–61).

The mobilization of the Alevis had already begun in Germany by in the early 1990s, but speeded up with the above-mentioned events in Turkey. Between 1993 and 1996, the number of membership organizations of the main Alevi federation, the AABF, grew from 32 to approximately 120. Not a festival takes place without commemorating the dead, and a special room in the buildings of the AABF is dedicated to the victims of the Sivas Massacre with photos of each victim on the walls (own observations). Another important factor in this mobilization was the situation in Germany, where the Sunni Muslim organizations were calling for further rights to Islamic practice for Sunnis only. One of the founders of the first Alevi organizations in Germany explained how he was upset when he saw his mother pretend to observe Ramadan in order not to be scrutinized by her Sunni colleagues – in Hamburg (interview with AABF, 3 December 1997).

Immigrant and homeland political activities cannot be separated when it comes to the Alevis. The aim of the AABF is, according to its own publications, to work for the recognition of Alevism inside and outside of Turkey. In practice, this means an extensive information campaign to portray Alevis as the 'good' Muslims who are easy to integrate because of their lack of adherence to Sunni traditions. From Germany, Alevis urge the Turkish state to officially recognize Alevism and abolish the Directorate of Religious Affairs because it caters only for Sunnis. Moreover, Alevis abroad support Alevi organizations and political parties in Turkey. Indeed, the chairman of the AABF stood as a candidate for the marginal *Barış Partisi* in the 1999 Turkish general election.

The AABF continues to be the main representative of Alevis in Germany, and their yearly cultural festivals attract crowds of up to 40,000 people (*Tageszeitung*, 26 July 1997). It is, however, not the only Alevi organization. Kurdish Alevi and other Alevi organizations who take a different stance towards the Turkish state have been set up in the 1990s. In particular, opinions have been divided on the issue of the funding of Alevi organizations by the Turkish state. Some Alevi movements argue that they will lose their independence if they accept money and thus become another DITIB. Others, like the small, but in Turkey well-connected, *Cumhuriyet Eğitim Merkezi* (Cem Vakfı), support this trend. It argues that it is only fair if Alevis get support for education in return for their tax money (interview with Cem Vakfı, 12 October 2000).

The Kurds

Kurds are the largest stateless ethnic group in the world and of the estimated 20–25 million Kurds approximately half live in Turkey and the rest in Iraq, Iran, Syria, and the former Soviet Union (McDowall 1996). The statelessness of the Kurdish people in Turkey has led to a number of uprisings throughout the twentieth century, and the formation of a range of Kurdish political movements and parties with different ideologies and priorities.[16] The Kurdish minority has become increasingly politicized since Second World War (Bruinessen 1991). Economic deprivation in the southeastern part of Turkey, the physical displacement of many Kurds to the West of Turkey, combined with ideas of ethnicity formed the basis for the late 1970s movements of resistance in Turkey. In the 1960s and 1970s, Kurdish activists were working within the Turkish left-wing parties, trade unions of Marxist–Leninist orientation as well as various student organizations (McDowall 1996: 404–15).

In the latter half of the 1970s, underground Kurdish parties began to be formed. Of these, the best known is the PKK, which has led an armed struggle against the Turkish military forces since the beginning of the 1980s. The PKK's political goal has shifted away from independence and towards less separatist ideas of self-rule and autonomy. The response of the Turkish state to the PKK was a complete ban of Kurdish organizations, the persecution of politicians from political parties supporting the Kurdish issue, and high sensitivity to any activity perceived as supporting the cause of the Kurdish activists, including academic research and literature.

Indeed, it is disproportional to describe the Kurdish issue on par with the other groups mentioned in this chapter. The civil-war-like situation in southeastern

Anatolia is estimated to have claimed the lives of more than 30,000 people, of which a vast majority are civilians, destroyed thousands of villages, and displaced hundreds of thousands of people. Thus, the Kurdish issue constitutes one of the most pressing political problems of present-day Turkey (Olson 1996; Steinbach 1996; Pope and Pope 1997; Barkey and Fuller 1998). The means by which the Turkish state has tried to deal with the Kurdish minority's opposition movements are by no means in accordance with international conventions on human rights. Accordingly, the issue of the Kurds forms a substantial part of the international relations between Turkey and western Europe, including Germany, as will be discussed further in Chapters 6 and 7.

The PKK has recently announced its transformation process from a military to a civil organization. Moreover, it is not the only Kurdish movement in or outside of Turkey. Some want an independent Kurdish state, others regional governance within a federation. Others again merely challenge the Turkish Kemalist notion of unitary national Turkish identity by demanding recognition of Kurdish distinctiveness in Turkish public space such as the right to use the Kurdish language in schools and in the media, and the right to use Kurdish names. However, the road to such recognition is halted by the lack of freedom of speech and political organization among Kurds in Turkey. Kurdish political activity is, still, regarded as a security threat and treated accordingly. The right to political Kurdish representation has in and of itself become an important first point on the agenda of all Kurdish organizations and those sympathetic to the Kurdish cause.

The size of the Kurdish minority from Turkey in Germany is a contested issue, but most estimates range from 500,000 to 700,000, of which 90 per cent are from Turkey. Many of these, as is the case in Turkey, do not emphasize their political and ethnic identity, but live as 'assimilated Turks'. 'Long distance nationalism' as defined by Anderson (1992) does not include all Kurds abroad and accordingly the Kurdish political organizations are only representative of parts of the Kurdish minority abroad.

Yet, a substantial number of political activists and supporters have emerged from among both refugees and descendents of Kurdish guest workers from Turkey. These Kurds form an integral part of the Kurdish movement, reflecting the freedom of expression available abroad. Moreover, refugees and asylum seekers continuously seek to mobilize Kurds who have arrived as immigrants, or their descendants, and lobby the governments of their respective new countries of settlement. Thus, the Kurdish conflict has 'spilled over' into Germany and attitudes towards the PKK have especially divided many Turkish and Kurdish organizations, even if only a minority of the Kurds in Germany are actually members or supporters of the PKK (see also Mertens 2000). The PKK's organization in Germany was until recently called the *Eniya Rizgariya Netwa Kurdistan* (ERNK), which was banned in Germany in November 1993.[17] The ban followed a decade of escalating violence culminating in two waves of attacks on Turkish businesses in 1993. These events will be further described in Chapter 5. The PKK is today estimated to have approximately 11,000–12,000 members in Germany

(*Verfassungsschutz* 2000: 188), and a wider number of supporters has risen steadily since the mid-1980s.

Two of the main *legal* federations of Kurdish organizations in Germany today are: the *Yekitiya Komelên Kurdistan* (KOMKAR) and the *Yekitiya Komelên Kurd li Elmanya* (YEK-KOM).[18] Founded in 1978, the KOMKAR is the oldest federative organization of the Kurds in Germany, which still exists under its original name. It started out coordinating workers associations which did not even use the word 'Kurdish' until much later (interview with KOMKAR, 19 February 1998). It has grown from the founding eight organizations to 40 membership organizations and approximately 4,000 members (NRW 1999: 97).[19] It is not a coincidence that the other main Kurdish migrant organization, YEK-KOM, was established in March 1994, in the aftermath of the German ban of all PKK-affiliated organizations. According to its own estimates, the YEK-KOM is slightly larger than KOMKAR with around 50 membership organizations (YEK-KOM 1997).

Kurdish organizations between migrant politics and homeland politics

Both the KOMKAR and the YEK-KOM claim to be working mainly for the plight of Kurdish immigrants and refugees in Germany. However, as is the case with the Sunni and Alevi movements, the immigrant political activities cannot be separated from the homeland oriented agenda of the Kurdish organizations. On top of the immigrant political agenda is the demand for German authorities to accept the Kurdish people as a different nation (from Turks) in Germany. Thus, an integral part of the immigrant political work is to carry out activities related to the recognition of Kurdish identity, such as cultural events celebrating Kurdish traditions, and demands for mother-tongue teaching in Kurdish. Given the sensitivity of expressions of Kurdish identity in Turkey, such activities send an important signal to the political authorities in Turkey.

While the immigrant political agenda of the different Kurdish organizations is largely the same, the two federative legal organizations of Kurds in Germany differ in terms of which political movements and parties in Turkey they support. Both organizations generally support human rights organizations in Turkey such as the *Insan Halkları Derneği* (IHD), and the more broadly based political parties such as the *Halkın ve Demokrasi Partisi* (HADEP) in Turkey. However, they support, and some of their members are also members of, different political parties and movements in Turkey. The KOMKAR supports the *Partiya Sosyalist a Kurdistan* (PSK), which was founded in 1974 by the now exiled leader Kemal Burkay. The PSK is illegal in Turkey, and has been described as one of the casualties in the rise of the PKK (Barkey and Fuller 1998: 80; see also Gürbey 1996). The PSK stands for a Turkish–Kurdish federation like that of Belgium; in that respect it does not differ from the more recent political agenda of the PKK. The official aim of the YEK-KOM is to 'work through peaceful means for the recognition of the identity of the Kurdish people in Germany as well as their cultural, ethnic, social and political rights' (YEK-KOM 1997). However, it is clear that its sympathy for the ERNK and the PKK is strong on both an organizational level and among its members (interview with YEK-KOM, 20 July 1997).

All three organizations try to support their compatriots in Turkey by providing German policy makers and the wider public with information on the situation in southeastern Anatolia. To that end, a vast range of material is produced and disseminated to German political institutions. The main point of the homeland political agenda is to urge the German government to put pressure on the Turkish government to find a political solution to the Kurdish issue. That is, the organizations are against military and economic assistance from Germany to Turkey, and advocate Germany taking a more critical stand towards the problems of human rights and democracy in Turkey. Furthermore, the Kurdish organizations are strongly against the deportation of asylum seekers, almost all of whom are Kurdish, to Turkey.

The violent campaigns of the PKK/ERNK in Turkey as well as in Germany in the 1990s have served to stigmatize other Kurdish movements as separatists in the eyes of the German public and have made the work of organizations such as the KOMKAR difficult (interview with KOMKAR, 19 February 1998). Yet, the KOMKAR has a wide range of contacts with German political institutions, and is perceived as being more 'intellectual'. This is related to the fact that while the membership organizations of the YEK-KOM are dominated by asylum seekers, the KOMKAR represents a large number of 'guest worker children' rediscovering their Kurdishness in the diaspora. While the YEK-KOM have more or less explicitly supported the armed resistance in southeast Anatolia, the KOMKAR demands recognition of Kurdish identity in Turkey and in Germany and arranged celebrations of the the first 100 years of the 'first Kurdish newspaper in the diaspora' – thus seeking to profile Kurdish diasporic identity as separate from the Turkish minority in Germany.

Patterns of mobilization

The developments of the landscape of Turkish and Kurdish organizations demonstrate that, despite the trend towards more immigrant political focused work in most organizations, Turkish politics still matters in various degrees. Opposition to political developments in Turkey has mobilized Turks and Kurds abroad. This can be opposition to the success of particular parties, or opposition to the state or government in general. Furthermore, the banning of political organizations and parties in Turkey have contributed to the organization of these groups in Germany. Most importantly, because of German rights to freedom of expression, more marginal political groupings have been able to act publicly. Inflows of asylum seekers have contributed to political mobilization in opposition to the homeland regime – notably the Kurds and the New Left. That such organizations still have relatively small followings reflects the fact that the vast majority of the Turkish citizens in Germany adhere to moderate conservative or social-democratic parties.

Many Turkish organizations are also pro-state or pro-government. In particular, the organizations from the moderate right-wing and the moderate left-wing seek to represent Turkish political agendas in Germany and defend Turkish interests *vis-à-vis* German political actors. The success of political parties in Turkey also mobilizes citizens abroad. The rise of the *Refah Partisi/Fazilet Partisi* and the developments of the *Milli Görüş* amply illustrate this.

The concomitant mobilization against and for the political regime of Turkey means that the communities are divided on the issue of Turkish–European or Turkish–German relations, and react differently to developments in these issues. Movements and organizations critical of developments in Turkey press for Germany to stop delivering weapons or deporting asylum seekers to Turkey; they argue that Turkey should be integrated with Europe, but only so that there is a continued demand for improvement of the situation of democracy and human rights. More pro-Turkish groups, such as the *Hür-Türk*, work for Turkey's EU candidacy and for Germany to employ a more sensitive stance *vis-à-vis* Turkish domestic political issues. Most Sunni Muslim organizations claim to be pro-European integration of Turkey, albeit emphasizing that Turkey should also utilize its 'eastern' connections in Central Asia and the Middle East.

That Turkish organizations promote the acceptance of Turkey in the EU is not disconnected from their own situation in Germany. Turkey's status as an EU-member state would change the status of Turkish citizens in Germany from third country nationals to EU citizens. They would thus obtain the much wider palette of rights granted to EU citizens, including freedom of movement and local voting rights. Also in other cases are homeland political and immigrant political claims-making closely connected. As described in the case of Alevis, Sunnis, and Kurds, minority rights in Germany are paralleled by claims for religious or ethnic rights in Turkey. As will be discussed further in the subsequent chapters, this mixing of demands is mostly not the result of a conscious strategic effort, but rather a reflection of the fact that these are inseparable categories for Turkish and Kurdish migrants and refugees in Germany.

Generally, homeland political mobilization is a complex mix of transnationalism 'from above' and 'from below' (Smith and Guanizo 1998). The perceptions and policies of Turkish political institutions, in particular changes in government policies towards citizens abroad, will be described in greater detail in Chapter 7. The following is, therefore, just a brief outline of their role in mobilizing Turks and Kurds abroad.

The state The large diplomatic representation of Turkey in Germany does not seem to constitute a mobilizing factor. Turkish diplomatic representation seek to encourage pro-state organization and curb dissidence as it is part of the task of the consular services to both represent the interests of the homeland and obtain information on the citizens and their organizations. Accordingly, the Turkish consulates have tried to establish networks of organizations, the so-called 'coordination councils', and are also thought to fund organizations such as the AADD. Turkish diplomats turn up for events held by organizations that are not critical of Turkey. Yet, a majority of the organizations wish, if not to oppose directly, then to keep an explicit distance from the diplomatic representation, in order not to be branded as the 'tool of Ankara'.

Political parties Besides the state a number of organizations such as the HDF, the *Türk Federasyon*, or the *Milli Görüş* are either initiated by Turkish political parties or have developed strong links with a party as in the case of the DIDF. In both cases, Turkish political leaders use the German-based organizations as platforms from which to convey the main agenda of the party, and ask for economic and political support.

Religious institutions Also, religious movements are competing for constituency abroad. To categorize these transnational ties as 'political mobilization' is not appropriate in all cases since most of the organizations stress their lack of political aspirations. Yet, because these organizations can discuss issues of Islamic practice in Germany to a much greater extent than they can in Turkey their missionary work may have a homeland political dimension.

The media More important, albeit not quantifiable, is the role of the media. As mentioned in Chapter 3, almost all Turks and Kurds follow the news of the their homeland through Turkish or Kurdish printed and electronic media. There is some Kurdish and Turkish media that have a critical view of Turkey, but the majority of the newspapers and television channels can be radical in their tone when defending Turkish domestic politics and when criticizing the treatment of Turkish citizens in German society and the German tolerance of organizations such as the PKK/ERNK (see also Chapter 7). Furthermore, notably *Hürriyet*, the most widely disseminated Turkish daily in Germany, frequently undertakes campaigns where Turkish citizens are urged to fax or call German or European politicians who have criticized Turkey or supported Kurdish groups. The Turkish media in general and its tone and campaigns, in particular, are frequently mentioned as the most important factor contributing to the reintroduction of Turkish politics among Turks and Kurds in Germany. Indeed, the media is seen as an obstacle to political integration of Turks in Germany. Yet, it has also been argued that Turks do not simply 'internalize' the messages conveyed through the media but read or watch Turkish news with a critical eye (Aksoy and Robins 2000).

An important dimension of homeland political mobilization is that the dynamics of mobilization 'take on a life of their own' within the groups of migrants and refugees abroad. The transnational mobilization is not just related to political developments in Turkey or in German–Turkish relations. The intra-group dynamics among various political, ethnic, and religious segments of the immigrant communities from Turkey affect their political agendas and activities. The mobilization of one group creates situations of counter-mobilization of other groups. For instance, the founding of the DITIB was a response of the Turkish authorities, who were discontent with the spread of the other Sunni Muslim groups in Germany. There is a 'conflict of representation' both inwards *vis-à-vis* the Turks and Kurds and 'outwards' towards German authorities, meaning that if one certain Turkish organization starts representing the Turks in Germany, others will be formed to challenge the representativeness of the first one. The main pairs of opposing groups are give below.

Radical left versus *radical right* In the beginning of the 1980s (and before), relations between the radical left- and right-wing organizations often led to violent clashes on German soil. Both wings agitated against each other, published material against each other, and sought to convince the German authorities to ban or control the activities of the other group. This hostility persists today in the sense that there is almost no cooperation between the organizations stemming from the radical and moderate left-wing organizations on the one hand, and the extreme right-wing organizations on the other. In practice, this means that the nationalist *Türk Federasyon* is rarely invited to meetings with other Turkish organizations.

Turkish versus *Kurdish* During the mid-1980s, the relationship between Kurdish and Turkish organizations became increasingly difficult. From the moment when organizations such as the KOMKAR were established, the Turkish right-wing organizations expressed a hostility to these organizations that has not abated. Initially, some Kurdish organizations also found the Turkish left-wing organizations to be sceptical of Kurdish mobilization (interview with KOMKAR, 19 February 1998). Kurds, they felt, should not work for a separate ethnic agenda but unite with Turkish workers in common struggle against fascism and capitalism. Yet, the radical left organizations have lost a lot of members to the Kurdish issue. The simultaneous developments of the fall of the Berlin wall and the Soviet Union and the worsening of the Kurdish conflict in southeast Anatolia have contributed to their decline. Currently, the leftist organizations such as the GDF and notably the DIDF work more closely with Kurdish organizations. For instance, the GDF was coorganizer of the estimated 80,000 participant Kurdish Festival in Cologne in 1997 (interview with GDF, 16 December 1997). However, the moderate left-wing organizations only rarely organize events with Kurdish organizations and their immigrant political demands for only Turkish mother-tongue teaching frustrate the Kurdish organizations.

Sunnis versus *Alevis* The German-based Alevis became mobilized not only because of events in Turkey, but also because of the mobilization of the Sunnis in Germany. When the Sunni Muslim organizations started to lobby for religious rights in Germany, the Alevis perceived this as a repetition of the situation of the Alevis in Turkey. The case of the Alevis demonstrates that homeland opposition is not a function of mode of migration. Most activists in the Alevi movement arrived as economic migrants or as refugees for other reasons.

Sunnis versus *Kemalists and left-wing organizations* The mobilization of Sunni Muslims in Germany has mobilized the moderate left-wing. For instance, the HDF has forwarded their concerns with Sunni Muslim organizations in Germany to their German interlocutors in the SPD, and both the AADD and the GDF have countered Sunni lobbying for lessons in Islam in German schools by proposing more general religious education emphasizing secularism (AADD) or general ethics (GDF).

Divided we stand: the influence of homeland politics on the attempts to cooperate on immigrant political issues

Immigrant political and homeland political claims-making are often inseparable entities in the day-to-day work of Turkish and Kurdish organizations in Germany. However, the homeland political outlook of the various organizations constitutes an obstacle to forming common platforms on which to voice common demands as Turkish citizens in Germany *vis-à-vis* German and Turkish authorities.

In the first half of the 1980s, joint immigrant political platforms were formed mostly within the left-wing groups. Since the latter half of the 1980s, and especially in the 1990s, there have been several attempts to form platforms across party-political, ethnic, and religious divides. Some of these were never viable, as the *Türkiye Göçmen Topluluğu* (TGT). The TGT was launched in 1985, with expensive folders and information material (TGT 1985). However, due to strife over who was to lead the organization it never made it past the founding general assembly (interview with GDF, 21 July 1997).

Other joint platforms find themselves only supported by certain parts of the organizations. Two such organizations deserve mention. One is the *Rat der Türkischen Staatsbürger* (RTS), founded in 1993 by 15 federations, which presents itself as the organization for all Turkish citizens in Germany and frequently meets with German and Turkish politicians to discuss relevant issues (interview with RTS, 9 December 1997). The RTS has, however, mainly managed to attract right-wing and Sunni Muslim organizations. More recently, with intense media coverage, the *Almanya Türk Toplumu* (ATT) was launched by members of mainly moderate left-wing organizations in December 1995. Officially, the platform was formed as a reaction to the fire attacks on Turkish citizens in Mölln and Solingen, and the aim was to fight for equal rights for all Turkish citizens in Germany. At the founding of the ATT, representatives from all German political parties, the Turkish ambassador to Germany, and many other prominent people were present and the organization was hailed as '*the* representative of the Turkish minority in Germany' (ATT 1996). However, the reactions from other organizations, notably the leftist and the Kurdish organizations, were very harsh. These organizations stated that no single organization can ever represent all the Turkish citizens, given the different ethnic, political, and religious divisions within the community. Indeed, opposition to the ATT brought otherwise distant organizations such as the Alevi AABF, the right-wing RTS and the Kurdish KOMKAR together to produce joint press releases accusing the leader, a founding member of the social democratic HDF and member of the Hamburg parliament for SPD, of being a nationalist and the 'tool of Ankara' (see *Frankfurter Allgemeine*, 1 December 1995).

Realizing the weakness of having two platforms, the RTS and the ATT have tried to bridge their difference and work together. One such attempt was to form an anti-racism forum, where the main organizations (except the nationalist *Türk Federasyon* and the New left) met three times. However, when the time came to define racism, a heated discussion broke out between the leader of the ATT and the representative from *Milli Görüş* on the one hand, and the representative of the KOMKAR on the other. The Forum has not met since (interview with GDF, 16 December 1997; interview with KOMKAR, 19 February 1998; interview with *Milli Görüş*, 25 July 1997).

The same dynamics served to hinder the only attempt to form a common Turkish political party to run for the German election in 1998. The idea of the *Demokratische Partei Deutschland* (DPD) was launched in late spring 1995 and the founding meeting took place at the end of October the same year. The incentive was that 'the current electoral law and the citizenship law are racist' and hence the initiator and leader of the DPD, Sedat Sezgin, advocated voting rights for foreigners with long-term residence (*Financial Times*, 10 November 1995; *Süddeutsche Zeitung*, 12 July 1995). There was, however, also a homeland political agenda in his initial statements. The DPD wanted to be a 'counterweight to the negative [German] critique of Turkey' (*Tageszeitung*, 16 May 1995), and to 'correct the wrong image of Turkish domestic politics' (*Süddeutsche Zeitung*, 10 August 1995). When the DPD was launched, it created a great deal of publicity, but mostly in the form of negative comments from migrant organizations. As in the case of the ATT, it was said that no single party can ever represent the Turks in Germany, given that they are a heterogeneous group with few common interests (Özdemir in *Süddeutsche Zeitung*, 10 August 1995; GDF in *TAZ*, 31 May 1995). One interviewee hinted that this initiative might originate in Ankara: 'Perhaps the Turkish government is trying to see how far they can go with their "disinformation campaign" in German domestic politics.' (Özdemir in *Tageszeitung*, 16 May 1995).

Since the mid-1990s, there have been no further attempts to form common umbrella organizations or parties. Realizing the futility of 'such unrealistic initiatives', the Alevi AABF invited members of all Turkish and Kurdish federations to a meeting in January 2000. The aim was to discuss common ground and to agree on exchanging publications, statements, opinions, solutions, criticisms, and thus 'sort out our misunderstandings so that we will not be wasting our energy' (AABF 2000a). In addition, the AABF made all the invited organizations support Alevi demands for equal status with Sunnis in Turkey and Germany. While this meeting was a success and managed to include both Kurdish and Turkish, left-wing and moderate left-wing organizations, the follow-up meeting, hosted by the ATT, was not. The ATT had decided to go further and invite also conservative liberal (RTS) and religious organizations (DITIB) and this was too much for both the Kurdish KOMKAR and leftist organizations such as the GDF and the DIDF. The GDF stated to the press:

> We would not be able to stay in the same platform with racist, fascist and fundamentalist Muslim organizations [...] there is no need and it is not correct to make an umbrella organization between organizations or persons who have different opinion, different interests and different missions.
>
> (GDF in *Evrensel*, 8 July 2000)

The KOMKAR was more precise, as they complained that they:

> Cannot understand a person who is supporting and defending Turkish mother tongue teaching in Germany but not supporting and defending education for Kurdish children in Kurdish language in Turkey. This is a kind of double-dealing policy.
>
> (KOMKAR in *Evrensel*, 8 July 2000)

The difficulties for the organizations to work together are, as is often the case in politics, also caused by personal strife and ambition. Moreover, the clashes between heads of organizations do not mean that individuals cannot work together. Still, the homeland political identity of the organizations, be it direct links to political movements in Turkey or more abstract support for a particular political line, is of overriding importance. As noted by the member of German *Bundestag* (MdB) of Turkish origin, Cem Özdemir: 'We still live with the feet in Germany, but the head in Turkey.' (Interview with MdB for *Die Grüne*, 11 February 1998).

This is, however, only half the story of the Turkish and Kurdish organizations in Germany. As will be shown in Chapters 5 and 6, these organizations increasingly have the head not only in Turkey but also in Germany as their information campaigns gradually integrate with the German political system and discourse.

5 From confrontational to multi-layered strategies

Turkish and Kurdish information campaigns in Germany

Broadly speaking, Turks and Kurds in Germany can try to influence political developments in Turkey in two ways: directly and indirectly. Direct influence may come through giving economic, political, or even military support to political counterparts in the homeland. Turkish citizens can go home to vote, Turkish and Kurdish organizations can collect funding among their supporters for political counterparts in Turkey, and some Kurdish organizations have even been known to recruit guerrilla fighters to join the armed Kurdish opposition in Turkey.

Yet, a large part of the homeland political work of Turkish and Kurdish organizations plays itself out in Germany, as the organizations try to influence politics in Turkey indirectly through discussions and information campaigns about Turkish politics aimed at the German public and policy-makers. Such information campaigns range from fly-posting at night to targeted lobbying of key policy makers. Why do different organizations work in such different ways? Why have some managed to negotiate their way into the political system while others have not?

The concept of 'institutional channelling' (see Chapter 2) suggests that immigrants' forms of political participation in Europe relate to the specific political opportunity structures which immigrants face. The more inclusive the political system is, the more the activities are 'channelled into' that system and shaped accordingly, rather than taking place 'outside the system' in more confrontational forms (Ireland 1994; see also Soysal 1994). However, these studies mainly focus on immigrants fighting for their rights in the 'host' society, and do not pursue the dimension of homeland politics in a similar systematic fashion. To what extent is the concept of 'institutional channelling' also applicable to the integration of homeland political activities into the political system of the receiving country?

In order to answer these questions, this chapter analyses the multi-level strategies with which Turkish and Kurdish political organizations carry out their information campaigns in Germany. It demonstrates how some groups employ 'confrontational' strategies, others more 'institutional participation', and many a combination of both. Kurdish and Turkish organizations' are certainly anchored in their local political institutional context. Germany is not a free haven for all kinds of activities, and the German tolerance and attentiveness to information campaigns span from banning organizations or ignoring them to actively lending support. Considering this, I argue that the choice of strategy is related to the movement/organization's agenda, its degree of opposition or support to the homeland regime, and the extent to which their agenda is compatible with that of political actors in the receiving country. This contention complicates the somewhat functionalist understanding of the significance of the receiving country's political opportunity structures. A key aspect of this analysis suggests that the concept of 'institutional channelling' presupposes a boundedness of the political dialogue between migrants or refugees and their 'host' state. Yet, it is the unboundedness, the transnational orientation and ties of the homeland political organizations, which are one of their defining features. Turkish and Kurdish organizations may draw on – or be dictated by – their political or religious counterparts in Turkey or elsewhere in Europe.

The following analysis presents four main dimensions of the interface between Turkish and Kurdish homeland political information campaigns and their multi-level political–institutional context: The first two dimensions describe how organizations engage in *confrontational participation*. Some organizations use German public space for extremist activities, such as violent campaigns, on the wrong side of German law, while others organize demonstrations, mass-meetings, fly-posting and graffiti, or hunger strikes. The next section describes instances of *institutional participation*, whereby lobby groups work with or sometimes even within host country political institutions or international organizations. Finally, I show how Turkish and Kurdish organizations utilize their transnational networks in their information campaigns or turn to lobbying international political institutions. The dialogue with Turkey will be dealt with further in Chapter 7.

Extremist and illegal activities

Only few Turkish or Kurdish movements have resorted to extremist or illegal activities. Moreover, the organizations within this category are not constant as organizations change tactics over the years. Here, the Turkish New Left, the Kurdish organizations supporting the PKK and Sunni Muslim groups of ICCB and *Milli Görüş* serve as three main examples illustrating how Turkish and Kurdish organizations have promoted their agendas on the wrong side of the German law or the wrong side of German perceptions of where general homeland politics ends and *Ausländerextremismus* begins.

In the early 1980s, there were continuous clashes between Turkish communists and right-wing nationalists in Germany. This took the form of Molotov cocktails, attacks on migrant organizations, and violent incidents when demonstrators clashed in the street. The use of violence was mainly intra-communal, and seemed more like an ongoing feud of retaliations. Thus, the organizations were watched by the Geman *Verfassungsschutz*, but otherwise received relatively little attention among the wider German public. Yet, the militant Maoist movement *Devrimci Sol* was banned after an incident where armed and masked members occupied the Turkish consulate in Cologne for several hours in November 1982, holding numerous people hostage. The aim was to protest against the Turkish national referendum on the proposed new constitution of Turkey, which the *Devrimci Sol* maintained, had not been drawn up democratically (*Verfassungsschutz* 1983: 175). While the Turkish right-wing nationalist organizations have later refrained from more violent activities, the small and marginal successor organizations to the *Devrimci Sol* (such as DHKP-C and THKP-C) were linked with violent campaigns in Germany and in Turkey leading to yet another ban in 1998, and the arrest of *Devrimci Sol* leaders throughout Europe (*Verfassungsschutz* 2000: 197–8).

Whereas the campaigns of the New Left have gone largely unnoticed by the wider German public, the larger and more extensive campaigns of the PKK in Germany have been widely publicized and scrutinized, and have served to stigmatize other more peaceful Kurdish movements in Germany. From the late 1980s, the PKK-related movements in Germany wanted to force the German government to press Turkish authorities for a solution to the Kurdish problem. Instead, notably two waves of violence in June and November 1993 led to the ban of the PKK-related organizations the same year. The attacks were mainly directed at Turkish diplomatic representations, travel agencies, and banks in different German cities. Most of the targeted property was completely destroyed and the damage amounted to hundreds of thousands of Deutschmarks (*Verfassungsschutz* 1993: 168–9).

The campaign was well coordinated with around 50 simultaneous attacks in June and 60 attacks in November. The PKK came under immediate suspicion as its leader, Abdullah Öcalan, had warned about the possibility of violence in Germany. After the ban there were more attacks on Turkish property in Germany and violent demonstrations in 1994 and 1996, until Öcalan ordered an end to the violence in Europe in relation to the wider attempt to reorient the PKK from a military to a political organization. However, with the dramatic capture of Öcalan in 1999, demonstrations, bombings, and occupations of embassies (Greek, Kenyan, and Turkish) broke out throughout the world within a day of the dissemination of the news. In Germany, there were no less than 46 demonstrations (of which 40 were peaceful), 10 actions against diplomatic representations of Greece and Kenya and a raid against the Israeli consulate in Berlin resulting in the death of three Kurdish activists. There were occupations of party offices and hostage taking. Twenty-seven German policemen were injured, 2,300 people taken into custody, and an arrest order issued for further 135 (*Deutscher Bundestag* 1999).

Still, in particular since the capture of PKK leader Abdullah Öcalan, the PKK has continued to promote itself as a civilian rather than militant organization, stressing issues like ethnicity and minority rights rather than promoting Marxist paroles. The PKK Central Committee's repeated calls for non-violence at demonstrations and other events are largely being followed by organizations throughout the diaspora.

Besides organizations whose members throw Molotov cocktails, destroy Turkish property, or stage violent demonstrations on German highways, a number of other organizations are watched closely by the German *Verfassungsschutz*. Although these organizations do not break the law through their activities, their ideology is viewed as subversive by not only Turkish, but also German authorities. On this list of organizations are Sunni Muslim organizations of the *Milli Görüş* and the ICCB. Each year, the *Verfassungsschutz* publishes quotes of particularly radical statements of an anti-semitic or fundamentalist character. For instance, the *Verfassungsschutz* in its yearly report of 1996, justifies categorizing the religious groups of the ICCB and the *Milli Görüş* as a threat because:

> The attempts to establish a certain societal order with fewer fundamental rights, less freedom and a another distribution of sovereign functions than is envisaged in the [German] constitution, are efforts against the free democratic basic constitutional order [in Germany].
> (*Verfassungsschutz* 1996: 198)

In other words, although the ICCB and the *Milli Görüş* have not actually been doing anything illegal, their vision/ideology is regarded as unwanted.

German reactions to extremist activities

In the early 1980s, Turkish and Kurdish organizations' illegal activities did not dominate the annual reports of the *Verfassungsschutz* the way they do now. Although they constituted approximately half of the estimated members of extremist organizations, their activities were not as violent as those of the Palestinians, Armenians, or Croatian extremists (*Verfassungsschutz* 1981: 149).[1] Nonetheless, the extremist activities of Turkish citizens did reach the attention of German policy makers. Indeed, concern with extremist groups dominates discussions of foreigners' organizations in the *Bundestag*, and therefore deserves mentioning in greater detail. Debates have centered on how to restrict extremist activities, rather than how to channel them into the system.

Back in the early 1980s, the *Bundestag*, representatives from the government, as well as the opposition expressed their concern with the threat such organizations were considered to pose to the domestic security of German society:

> The political *Ausländerextremismus* has secured a solid organizational and financial basis in Germany through the foundation of associations and thereby increased their dangerousness considerably.
> (*Deutscher Bundestag* 1982a)

Accordingly, parliamentarians repeatedly requested the closure or restriction of the most profiled organizations such as those affiliated with the *Türk Federasyon* or the extreme left-wing organizations. The government stance was that 'Turkish extremism, as before, must be watched with the greatest attention and that all legal possibilities must be used in fighting extremism on the part of foreigners' (see among others, *Deutscher Bundestag* 1981b).[2]

It is the Federal Ministry of the Interior which is responsible for banning organizations that operate illegally throughout all of Germany. As mentioned, such bans have been declared several times in the case of Turkish and Kurdish organizations.

Such drastic measures against extremist activities have fed into the perception that these groups did not belong in Germany in the first place. In several motions and questions from the CDU in particular, violent behaviour of foreigners was formulated as a misuse of the *Gastrecht* – that is, rights as 'guests' granted to foreigners by their 'host', Germany. Similarly, statements from the Ministry of Interior confirmed that there were great difficulties in surveying the groups of extremist Turks, since 'we are dealing with people who do not have their roots in our country, who do not speak our language, and who often are controlled from abroad.' (*Deutscher Bundestag* 1981e).

In the late 1980s, as the clashes between extremist groups of right- and left-wing were gradually replaced by the Turkish–Kurdish conflict, the use of *Gastrech* was increasingly used in debates in the *Bundestag*. The perceived misuse of the *Gastrecht* by immigrants and refugees, it was felt, should lead to expulsion and deportation of the perpetrators. For instance, in the aftermath of the violent Kurdish demonstrations around Nevruz in 1994, Foreign Minister Kinkel appealed:

> To all the Kurds living in Germany: Do not bring your conflicts to Germany and do not think that violence is the way to realize legitimate political aims, such as the protection of minorities in your homeland.
> (*Deutscher Bundestag* 1994)

Five years later, more or less exactly the same wording was used by his successor, Otto Schily of the SPD, in the aftermath of the violent demonstration against the capture of Abdullah Öcalan (*Deutscher Bundestag* 1999).

Other confrontational strategies

The vast majority of Turkish and Kurdish organizations use German public space to stage peaceful events. The two examples of such activity are demonstrations and large-scale political meetings. These are not the only examples. Notably hunger-strikes, a symbolically violent act, occur frequently among leftist and Kurdish activists who protest against treatment of prisoners in Turkey or deportation of asylum seekers back to Turkey. Another example is political graffiti. In particular, leftist organizations are known to organize nightly excursions to put up posters and write on walls. For instance, the Turkish-dominated area around Kottbusser Tor in Kreuzberg in Berlin is covered in elaborate Maoist slogans, pictures, and a multitude of posters. Turkish friends sometimes speculated with amusement on the extent to which one may deduct the power hierarchy of organizations, by who dares to put their posters on top of the others. Yet, demonstrations and political mass-meetings are more interesting in the context of this analysis since they are used by a much broader selection of organizations, and has a higher profile in the Turkish and German public.

Demonstrations are a classic way of public manifestation, and Turks and Kurds have been marching the streets in Germany for decades. In the aftermath of the

Turkish coup in 1980, the *Türk Federasyon* protested against the military government of Turkey and the imprisonment of the MHP leader Alparslan Türkeş (*Verfassungsschutz* 1981: 159). The leftwing organizations, for once, put their internal strife in the background and organized protest demonstrations, which urged for German opposition to the 'military dictatorship' (*Verfassungsschutz* 1981: 147). The next two decades witnessed demonstrations organized by Turkish and Kurdish organizations in protest against German migration policies, Turkish politics or in solidarity with minorities in other countries. For instance during a nationalist demonstration in Cologne, March 1992, banners advocating solidarity with Azerbaycan 'Berg-Karabach is Turkish and will remain Turkish' were displayed (*Verfassungschutz* 1992: 154).

Yet, some organizations organize more demonstrations than others do, and while Turkish groups have increasingly protested against German policies, it is the Kurdish groups which have continued to organize large-scale demonstrations. Since the mid-1980s, their events have attracted larger crowds with often more than 50,000 participants. For instance, a demonstration in Bonn, June 1995, attracted an estimated 70,000 supporters (PKK themselves estimated several hundred thousand) assembled under the Motto: 'For a political solution in Kurdistan – No to the PKK ban' (*Verfassungsschutz* 1995: 215).

Political mass-meetings are of a different nature than demonstrations. While large-scale demonstrations are clearly aimed at German policy makers and public, political mass-meetings seem primarily geared towards mobilizing the migrants and refugees themselves. Indeed, not all examples of this type of activity are distinctly 'confrontational' as Kurdish and Turkish organizations increasingly include German speakers in their programmes for these events. This type of political activity deserves special attention since it constitutes a highly visible dimension of organizational activities and has developed into a particular form of migrant and homeland political expression among Turks and Kurds. These meetings span from annual meetings/party conferences and cultural festivals, to commemoration of founders, martyrs, or defining moments in Turkish history.

Despite the very different ideological content among the different organizations, mass-meetings are remarkably similar in their form. In a sports hall, 5,000–15,000 participants are expected, and at a stadium up to 50,000. There is usually a fairly high entrance fee (with a concession for members of the organization hosting the event). Even considering the costs such as the rent of the premises and the security personnel, a considerable profit is left for the sponsoring organization. In the lobby, the hosting organization displays stands with material and books, music cassettes, and expensive 'political souvenirs' such as emblems, postcards with heads or statuettes of organizations/movements, headbands with the name of the organizations or its political counterpart in Turkey, flags, banners, and T-shirts. These meetings usually attract participants from all over Germany and even Europe, and in the lobby old friends meet and new contacts are made.

The official programme of political mass meetings is also curiously similar, following the same pattern of alternating between political speeches and statements and cultural performances. First are usually political speeches by the leaders of the host organization in Germany, followed by invited speakers from other German or Turkish organizations, and concluded by a speech from the leader of the organization or party in Turkey, with which the particular organization or movement is affiliated. Usually, the Turkish speaker is placed late in the programme in order to ensure that the audience will stay, indicating that this is one of the main attractions. In the case of *Türk Federasyon*, the cult-like status of MHP leader Türkeş is among the more extreme examples. One Turkish journalist reported from a meeting organized by *Türk Federasyon* that:

> When Türkeş came to the yearly meetings of *Türk Federasyon* in Germany, there would be a standing ovation of ten minutes before he could even begin to speak. Then he would say one sentence and the screaming would begin again for another ten minutes.
> (Interview with *Türkiye*, 17 February 1998)

Admittedly, the meetings I have attended have reached fairly emotional stages as the crowd chants slogans and cheers the speakers along.

With a few exceptions, the organizations which host mass-meetings are those with not only an explicit homeland political agenda, but also clear ties to a specific political movement or party in Turkey, and a large enough following to support such events. Other studies on exile movements have noted how 'a ceremonial calendar' is a common device for evoking loyalty among refugees. A diaspora political movement may celebrate ritual marking points, commemorate fallen martyrs or founding fathers, or some event leading to exile (Shain 1989: 60). Also in this case such symbolism serves to impose an important yearly homeland-related 'calendar' on the diaspora, thus subtly maintaining the emotional homeland connection. For instance, the KOMKAR and organizations supporting the PKK celebrate Nevruz in Germany. The latter set of organizations has also been known to encourage annual celebrations marking the first day of their armed struggle against the Turkish state (*Verfassungsschutz* 1993: 169). The extreme left-wing commemorates the death of its founder Ibrahim Kaypakkaya; Sunni Muslim organizations such as the ICCB have celebrated the Sunni Muslim New Year with big meetings. Such celebrations are of course not the monopoly of the dissident movements. Pro-Turkish groups and the diplomatic representations similarly celebrate Turkey's national days.

While these meetings, usually organized on an annual basis, clearly serve the purpose of mobilizing supporters among migrants and refugees, they also send a message to both the Turkish and German policy makers and public. Journalists are invited, and press releases are sent before and after the meeting to mainly the Turkish, but increasingly also the German press. In the statements released by the organizations, the number of participating supporters is highlighted in order to convey their representativeness and, thus, give weight to their messages. For instance, the Alevi AABF organized an event called the 'Saga of the Millenium in 2000', which was preceded and followed by carefully prepared material in not only Turkish and German, but also English. The leader of the

AABF recalled:

> So we have concentrated on public relations and it has gone well. We did a giant event with 1200 Sass players and 700 Semak dancers. We wanted to break the record! It was in the Köln Arena. This event has motivated us a lot. We told the Alevi history and with lots of different musical groups: Greek, African, Kurdish, German. There were nine languages in the event. There were 18,000 people. The Köln Arena is the biggest place in Europe. There were lots of reports in TV and the news.
>
> (Interview with AABF, 10 October 2000)

As the above examples of confrontational information campaigns illustrate, the legal organizations with the most extreme agendas and strategies interact the least with German political institutions. Demonstrations or large-scale mass-meetings organized by the New Left or Islamic organizations such as the ICCB rarely includes German organizations or policy makers. By contrast, organizations like AABF, invite German politicians to speak or support the event. There is, however, not a uniform attitude towards confrontational activities among German political parties. This issue will be discussed further in the next chapter, but for now it should be mentioned that while all German political parties are against *Ausländerextremismus*, there is a party-political division dictating the tolerance of certain parties towards certain migrant organizations.

Perhaps not surprisingly, German left-wing parties have criticized the Turkish right-wing while the German right-wing has wanted to tighten the control of the Turkish left-wing. Indeed, in the early 1980s the SPD was very concerned by the nationalist *Türk Federasyon*, and it scrutinized the organization's radicalism and its links to the Turkish party MHP. For instance, members of the SPD repeatedly questioned the fact that Alparslan Türkeş, leader of the MHP, was allowed entry visas to participate in the annual meetings of the *Türk Federasyon* (*Deutscher Bundestag* 1981c). However, the SPD never asked critical questions about the extreme left-wing organizations in the early 1980s, most likely because of the close links with the Turkish left-wing through the HDF and the trade unions. Parallel to this, the CDU has never posed a question specifically on the Turkish extreme right-wing, but has raised a number of critical issues regarding the left-wing (see among others, *Deutscher Bundestag* 1982b). A main contributing factor was probably that the radicalism of the Turkish left-wing during the Cold War era in and of itself was perceived as provocative by CDU/CSU parliamentarians. As formulated by Regenspurger, MdB for the CDU: 'For how long are Turks here going to be allowed to take advantage of public streets and places for demonstrations and parades under hammer, sickle and Soviet star?' (*Deutscher Bundestag* 1983).[3]

More recently, both the SPD and CDU have united in their criticism of all radical movements. Only the *Bündnis 90/Die Grüne*, and even more so the PDS, have continued to raise critical questions on the activities of right-wing organizations while more or less defending the existence of extreme Kurdish organizations.

Die Grüne and, in particular, members of the PDS have argued for lifting the ban of the PKK, and they turn up for demonstrations and meetings organized by Kurdish organizations. Indeed members of the PDS are explicitly pro-PKK and anti-*Türk Federasyon*, and lately remain the only party continuously raising the issue of the extremism of the latter.

Closer cooperation with German authorities

Besides marching on the streets or filling stadiums, there are a whole host of activities which are organized with German counterparts on a more cooperative than confrontational basis. The main activities in this respect are the more elite level seminars and panel discussions to which German politicians, leading intellectuals, and journalists are invited, or which are organized in cooperation with or sponsored by the German Party Foundations or other German NGOs. These events provide an immediate means to convey concerns and opinions to the German or Turkish politicians present. At events attended by this author, these events rarely attract the wider German public. The Kurdish movements constitute an exception to this. They successfully cooperate with German NGOs, in particular human rights organizations, to a much larger extent than other organizations.[4]

In addition, both Kurdish and Turkish organizations are increasingly seeking consultations with German or European politicians. Notably, a Kurdish organization like the KOMKAR is very active in this respect, as are the Alevi AABF, and the wider platforms such as RTS and ATT. Organizations interviewed place great emphasis on this dimension of their work. As formulated by a member of the board of the KOMKAR:

> We think about which actions are most effective. We must be very careful in order to retain our legitimacy. One good talk with a politician or a journalist on for instance the subject of village burning in Turkey is often much more worthwhile than a demonstration of a 1000 people in town. The methods must always be carefully considered.
>
> (Interview with KOMKAR, 23 July 1997)

Organizations engaging in this type of activity have become more concerned with finding the most relevant and influential policy makers to consult. Those organizations with links to smaller NGOs or political parties are now seeking interlocutors from the bigger and more influential parties such as the SPD and the CDU. These parties are, however, carefully monitoring which events they support or participate in. The suspicion that certain organizations may represent a political party in Turkey rather than migrants or refugees in Germany or have closer links to radical migrant organizations sometimes make them decline invitations. In interviews, several members of the *Bundestag* recall how they say no to invitations to larger arrangements organized by Turkish or Kurdish organizations because they are not sure if they can endorse what is being said by speakers in Turkish. This uncertainty has been addressed within a working group in the SPD.

From confrontational to multi-layered strategies 79

For instance, Leyla Onur, Turkish descent member of *Bundestag* from the SPD known for her knowledge of and engagement in Turkish migrant affairs, told me that she refused to go to either events organized by certain Sunni Muslim or Kurdish organizations, because:

> There is no point in going to tell them that they are wrong [...] But I can recognize these organizations because of my long experience. Others cannot. We have worked on this within the party [...] there is no point in writing lists because these organizations change name like they change underwear. We have to help our members [SPD parliamentarians] to ask questions so they can identify these organizations. Then they can still go, but they know with whom they are dealing.
> (Interview with MdB for SPD, 12 October 2000)

Significantly, most Turkish and Kurdish organizations, in particular those in closer and more regular contact with German political institutions, display signs of adjustment to German political 'discourse'. Within this category especially, are examples of organizations formulating homeland politics as immigrant politics in a wide sense. Religious organizations which keep a low profile in Turkey demand to be recognized as official representatives of Islam in Germany. Kurdish organizations such as YEK-KOM and KOMKAR emphasize the right for Kurds to be recognized as a minority separate from Turks in Germany. In particular, they promote 'the right to Kurdish language' in the form of Kurdish mother-tongue teaching in German schools. This is presently only offered in a few *Länder*.[5] Both sets of claims-making are certainly immigrant political claims in and of themselves, but they also send a strong signal to Turkish political authorities. As it is formulated in a petition written by several Kurdish organizations to the *Bundestag*:

> 500,000 people of Kurdish descent live in Germany. Every third of us is a German citizen. We are 150,000 German citizens of Kurdish descent and have a right to respect and recognition of our culture, our language and our national origin [...] We live in a democratic Europe. We do not want that our nationality, our language and culture is just as suppressed here as it is in our regions of origin. There we are terribly suppressed, our language is forbidden, our parties, newspapers and journals are persecuted. [...] A signal must be sent from Europe that this persecution of Kurds can no longer be tolerated. 150,000 Kurds with German citizenship have the same rights to respect and support of their nationality, tradition, language and culture as the Sorbic, Danish, and Frisean minorities [...]
> (Deutsch-Kurdischer Freundschaftsverein, October 2000)

Besides these examples, one could add how both leftist, Kemalist, Alevi, and Sunni movements have put forward their particular version of how Islam or Turkish history should be taught in German schools. Sunni Muslims propose Koran lessons, Kemalists warn against this, Leftists propose teaching 'ethics of life' and Alevis want Alevism to be taught on par with other religions. Yet, these instances do not have an indirect message to Turkish authorities, but rather reflect how migrant political initiatives can have a homeland political frame of reference.

In addition, organizations may use seminars or meetings organized around other subjects to inject their views on Turkish politics or Turkish–German relations. For instance, a seminar organized by the Turkish organization ATT and the German Friedrich Ebert Stiftung in 1997 on 'The Turkish and German Media and Integration' gave ample opportunity for the ATT executive to specify where he felt the German press conveyed a wrong or insufficient impression of Turkish political affairs. Indeed, at this particular event, the leader of the organization opened the seminar with a lengthy speech on German–Turkish relations including a plea to German authorities not to accept asylum seekers from Turkey whose claims of state persecution are unfounded and who use their asylum in Germany to carry out subversive activities against the Turkish political regime.

Significantly, there is also an increased use of German language in the publications of the organizations. To some extent this is to accommodate those second or third generation Turks and Kurds who do not speak Turkish or Kurdish, but it is also to reach a wider audience. Thus, most organizations have begun publishing their membership journals in Turkish and German (in some instances, only in German), as well as issuing press releases and pamphlets in both languages. Moreover, most Turkish and German organizations have made an active effort recruit younger members the executive board. For instance, the GDF proudly announced in its membership journal that the average age of its new board had fallen from 48 to 33 years (GDF 1997). When contacting the organizations, I was often immediately allocated to a member of the executive board, who had grown up in Germany, was highly educated and spoke fluent German. Such a strategy is, of course, used to accommodate the fact that few non-Turkish researchers or journalists speak Turkish. However, it also serves to accentuate the 'immigrant political' image of the organization.

Another trend is how Turks and Kurds with a very critical homeland political attitude towards Turkish politics moved from a more anachronistic rhetoric of old revolutionary movements (more closely associated with Turkish left-wing Maoist or Marxist–Leninist movements) towards a more human rights-based rhetoric. Thus, Turkish left-wing or Kurdish seminars and panel discussions deal with particular dimensions of human rights abuse by the Turkish state or conceptual definitions of nationhood and state formation. Pamphlets refer to Human Rights Conventions, scholarly work on the subject, and recent inter-governmental or supranational summits. Left behind is the more unfocused meeting where the participants are encouraged through paroles of anti-fascism and anti-imperialism to fight against the general oppression in Turkey (see also, Østergaard-Nielsen 2002a). Similarly, religious organizations are making more references to human rights conventions and less to religious text when arguing for rights to bear headscarves, build mosques, or organize koran courses (see also, Soysal 2000). For instance, on the website of the *Milli Görüş*, one can find documentation written by their 'Human Rights Department' on the subject of 'Freedom of religion and conscience in Turkey'. In this document, the *Milli Görüş* describes how the Turkish State, in its opinion, violates the European Human Rights Convention on religious rights in many instances (IGMG 2000).

Transnational networks with organizations in other European countries

While most information campaigns are formulated and carried out at the level of the nation state, there is an increased salience of homeland political activities which are aided by or take place through means unbounded by national borders. In order to reach the attention of relevant policy makers – and at the same time mobilize Turks and Kurds abroad – organizations may draw on their networks with counterparts elsewhere in Europe.

Indeed, the very institutionalization of most homeland political movements at the European level strongly indicates the unboundedness of homeland politics. During the last two decades in particular, Turkish and Kurdish migrant organizations have set up European federations. In a few cases, such as the Alevi AABF, such attempts have been aborted as the various national Federations could not agree on who to appoint as the European executive. Otherwise, almost all the organizations, mentioned in Chapter 4, now have European headquarters. In some cases, such as the Kemalist AADD, this 'Europeanization' seems the initiative of the migrant organizations themselves. Both the AADD and the AABF have assisted in setting up organizations among more recently mobilized groups in other countries. In other cases, such as the *Türk Federasyon*, most of the Sunni Muslim organizations, the more extreme left, and the Kurdish organizations, the networks are also facilitated by the fact that there are organizations in different European countries with the same Turkish political counterparts. In such cases, the German-based federations, with their larger support structure, serve as a bridgehead between political parties or movements in Turkey and organizations in other European countries. Organizations without a European headquarter may have links of a more informal nature, often based on personal contacts. Indeed, one gets the impression that there can be more contact and cooperation within the various Kurdish or Turkish groups at the European level than among movements within the same country.

Turkish and Kurdish organizations draw on these transnational links and connections with other organizations in countries outside Turkey in a variety of ways. Organizations banned in one country can open offices in others where such bans have not been imposed. The ERNK's opening of an office in Copenhagen in 1995 following the closure of its offices in Germany is a case in point. More usually, transnational links are used to exchange press releases, information pamphlets, and other relevant material. The fact that an increasing amount of material is in English (the *Milli Görüş* and AABF) or French (the New Left) means that such material is not produced by or for German organizations only. Moreover, they share information on demonstrations and other large-scale events which in turn attract supporters from all over Europe. Once, at a Kurdish demonstration in Hague in 1999, I was looking for Kurds from Holland to interview, but the first five Kurds I approached were from various German cities, transported to the Hague in buses. Similarly, delegates of organizations from different European countries meet at the annual mass-meetings; outside are parked buses with signs testifying to European countries of origin. Moreover, particular Kurdish movements supporting the PKK have used their European networks to coordinate demonstrations to happen simultaneously in different cities. As already mentioned, Kurds protested against capture of the PKK leader, Abdullah Öcalan in November 1999, throughout Europe, the US, Russia, and Australia. Apparently mobile phones were used to update protesters throughout the world (Østergaard-Nielsen 2002a).

Transnational networks are clearly aided by modern means of communication. Some organizations, in stark opposition to Turkish policies, have set up TV stations to produce programmes for Turks or Kurds both inside and outside of Turkey. The Kurdish MEDYA-TV produces a vast range of programmes in Kurdish including children's programmes and political debates. However, up through the 1990s, the MEDYA-TV has struggled to find hosting satellites which could withstand the Turkish government's pressure for a ban of the channel (*Verfassungsschutz* 2000: 193; Rogers 1999).[6]

More generally, faxes, phones, and lately e-mail and Internet are part of the equipment in all Turkish or Kurdish organizations in Germany. In particular, the use of the Internet is becoming an increasingly important vehicle for transnational communication by most Turkish and Kurdish organizations. This author used to receive press releases and newsletters by fax, but now most material arrive via e-mail. All organizations have set up web pages over the last five years with their aims, code of practice, virtual libraries, relevant press cuttings, and press releases, announcement of coming events, and links to membership organizations and other relevant NGOs, and political parties. Obviously, this is a particularly useful resource for those organizations which otherwise operate underground with no public address or office building. In particular, organizations from the New Left are active on the Net. Their sights are monitored by the German *Verfassungsschutz*, which include an increasing amount of web material in their annual reports on foreigners' extreme activities.

A European network or even federation lends legitimacy to lobbying at the level of European supranational or inter-governmental institutions. However, only a few organizations utilize these links to advocate homeland political agendas at the level of European political institutions, such as the European Parliament. In terms of homeland politics it is mainly the Kurdish movements, the Alevis and the employers' associations, such as the ATIAD, which lobby at this level. Other organizations' European-level lobbying consists of sending letters to the European parliament expressing discontent with or approval of their various decisions on EU–Turkish relations. That far from all organizations are engaging themselves in political activities at the level of European political institutions is most likely related to the fact that European level lobbying requires additional resources and knowledge, which only a small fraction of the migrant organizations can mobilize. For instance, the ATIAD, which undertakes extensive lobbying at the level of EU institutions, is at the same time a very financially resourceful organization, as illustrated by the range of activities undertaken to influence the decision of the European Parliament to agree to the Customs Union with Turkey in 1995 (ATIAD 1996).[7] More usually, international or supranational institutions, such as the European parliament, serve as a frame of reference for lobbying at national level. European Parliament decisions in favour of minority, cultural, and religious rights are evoked in campaigns for Kurdish rights in the same manner as human rights norms and conventions are.

From confrontational activities to multi-layered strategies

The above descriptions illustrate the scope and width of Turkish and Kurdish organizations' homeland political information campaigns in Germany. They also highlight trends and developments within the field of Turkish politics in Germany over the last two decades.

Few movements and organizations seek to provoke political change in Turkey directly through military, economic, or political means. Rather, there is a tendency to make a detour through German political institutions, and to seek to influence the German government to pursue a particular policy towards Turkey. Homeland opposition aims to use German channels to bring about changes in Turkey, and pro-Turkish forces try to engage themselves in bettering the relationship between their homeland and their receiving country. To this end, a variety of strategies and activities are employed spanning from illegal violent activities to selective lobbying of parliamentarians. Over time, there has been a change in the various political channels used. Most Turkish and Kurdish political organizations in Germany have added institutional participation to their confrontational strategies. And in both instances they may draw on their transnational networks throughout Europe. Confrontational strategies are still being used, but increasingly mass rallies and meetings involve speeches by German politicians, and are co-organized with German institutions. Thus, a process of institutional channeling has taken place whereby the forms of Turkish and Kurdish political activities have adapted to their German political institutional environment. Indeed, many organizations are increasingly employing a multi-stranded approach to advocating their agendas, combining large-scale public events with seminars, and using the Turkish press and meetings with individual politicians. This development has clearly come to stay, although some organizations occasionally express their frustration with the lack of visible results. As stated by a representative from the KOMKAR in an interview in an Alevi membership journal:

> For years we have been defending democracy and peace while armed conflict was continuing in Turkey, but nobody heard our voice. They only heard the voice of those who were supporting the armed struggle.
> (The KOMKAR in AABF 2000)

The question remains, why some organizations and movements choose more institutional participation while others continue to employ confrontational strategies. The field of agency is complex, as organizations are using multi-layered strategies. Certainly the choice of strategy and method of working depend on the particular organization or network's social, economic, and political resources. Moreover, a pattern emerges whereby the degree of inclusion is related to the degree to which the organization presents itself as homeland political (as opposed to immigrant political). In other words, inclusion is related to the extent to which the goals of the organization comply with political norms and agendas of political actors in Germany, and this tends to be a self-reinforcing process. The more an organization is included in the political system, the more compromises are made in terms of goals and activities, and the less radical this organization becomes. The less an organization or movement is included in the political system, the fewer compromises are made in terms of goals, and the more radical it may be. In general, Turkish citizens in Germany, because they are without voting rights in Germany (and Turkey), have been forced to operate as 'outsiders'. Some groups have departed their more radical agendas and rhetoric in order to cooperate with German authorities, while others have not and their agendas have remained beyond the realm of compromise with policy makers, either in their receiving country or their homeland.

Thus, including both the political system of the receiving country *and* the homeland complements the understanding of the extent to which immigrants and refugees cooperate with political institutions while residing in their receiving country. Most importantly, the relationship between the diasporas and their receiving country and homeland, respectively, constitutes a 'mirror effect'. Political mobilization by a Turkish political party in the diasporas may for that very reason keep that group outside of the system of German politics. For instance, the *Türk Federasyon* is, due to its close relations with MHP, not attractive for any German political party. Similarly, the *Milli Görüş*, closely associated with the Turkish *Fazilet Partisi* is, despite its strong position among migrants in Germany, by no means wooed by German political parties. One way of overcoming these barriers is to formulate information campaigns in more immigrant political terms or link them with human rights norms and conventions. A much less used strategy is to turn to European institutions.

Thus, development of strategies to advocate homeland-related agendas does not parallel the patterns of the diasporas' political activities aimed at bettering their situation in the receiving country. While immigration politics are increasingly being negotiated within the system, German political institutions or authorities do not welcome homeland political issues to the same extent. Yet, one cannot say that diaspora politics are taking place outside the system while immigrant politics are on the inside. Rather, they are not being integrated at the same pace. An important factor in this respect is the great reluctance within German political institutions to accept homeland politics of the communities from Turkey as part of the political affairs of Germany. This reluctance will be dealt with further in the next chapter, where an analysis of reactions to diaspora politics by German authorities and political institutions complements the understanding of the relationship between patterns of participation and the receiving country's political structure of opportunity.

6 Thresholds of tolerance
Turkish politics within
German political institutions

Migrants' transnational political practices raise the question of what interests are at stake for the receiving country. While issues of immigration and integration of Turkish citizens in Germany are being recognized as increasingly significant for Turkish–German relations, the homeland political efforts of the communities themselves are still viewed with some scepticism. There is a reluctance to deal with homeland political agendas, to have Turkish politics play itself out on German soil, and to represent the Turkish citizens as Turks or Kurds, Sunnis or Alevis, rather than as immigrants, in German politics.

Accordingly, two main issues are addressed in this chapter. The first is the extent to which German political institutions tolerate Turkish politics within their realm. In tandem with the first is the second issue, the effectiveness of transnational political activities. To what extent do the various Turkish and Kurdish groups succeed in introducing issues related to Turkish domestic and foreign politics to the policy makers of their country of residence? In explaining why some information campaigns get more notice from policy makers than others, it will be shown how 'host' state politicians try to weigh the following two considerations against each other: (a) the 'degree of institutionalization' of the issue at stake and its compatibility with international norms (legitimacy of political agenda); and (b) national interests such as the relationship with the homeland and the 'harmonious coexistence' of ethnic minorities in Germany. In this discussion, the main emphasis will be on the agendas of the Kurdish and Sunni Muslim movements, with the Alevi movement as an intermediate case.

General perceptions of homeland politics

Already in 1984, German authorities took note of the fact that not only were the activities of foreigners' organizations influenced by events in the homeland, but also the foreign policy decisions of the German federal government played a considerable role in the mobilization and engagement of these organizations (*Verfassungsschutz* 1984: 175). Since then, the presence of more than 2 million Turkish citizens in Germany has heightened the awareness of Turkish domestic political issues, as well as German–Turkish relations, among German political parties. Increasingly, German politicians are making an explicit link (in parliamentary debates and documents, and statements to the press) between the Turks and Kurds in Germany and the developments in Turkey. They are mainly concerned with how domestic political developments in Turkey may effect the activities of the German-based homeland political opposition to the Turkish state and government. Notably, there has been a concern that changes in Turkish domestic politics may radicalize the communities from Turkey in Germany (see among others, *Deutscher Bundestag* 1981b, 1999).

Moreover, in particular in 1997–8 there was an increasing concern that a deterioration of European–Turkish relations would make those of Turkish origin feel unwelcome in Germany. As stated by Thomas Kossendey, member of Bundestag for the CDU who is also previous chairman of the Turkish–German Parliamentarian group:

> It is very hurtful for Turks to see how their country is discussed in Germany [...] we have a difficult situation in which the foreign policy relations with Turkey have become a domestic political conflict.
>
> (Interview with MdB for CDU, 11 December 1997)

Similarly, Leyla Onur, member of *Bundestag* for the SPD, found that in speeches and statements about Turkey every 'word is weighed very carefully because each word may be taken personally by the Turkish community in Germany', she continued:

> Turkey is no longer just important in terms of foreign policy, but has become a domestic political issue because of the more than 2 million people of Turkish descent living here. When we say something critical about China or India we have no idea if they get upset. But with Turkey we do.
>
> (Interview with MdB for SPD, 11 December 1997)

Consequently, German parties follow Turkish politics relatively closely. There are consultative networks between parties and parliamentarians from both countries, and several institutions have been created to deal with Turkish politics in particular. Among others, the SPD has set up a unique coordination group on Turkey consisting of SPD members of the Landtag, Bundestag, European Parliament, and the Friedrich Ebert Stiftung (interview with MdB for SPD, 12 December 1997). Also, the establishment of the German–Turkish Parliamentarian Group in 1994 is a reflection of the inextricable connectedness between the two countries. This group, led by a German and Turkish parliamentarian, deals with all aspects of German–Turkish relations including the role of Turkish citizens in Germany. The group is lobbied by organizations spanning from the Kurdish KOMKAR to the employers' association ATIAD, and its chairman finds that it has functioned as an important source of information for German politicians on Turkish domestic political issues and on the plight of the migrants and refugees (interview with MdB for CDU, 11 December 1997).

Patterns of dialogue

Beyond German politicians acknowledging the fact that foreign policy towards Turkey matters to resident Turks and Kurds, it is difficult to trace how foreign policy towards Turkey actually changes due to the efforts of the various homeland political movements. The passive presence of a minority of one country in another may be taken into consideration in bilateral relations. However, it is rarely feasible to measure the effect of homeland political lobbying on the receiving country's foreign policy. The position of this analysis is that if a position on policy is not in the receiving country's interests then the foreign policy lobbying of an ethnic minority is usually not successful. Yet, there may be instances in which a country's foreign policy may be guided in a particular direction or the attention to the issue is 'scaled up' because of such lobbying. Here, it helps if the ethnic minority is a substantial part of the electorate, or if it constitutes a powerful economic interest. However, neither of these features characterizes the communities of Turkish citizens in Germany. The vast majority of Turks or Kurds in Germany cannot vote, and, despite the rapid growth in 'Turkish business' in Germany, the communities of Turkish origin are still far from being as economically significant as the Chinese, Indian, or Jewish diasporas in the US.

Nonetheless, as described in the previous chapter, homeland political issues have been persistently put forward by various ethnic, religious, and party political movements in Germany. The effectiveness of such efforts may be assessed by standards other than actual changes in German foreign policy. As discussed in Chapter 2, one such measure of effectiveness may be the extent to which German politicians engage in dialogue on homeland political issues. This dialogue relates to the extent to which transnational political movements succeed in framing debates, putting issues on the agenda, and establishing channels of communication with central policy actors.

Therefore, it is of interest which groups the politicians consider legitimate interlocutors. The following section will focus on how homeland political issues unfold within a selection of German political institutions (trade unions and political parties).[1] These cases also have a chronological aspect. First came the trade unions, which were the main German political institutions within which Turkish guest workers expressed their homeland political concerns; then came the closer dialogue with German political parties. Note that the primary incentive to become a trade unionist or to join a German political party is, of course, not necessarily to further a homeland political agenda but to work on immigrant political or other issues. However, issues pertaining to Turkish domestic politics have been unfolding within these institutions in ways that allude to the complex ways in which national political institutions perceive and react to migrants' transnational political practices.

The trade unions

The trade unions were one of the main political fora in which Turkish citizens in Germany were organized, especially in the 1960s and the 1970s.[2] As formulated by one former Turkish trade unionist in Germany: 'Unions were our organizations, there we had a say. They dealt with our day-to-day life and our future.' (interview with IGMetall, 13 October 2000). Given their lack of earlier trade union affiliation, the level of trade union organization among Turkish workers in Germany was surprisingly high.[3] In 1974, 34 per cent of the Turkish citizens employed in Germany were organized in one of the trade unions belonging to the *Deutsche Gewerkschaftsbund* (DGB), which is one of the main federations of trade unions in Germany. This figure rose to more than 50 per cent in 1983 and has fluctuated between 40 and 45 per cent since 1989.[4] That means that the level of organization of Turkish workers was, and is, higher than the average level of organization of foreign workers in trade unions in Germany.

Turkish workers, in particular, were very willing to fight for their rights as workers alongside their German colleagues (Aslantepe 1990). With the change in the code of industrial relations in 1972, foreign workers gained the right to be elected to positions in trade union committees within German trade unions. Already in the first election in 1972, 769 Turkish workers were elected as trade union committee members. In the following election in 1975, this figure more than doubled to 1,589, and since then the level of Turkish citizens in trade union committees has been steadily rising, reaching 3,545 in 1994.[5] Similarly, foreign workers have been elected as trade union representatives on an increasing scale. However, relatively few Turkish citizens have risen to high positions within the ranks of the unions. It was not until 1992 that Yilmaz Karahasan, former worker at the Ford Factory in Cologne, was elected as the first foreigner to the Federal Executive Board of the trade union for metal workers, IGMetall (*Tageszeitung*, 14 October 1992).

According to one interviewee, political conflicts in Turkey began to spill over to the trade unions in Germany from the early 1970s, as 'every political group sought to use the trade union as a platform' (interview with IGMetall, 17 December 1998). Thus, in the 1970s and the 1980s the right- *versus* left-wing clashes in Turkey were replicated within the trade unions. In elections for trade union committees or trade union representatives, supporters of the nationalist MHP supporters would run against supporters of the communist TKP (interview with IGMetall, 27 May 1998).

The extent to which Turkish colleagues' influenced their trade unions' political stance towards Turkey is difficult to discern. Throughout the 1980s, the stance of the DGB and IGMetall was largely similar to that of the German left-wing opposition. The DGB urged the German government to halt military aid and weapon supplies to Turkey and to put pressure on the Turkish authorities to re-install democracy after the coup in 1980, and respect human rights.[6] Trade unions also put forward their opinion on human rights problems in other parts of the world, but both the DGB and IGMetall took a relatively large interest in Turkish domestic political affairs in the first half of the 1980s. Moreover, the trade unions concerned themselves with the situation of trade unionists in Turkey, many of whom were hard hit by the military coup in 1980.[7] Not surprisingly, the DGB and IGMetall, along with trade unions throughout Europe, criticized the imprisonment of the leader of the confederation of socialist trade unions in Turkey (DISK), Abdullah Baştürk, and 51 other trade unionists.[8] They also urged the German government to welcome asylum seekers fleeing Turkey due to their union-related or other political work. It is likely that the numerical presence of 'Turkish colleagues' added to the traditional agenda of international workers' solidarity. Indeed, a relatively large number of Turkish workers in Germany were arrested upon return to Turkey because of their political activities abroad, and trade unions went far to help these people (see Chapter 7).

Workers of all kinds of political or religious persuasion were organized in German trade unions. Yet, perhaps not surprisingly, trade unions such as the DGB and IGMetall had a somewhat one-sided perception of Turkish political organizations in Germany. Both trade unions expressed great concern over the violence and extremism of right-wing movements such as the Grey Wolves (MHP), whereas the activities of extreme and violent left-wing movements such as the *Devrimci Sol*, were passed over in silence.[9] For instance, demands for a ban of the organization of the Grey Wolves were included in a motion, which urged the countering of wider fascistic and neo-fascistic tendencies in Germany (DGB 1982). Similarly, in the membership journal of the IGMetall at the beginning of the 1980s, there were many critical articles on the political situation in Turkey and the activities of MHP-related organizations in Germany. Indeed, almost all of the articles on Turkish politics addressed the organization of MHP in Germany in the years 1980–2. Also, the DGB compiled and wrote 'background material' on so-called 'fanatic' religious movements – such as the Nurcular, Süleymancilar, and MSP (later *Milli Görüş*) – seeking to expose the anti-Kemalist and anti-laic elements within these movements (DGB 1980).

Yet, at the same time, the presence of radical homeland political groups in Germany in general, and within the trade unions in particular, was criticized in more general terms, as in the following example:

> Time and time again, the DGB has warned against the fighting out of domestic political disputes from other countries in Germany. The DGB has encouraged the foreign workers to be on their guard against groups from their homelands which try to transfer party-political problems to their host-country and misuse the foreign workers as vehicles to transport extremist political ideas. Political groups which are recognized and proved to represent radical political ideas and who are not in accordance with the constitution of Germany, and are misusing the opportunity to be politically active in Germany, should be banned as soon as possible.
>
> (DGB 1983)

The statement concludes that such attitudes are also in the interest of the Turkish workers since such activities strain the relations between Germans and foreigners (DGB 1983).

Similarly, Yilmaz Karahasan, member of IGMetall's federal executive board, recalls how the IGMetall did not want to touch the issue of its Turkish members' homeland political affiliation:

> The Turkish fascists were very active. There were no confrontations, but they directed their criticism against persons like me. Back then we ran a newspaper in Turkish and it was often criticized for being communist propaganda. So at one point we wanted to make a survey among the foreign workers to find out what we could do better in terms of the newspaper, the union, and so on. Among other things, I wanted to add a question to see if they were members of a German party or a Turkish party, and I wrote the names of the parties [...] and included the MHP, because I wanted to know if there were many fascists among the Turks. But then some fascists complained and I was suspended [...] until all accusations were cleared. They [the IGMetall executive] translated all my writings in the newspaper. After two or three weeks I was allowed back. So it was difficult to do Turkish politics in German unions. Because if the members complained or threatened to leave then money would be lost and the union got cold feet. And unions are not revolutionary organizations. In particular in Germany.
>
> (Interview with IGMetall, 13 October 2000)

Since the late 1980s there have been no motions, press releases, or events to advocate human rights in Turkey from the DGB or IGMetall. Both trade unions are continuously approached by Kurdish organizations and members to support their information campaigns. But while executive members may lend their support, this has only resulted in a few wider calls for a solution to the Kurdish issue (DGB 1992; IGMetall 1994). Instead, German trade unions engage themselves in immigrant political issues.

Homeland politics at the ballot box?

German political parties and the potential electorate of Turkish origin are showing a growing mutual interest in each other. In general Turks in Germany feel more represented by the Turkish than by the German government or German political parties (ZfT 2001: 135). Still, an increasing number of voters of Turkish descent, an estimated 160,000 in the German election in 1998, support, join, or even run as candidates for the various German parties. Electoral polls are periodically published to show the party political preference of Turkish citizens. When one such poll was conducted in the run up to the Federal election in 1998, half of the respondents were not clear on their German political preferences but for those who were clear, the distribution is described in Table 6.1.

This clear preference for the SPD has its historical legacy in the organization of Turkish workers in German trade unions.[10] It shows that voters of Turkish or Kurdish descent support a German political party because of its policies to further equal rights for migrants. In general, Turks are still more interested in Turkish politics than in German politics, although the balance is slowly changing (ZfT 2000b: 134). Yet, when they vote in German elections they vote with their

Table 6.1 Party political preferences of German and Turkish citizens

German political party	Support in per cent		
	1998		2000
	Germans	Turkish citizens	Turkish citizens
SPD	40.9	70.4	67.1
Bundnis90/Die Grüne	6.7	16.9	15.0
CDU/CSU	35.3	7.6	10.5
FDP	6.2	1.5	4.5
PDS	5.1	3.2	1.3
Others	5.8	0.4	1.3

Sources: ZfT, 1998b, 2000c; *Deutscher Bundestag*, Infothek, www.bundestag.de/info/wahlen.

Note: For 1998 (and 2000) the Turkish data is from a sample of approximately 1,000 Turks taken before the Federal election, while German data is from the overall results of the Federal election, September 1998.

situation in Germany in mind. In particular, the SPD's electoral promise to introduce dual citizenship was a major attraction for 65 per cent of its Turkish descent voters in 1998 (ZfT 1998b).

Yet, homeland political issues also appear in the interface between German parties and the Turkish or Kurdish descent electorate. Indeed, in 1998, Cem Özdemir, MdB for *Bundnis 90/Die Grüne*, complained that:

> The question of how does party x or y stand on my situation in Germany is being overshadowed by the question of how the party stands vis-a-vis Turkey not least due to the influence of the media.
> (Interview with MdB for *Die Grüne*, 11 February 1998)

The following examples of discussions on Turkish politics in German parties shows that in general these issues do not overshadow immigrant political issues, but they do unfold at times when Turkish members of German parties are dissatisfied with the particular line of the party towards Turkey. Most of these examples are drawn from dialogue between German political parties and their Turkish membership organizations. These organizations provide an interesting prism through which the various common viewpoints and tensions regarding homeland politics may be viewed. Membership of these organizations has also been referred to as the 'detour' Turkish citizens take to get to German political parties (*Tageszeitung*, 17 September 1994). These organizations perceive themselves as bridges between German parties and the wider Turkish electorate. Indeed, in many instances they serve as hothouses for candidates of Turkish descent in local and federal elections.

Such candidates, however, often have a very ambiguous relationship with Turkish politics. The Turkish or Kurdish descent German politicians interviewed can be divided into two main groups. First, those who are actively engaged in Turkish politics. In particular, the Kurdish descent German representatives in local councils and national parliaments partake in or even initiate campaigns for further Kurdish rights in Germany as well as in Turkey. By contrast, in particular younger Turkish descent policy makers seek to distance themselves from Turkish politics because they want to concentrate on local or national German politics only. Moreover, they find the factionalism among migrant and refugee organizations frustrating because going to one organization shuts the doors of another. There are more votes to be lost than gained by taking a strong stand on Turkish domestic politics or German–Turkish relations. Yet, in some cases Turkish politics can be hard to keep at bay. A prime example is Cem Özdemir who have found himself at the centre of a long-lasting debate in the Turkish press about how loyal to Turkey, Turkish descent politicians in Germany should be (see also Chapter 7). Özdemir himself claims that he had to learn about Turkish politics *after* he entered German politics (interview with MdB for *Die Grüne*, 11 February 1998).

The Social Democrats

As already mentioned, the SPD enjoys widespread support among the Turkish descent electorate. The changes in German citizenship law in early 2000 disappointed Turkish supporters' hope for dual citizenship, but there has been widespread appreciation of the fact that the SPD government supported Turkey's EU candidacy at the Helsinki Summit in 1999. However, during the 1990s, the SPD's critical attitude towards Turkey led to conflicts with their Turkish peers in general, and members of the organization of Turkish social democrats, the HDF, in particular. As opposed to the other Turkish membership organizations of German parties, the HDF was founded on the initiative of the Turkish social democrats (CHP) and not the German social democrats. Yet, many members of the HDF are also members of the SPD, and while the SPD does not fund the HDF, the SPD party foundation, the Friedrich Ebert Stiftung, co-organizes and funds the seminars of the HDF. In terms of Turkish politics, the HDF warns against Islamist and separatist forces and hopes to modify the attitude of SPD towards Turkey's EU candidacy (interview with HDF, 5 August 1998).

The tension between the HDF's views on Turkey and those of the SPD peaked in April 1994, when Rudolph Scharping, then leader of the SPD, remarked that 'the federal government, EU, and NATO have been passively watching the genocide against the Kurds in Turkey' (*Tageszeitung*, 13 April 1994). The reactions in the Turkish media and among Turkish social democrats was strong. With the headline 'Worse than Shririnowski', the *Hürriyet* sharply condemned the statement and also reprinted an open letter from the HDF executive committee to Scharping, which expressed disappointment with such 'thoughtless and malicious' remarks (*Hürriyet*, 7 April 1994). HDF members wrote:

> Your public statement [...] has disappointed the Turks living here and the members of the SPD [...] The most important task for a state is the protection

of its people and its territory. What the Turkish state is doing against the PKK is nothing else but that. There cannot be used such expressions as 'extermination' or 'segregation' in a country where a third of the Parliamentarians are Kurds, and where these are given high office and can even be President.

(The HDF in *Tageszeitung*, 13 April 1994)[11]

There is a common belief that the SPD lost Turkish members during this period (interview with HDF, 5 August 1998; interview with MdB for SPD, 11 December 1997). However, this cannot easily be verified as the SPD does not register members according to nationality. In any case, it is clear that the perceptions of Turkish citizens in Germany increasingly matter to the SPD. For instance, in the aftermath of Scharping's comment, there were 'long discussions at the highest level' in the SPD. After that a policy paper on Turkey was formulated, which clearly stated the opinion of the SPD (interview with MdB of SPD, 11 December 1998).[12] At the 1997 federal party meeting, the Jusos (the youth group of the SPD) put forward a very critical motion on the Kurdish issue in Turkey and Germany. In order to avoid further polarization within the party on policies towards Turkey, an alternative motion was swiftly formulated, which, while still critical of Turkish policy, was far more constructive in terms of Turkey–European relations. Accordingly, a heated debate was avoided, as both motions were referred to the SPD Commission for Foreign and Security Politics. Thus, this account indicates an attempt within the SPD to word criticism of Turkey more carefully. While it is impossible to say that this shift is due to the influence of its Turkish members, it is significant that it has been justified in this way.

Bundnis90/Die Grüne

Die Grüne may have less electoral support by Turkish descent voters than the SPD, yet they have more Turkish or Kurdish origin candidates than any other party. They are attractive for Turkish voters because of their engagement in immigrant political issues, such as support for dual citizenship, and stronger measures to fight discrimination. In terms of Turkish politics, *Die Grüne*, in particular when they have served in opposition, takes a more critical line towards Turkey, concentrating on human rights, asylum seekers, and arms deliveries.

In 1992, Turkish members of *Die Grüne* established the organization *Yeşiller* (meaning 'the Greens' in Turkish). Its main aims were to further the political influence of immigrants in the light of increasing exclusion and discrimination, to recruit members of Turkish descent for *Die Grüne*, and to build a lobby within the party (*Hürriyet*, 2 March 1992; Özdemir 1997: 96). However, this organization did not survive long because it proved impossible to overcome political differences related to Turkey between Kurds and Turks. Instead, *Yeşiller* was replaced by an immigrant organization, *Immigrün*, which is open to foreigners of all nationalities and in which 'debates on Turkish politics are taboo' (*Tageszeitung*, 17 September 1994). These developments largely reflect the main dilemma for *Die Grüne*: how to maintain their critical stance towards Turkey while at the same time not distance those Turkish descent members and voters who support *Die Grüne* for their policies on integration. As stated by Özdemir:

> The bitter lesson: Not only could we not bridge, overcome or keep out the various differences between us. The conflict between Turks and Kurds [...] was also instrumentalized in personal and political questions. For some we were too close to Turkey, for others we were too critical.
>
> (Özdemir 1997: 97)

However, *Die Grüne* increasingly formulate their questions and speeches more carefully and do not defend the PKK in the way that PDS does. Moreover, they and their candidates mainly focus on immigrant politics in their dealings with their Turkish descent electorate. For instance, a Berlin Senate member of Turkish descent describes how he overcame the homeland political obstacles to his election campaign:

> [For some] we were the anti-Turkey party, that is, the pro-Kurdish party, because of the human rights situation and our statements. Yes, and that had the consequence that I had difficulties in going to the Turkish organizations, because I was from *Die Grüne*, because they would not have anything to do with *Die Grüne*. Then when I made clear what I do and what I have done [in terms of migrant politics] the doors were slowly opened. When they brought up this Kurdish issue, I have always said: "We are in Berlin, in Germany, we are not in Turkey; we should not keep what is happening in Turkey a secret, but I have not come to talk about that. I have come to talk about Berlin, about Kreuzberg, about your problems." Or I would say: "If we were really a pro-Kurdish party, then why have I founded a German–Turkish school in Berlin? Why not a German–Kurdish school?"
>
> (Interview with member of Berlin Senate for *Die Grüne*, 11 September 2000)

The Socialists

Of the left-wing opposition, it is the PDS which continuously promotes the most critical attitude to the Turkish state and government. Whereas both the SPD and *Die Grüne* have softened their stances towards Turkey, the PDS continuously proposes that Germany stop military aid and help find a solution to the problems of human rights and the Kurdish problem. The PDS also has several representatives of Kurdish descent, such as in the Berlin Senate and the Cologne city council, who actively work for Kurdish minority rights in Germany. As commented by one of them:

> I do not agree with everything that the PDS stands for, there are always things with which one cannot identify fully. PDS does good work for the Kurds, but PDS also needs the Kurds.
>
> (Interview with representative for the PDS in Cologne local council, 12 October 2000)

The PDS representatives in the *Bundestag* and *Landstag* are in closer dialogue with more radical Kurdish organizations, such as the PKK, than any other party. One of the PDS representatives in the Bundestag, Ulla Jelpke, has asked more than a thousand questions in the 13th election period, many of which urge for the lifting of the ban on the PKK. Indeed the representation by the PDS of this part of the Kurdish movement led to the following comment during a debate on the PKK in the *Bundestag*: '[...] one gets the impression that we have given the time for speaking to the PKK rather than to a member of the German *Bundestag*.' (*Deutscher Bundestag* 1996).

However, since the capture of PKK leader Abdullah Öcalan and the PKK's changing of tactics from active military insertion to more peaceful information campaigns, there have been problems between the PDS and PKK supporters in Germany. PDS representatives, in particular Ulla Jelpke, were dissatisfied with the PKK's focus on freedom for Öcalan rather than general freedom for Kurds in Turkey. In Spring 2000, she published an open letter blaming the PKK for the death of 34 dissenting PKK fighters in southern Kurdistan. This led to widespread mutual accusations between Jelpke and PKK supporters in Germany, a development which has disappointed PDS politicians of Kurdish descent.

The Christian Democrats

The CDU only began to show an interest in voters of Turkish descent in the 1990s. Since then the party has experienced an increase in Turkish supporters and members and recently the CDU has put forward Turkish descent candidates.[13] Besides the Turkish organization Hür-Türk, several organizations have been founded by Turks close to the CDU since: 'Hundred of thousands of citizens of Turkish origin feel close to the basic values of the CDU.' (The DTU 1996). Of these, the *Deutsch–Türkische Union* (DTU) was founded in 1996 in Berlin and the *Deutsch–Türkiche Federasyon* (DTF) in 1997 in Nordrhein-Westfalen. The explicit aim of the DTU and DTF is to reach out to German citizens of Turkish origin in an attempt to attract their votes and for the organizations to contribute to policy formulation within the CDU.

Why do Turks support the CDU, when the party's exclusive policies of integration and migration are so far from the stance of most immigrants in Germany? An immediate explanation can be sought in the fact that a substantial part of the citizens of Turkish origin are conservative regarding Turkish political parties. Forty-one per cent of Turkish citizens would have voted for ANAP and DYP in 1994 (Şen and Karakaşoğlu 1994) and hence, this 'right-wing' affiliation is transferred to their German political alignment. However, the reasons for joining the CDU are far more complex; they also reflect the changing social composition of the migrants from Turkey in Germany. The Turks who join the DTU and DTF mainly belong to the rapidly increasing group of Turkish employers, lawyers, and bankers. This group prefers not to be represented by left-wing German parties. The DTU was launched under headlines such as 'The CDU will cultivate fallow land' (*Tagesspiegel*, 23 March 1996); 'Immigrant policies are no longer the monopoly of the left-wing' (*Tageszeitung*, 25 March 1996); and 'Only few Turks can deal with the multicultural soup' (*Die Welt*, 21 August 1996). As phrased by the leader of the DTU, Uzun:

> Those of Turkish origin in the CDU want to leave the 'minority-themes' behind since these rather represent the 'utopia of left-wing party politicians' than the foreigners living in Germany [...] That more and more Turks are joining the CDU is also an indication of the fact that they no longer have any desire to be dictated to by the left-wing.
> (Uzun in *Das Sonntagsblatt*, 16–19 April 1995)

Thus, in terms of common values shared by the CDU and its Turkish members, the meetings and press releases reveal that the main common denominators are a 'conservative liberal outlook of family values, patriotism, order, and private initiative' (*Frankfurter Allgemeine Zeitung*, 22 March 1996).

In addition to immigrant policies, the issue of homeland politics remains. Many Turkish citizens in Germany are not against the regime in their homeland. Indeed, it may be argued that living in Germany furthers a defensive attitude towards domestic political issues in Turkey. One might think that the CDU would not be so attractive in this respect either, as leading CDU parliamentarians have envisaged little room for an Islamic Turkey in a Christian Europe. Yet, the CDU is attractive in terms of homeland politics because it has not criticized Turkey's domestic political problems in the same way that the SPD, *Die Grüne* and the PDS have. The DTU (like Hür-Türk) states in its working programme that it aims for a better relationship between Germany and Turkey (DTU 1996). Statements from the DTU in 1996 reiterate CDU policy: the PKK ban should be upheld and Germany should not interfere with the Turkish way of dealing with the PKK (*Tageszeitung*, 23–24 March 1996). The DTU has also argued that Germany should continue to regard most asylum seekers from Turkey as job seekers, left-wingers, Kurdish agitators, or criminals who:

> [...] seek to damage the situation of the immigrants in Germany and should be deported [...] The PKK is building a base in Germany by misusing the right to asylum. The victims of their attacks are again and again the Turks.
> (Uzun in *Wochenpost*, 8 August 1996)

Accordingly, the DTU has also demanded better security for the Turkish citizens in Germany, not against racist and xenophobic attacks as demanded by more left-wing organizations, but against the Kurdish separatists and left-wing extremists operating on German soil.

The CDU sees this dimension of homeland politics as the 'sugar on the pill' in its relationship with Turkish peers. Those politicians and party officials in closest contact with the DTU are not those CDU representatives who more or less explicitly reject Turkey's EU candidacy on grounds of religious differences. Instead they take a more inclusive stance towards Turkey's EU candidacy. At the launching of the DTU in 1996, Peter Kurth, CDU Secretary of State for Finance in Berlin, said that 'One should not under-estimate the dimension of foreign policy' in the relationship between the CDU and its German voters of Turkish descent (*Tageszeitung*, 25 March 1995). Accordingly, several high-ranking CDU politicians mentioned Turkish politics during interviews regarding the DTU. For instance, Thomas Kossendey, MdB for CDU and leader of the German–Turkish Parliamentarian group, stated, in connection with the founding of the DTU, that hard measures should be taken to curb the PKK (see *Hürriyet*, 8 July 1996 and *Sabah*, 8 July 1996).

Still, the dimension of homeland politics is also regarded with much scepticism within the CDU. This is best reflected through the attempts of the DTU to institutionalize its ties to the CDU. In the beginning, the DTU was not a formal part of the CDU, and at its foundation in 1996, the DTU applied to the CDU to be recognized as an official German–Turkish Forum within the party. However, from the CDU General Secretary Hintze in Bonn, the reaction was cool: 'I do not think we have such an organization and I do not find it right either.' (*Frankfurter Allgemeine Zeitung*, 27 March 1996). Over the summer of 1996, there was growing uneasiness in parts of the CDU at the prospect of having a Turkish membership organization on par with the Women's organization or Youth organization (*Tageszeitung*, 6 August 1996). Indeed, the concern with a 'Turkish lobby' within the CDU surfaced with comments such as: 'One should not forget, that Ankara views its Turks abroad as a part of its foreign policy' (Hapel in *Frankfurter Allgemeine Zeitung*, 7 August 1996).[14]

Thus, while the CDU is tempted by the thought of voters of Turkish descent, they also fear a backlash in terms of German voters. The issue of Islam may serve to further illustrate this. Initially, what could have been perceived as an immediate obstacle on both sides, the 'C' in CDU, was actively played down by the DTU and not presented as a problem: 'The Christian values of the CDU have their counterpart in a modern enlightened Islam.' (Interview with DTU, 9 October 1996). However, in September 1996, a DTU member, Taskiran, set off yet another difficult dispute between the CDU and DTU. Taskiran was a member of the DTU, but was also portrayed as a member of *Milli Görüş* in an article in the widely disseminated German weekly, *Der Spiegel*. Under the heading 'With Kohl and Koran', Taskiran was depicted as but one of many Sunni Muslim fundamentalists who are trying to act as a fifth column in the ranks of the CDU (*Der Spiegel*, 7 October 1996). The article warned against a 'party-political lobby' in the making. Taskiran was swiftly removed from the ranks of the DTU.

Most of the homeland political ground between the CDU and its Turkish descent voters was tested through the formation of the DTU. When the next membership organization, DTF, was founded, the initiators 'did not want to repeat the mistakes of DTU', meaning that homeland political agendas had been weeded out. The 'call for the foundation of the DTF' focused on integration and on the role of the DTF in making Turks more sensitive towards German politics in general and the CDU in particular. There was no mention of the relationship between Turkey and Germany (DTF 1997). Indeed, Karl Lamers, spokesman of the

CDU/CSU *Bundestagsfraktion*, released a statement in connection with the founding of the DTF, saying that: 'One would like the citizens of Turkish origin to be interested not in the politics of their homeland but in those of their new country (*Frankfurter Allgemeine Zeitung*, 6 December 1997).

Between integration policy and foreign policy

Different groups from Turkey seek to find leverage in German policies towards Turkey in order to take aim with their demands for accountability and policy change. Most Turkish and Kurdish homeland political movements and organizations have found attentive German political interlocutors. Yet, some agendas have generally found more sympathy than others. In Chapter 2 it was suggested that governments, in their response to such political lobbying, balance national interests with concerns about wider humanitarian and human rights issues. Thus, to what extent is the German government's attentiveness to homeland political demands affected by German national interests? National interests include foreign policy concerns with an important trade and security political partner like Turkey, concerns with threats to domestic security in Germany posed by more radical dissident homeland political groups, or general concern with harmonious coexistence among Turks, Kurds, and Germans. And to what extent are these foreign and domestic policy concerns tempered by a consideration of the extent to which homeland political demands are backed up by human rights conventions and norms to which also Germany adheres.

The cases of Kurdish and Sunni Muslim lobbying in Germany highlight these points. The Alevis serve as an intermediary case, which emphasizes the discrepancies between the Kurdish and Sunni Muslim cases.

The Kurdish issue

The Kurdish issue, as outlined in Chapters 3 and 4, constitutes one of the most pressing political problems of present-day Turkey. Since the mid-1980s, Kurds in Germany have worked for Kurdish rights in Turkey and, increasingly, in Germany. The Kurdish movements in Germany have been very active in trying to persuade German politicians to put more pressure on Turkish political authorities to find a political solution to their problems. Such pressure, they argue, should be in the form of freezing military (and sometimes economic) aid from Germany to Turkey as well as taking a sterner stance towards Turkish partnership in European intergovernmental cooperation. Finally, Kurdish movements have held Germany accountable for contributing to the conflict by delivering arms to Turkey.

In the German *Bundestag*, the Kurdish issue has been debated to such an extent that one the then State Minister in the Foreign Office, Helmut Schäfer, once commented:

'Because of my long service in this parliament and also as State Minister, I think I can say, that statistically there is no group of people [*Volksgruppe*]

that the German *Bundestag* has discussed so intensively and so considerately as the Kurds – None! ... unfortunately this does not mean that the Kurds in Germany, not even to a small degree, have begun to recognize that no other parliament in the world has taken up their cause as has the German.'
(*Deutscher Bundestag* 1996)

The harshest criticism of Turkey has come from the German left-wing parties and organizations, in particular when in opposition. German governments have, as outlined in Chapter 3, repeatedly urged Turkey to find a solution to its problems with the Kurdish minority, while at the same time trying not to upset an important trade and security-political partner. Thus, the German CDU/FDP government stated that it did: 'recognize the legitimate right of Turkey to curb terrorism with constitutional [*rechstaatliche*] means' (*Deutscher Bundestag* 1993a). But at the same it called for a solution, temporarily froze military aid, and periodically halted deportation of asylum seekers to Turkey. In line with EU foreign policy, the SPD/*Die Grüne* government has continued a critical, but also more constructive policy line, making Turkey's EU membership conditional upon, among other things, Turkey's respect for human rights conventions in dealing with the Kurdish minority.

The seamless web of factors influencing the bilateral relations with Turkey makes it difficult to isolate the significance of German-based Kurdish lobbying for German foreign policy towards Turkey. When calling on Turkey to solve its Kurdish problem, Germany refers to general respect for norms and conventions of human rights and democracy. Moreover, a solution to the Kurdish problem is a foreign policy interest for Germany because it would remove a major obstacle to genuine improvement in EU–Turkey relations. A solution would also halt the inflow of asylum seekers from Turkey, almost all of whom are Kurdish. Last, but not the least, clearly, the presence of 500,000–700,000 Kurds in Germany is of significance. First, Germany views the PKK as a domestic security threat. Parliamentary and public debates on the Kurdish issues have increasingly been linked with the issue of the Kurdish minorities in Germany and the concern with Kurdish–Turkish conflicts replicating themselves on German soil. When PKK leader Öcalan was held in Rome, Germany did not execute its international arrest warrant for him for fear of Kurdish unrest on its soil. Second, German policy makers are aware that only a minority of Kurds in Germany support the PKK or, indeed, violent information campaigns. Yet, it is believed that a solution to the Kurdish issue in Germany would take the homeland political air out of Kurdish migrant organizations leaving more room for immigrant political activities and cooperation with Turkish organizations.

At the same time, German authorities are slow in recognizing Kurdish minority rights in Germany. Kurds from Turkey arrive in Germany as Turkish citizens, and therefore only figure in German statistics in the accompanying explanatory text. This has concerned parts of the Kurdish community in Germany, in particular those who have arrived as asylum seekers. For these Kurds, German policies have felt like a continuation of Turkish minority laws. For instance, it has been the practice of German authorities only to recognize names from a Turkish official list, thereby forcing Kurds to name their children in Turkish and not in Kurdish (*Deutscher Bundestag* 1986b). After extensive lobbying, this curious practice has now been abolished.[15] Another example comes out of Berlin. As the city with the largest Turkish population outside of Turkey, Berlin has an estimated Kurdish population of between 25,000 and 50,000. Yet, until 1998 there was no separate information material on the Kurdish minority at the offices of the Office for Commissioner for Foreigners, despite the fact that other much smaller immigrant groups such as the Korean, Latin-American, and Vietnamese communities had their own separate leaflets. Several times information material was commissioned, but never published. The fact that it was never published was questioned by a member of the Berlin Senate of Kurdish origin for the PDS, Giyasettin Sayan. The answer from the Senate Department of Health and Social Issues stated that the manuscripts submitted in 1992–3 and 1996 were not:

> Fit for publication since on the background of the known conflicts, especially the one in Turkey, such a presentation must not strain the living together of Turks and Kurds in Berlin.
> (Berlin Senate's Department for Health and Social Issues 1996)

Later, a booklet called *Das Türkische Berlin*, co-edited by a German, included a lengthy section on the Kurdish minority, their situation in Turkey and their organizations in Germany (Greve and Çinar 1998: 21–3). This did not, however, satisfy the Kurdish organizations, which have produced their own information booklet *Kurden in Berlin*. But again this was not accepted as an official publication by the Foreigners Commission (interview with member of the Berlin Senate for PDS, 29 September 2000).

The lack of comprehensive recognition of a Kurdish minority separate from the Turkish minority is interpreted by Kurdish migrant organizations as the result of persistent pressure by Turkey and Turkish organizations in Germany. They argue that German responses to immigrant political demands by Kurdish movements reflect broader policy decisions not to support their homeland political cause. Certainly, both Turkey and Turkish migrant organizations have lobbied for Germany not to 'support separatist organizations'. Yet, the general response of German authorities should also be seen in the context of wider German integration policies which are based on national rather than ethnic minorities.

Still, both domestic security concerns and wider considerations of relations with Turkey have played into relations between the German authorities and Kurdish organizations in Germany. There have been instances when Kurdish organizations in Germany were unable to obtain *ABM-kräfte*, that is, state-subsidized assistants. When politicians from *Die Grüne* demanded an explanation, the government replied that German authorities take the relationship with Turkey into consideration when dealing with Kurdish organizations in Germany. For instance, the Foreign Ministry stated that the activities of Kurdish organizations in

Germany must not be supported by resources from federal authorities, because such organizations view themselves as 'political combat units' (*Deutscher Bundestag* 1995b). Even if immigrant political demands for support for cultural activities are put in the foreground, such demands 'sow seeds of discord' and lead to intra-communal struggle. Furthermore, the Turkish government would 'perceive it as interference in Turkey's domestic affairs and as the support of separatist tendencies' (*Deutscher Bundestag* 1995b).

The issue of Sunni Islam

The issue of Islam, or rather, the issue of the principle of laicism as institutionalized with the foundation of the Turkish Republic, constitutes a significant issue in Turkish domestic politics. As outlined in Chapter 4, the principle of laicism as defined in Turkey is among the strictest versions of secularism in any Muslim country. The practice of religion in public space is controlled, and several religious movements are perceived by the state as a threat to the republic's foundations. Hence, 'the rise of Islam', including the electoral success of the *Refah Partisi* in 1995, was viewed with much concern by Turkish authorities. The *Refah Partisi* was banned in 1998 and several party leaders were prosecuted. At the time the party was the largest in the Turkish Grand National Assembly and was in a coalition government with the DYP.

Sunni Muslim groups in Germany argue that freedom of religious expression constitutes a fundamental human right in Germany as well as in Turkey. They criticize the strictness of the Turkish principle of secularism (see Chapter 4). This is not to say that all Sunni Muslim organizations in Germany wish for the *Şariat* to be introduced in Turkey. Indeed, apart from the ICCB, this is not the official policy of any of them, and such political aspirations are pro-actively denied in all Sunni Muslim organizations. Instead, these organizations do wish for more opportunities to express religion in Turkey, such as for women to be able to wear head-scarves in universities and while carrying out work in public office, and for Koran schools to be legalized.

However, while this homeland political standpoint can be found in Sunni Muslim migrant organizations' written material, these organizations in Germany have been explicitly reluctant to advocate a homeland agenda *vis-à-vis* the German government and German political institutions. Instead they concentrate on the role of Islam in Germany. Indeed, when the issue of homeland political lobbying was introduced in interviews with heads of Sunni Muslim organizations in Germany, several interviewees initially ignored the question and went on to address other issues, such as the mis-perception of Islam in Germany. Accordingly, it is difficult to identify any dialogue or attentiveness on the part of German policy makers or organizations, in terms of the homeland political agendas of the Sunni Muslim organizations. While the Kurdish movements have found attentive interlocutors within the German left-wing opposition, there is no such dialogue between the conservative Sunni Muslim organizations and any political institutions in Germany.

Similarly, compared with the Kurdish issue, the German government has only sporadically commented on the role of Islam in Turkey. In short, to support Sunni migrant organizations' homeland political agendas is not in the interest of the German government. *First*, there are no human rights concerns on par with the Kurdish issue. The ban of the *Refah Partisi* was regretted for its violation of principles of democracy, but then again the electoral success of the party had not been welcomed in the first place. Indeed, after the 1995 Turkish elections, the German government expressed its concern with the development in Turkey of more widespread and radical political Islam. Foreign Minister Kinkel depicted the 'danger of fundamentalism', as one of the 'main domestic political difficulties of Turkey' (*Deutscher Bundestag* 1995a). However, at the same time he emphasized that: 'Not Germany, but the Turkish constitution and electorate alone decide on the borders for religious influence on state and society in Turkey.' (*Deutscher Bundestag* 1995a).

Second, a further Islamization of Turkey is not viewed as helpful for Turkish–EU relations. There is a widespread perception in Turkey, as well as among Turks in Germany, that Turkey is being excluded from the 'Christian club of Europe' on the grounds of its religion, and that Germany plays a significant role in taking this stance (see Erbakan in *Der Spiegel*, 1 May 1997). Indeed, German politicians from the CDU or CSU have occasionally stated that Turkey is not a part of Europe because of its 'cultural differences' (*Frankfurter Allgemeine Zeitung*, 12 May 1997). More frequently, however, the German government has an 'objective stance' on Islam and has emphasized that Turkey is *not* excluded from the EU because of its religion (Kinkel in *Frankfurter Allgemeine Zeitung*, 13 May 1997; *Türkiye*, 14 May 1997). *Third*, the presence of a large Muslim minority in Germany, most of whom are Turkish, adds a domestic-political concern to the foreign political stance towards Islam in Turkey. To support Sunni organizations' call for a relaxing of the principle of secularism in Turkey could, in particular in the opinion of German right-wing parties, serve to legitimize more radical Sunni organizations in Germany. The role of these as integration political spokespartners is already perceived as ambiguous.

Thus, while numerous debates and statements from the German government and parliament have called for an immediate solution to the Kurdish issue, the stance on Islam in Turkey has been very cautious. A similar reluctant stance is reflected in the relationship between German authorities and the Sunni Muslim communities in Germany. Just as the Kurds have demanded freedom to express their cultural rights in Germany, the Sunni Muslim organizations have lobbied for the recognition of Islam as an official religion in Germany for more than three decades.[16] The German authorities have not complied with these demands, but generally there is a significant trend towards more cooperation and dialogue with Sunni migrant organizations. Licences to build mosques are increasingly granted, and Islamic lessons are occasionally permitted in German schools. Still, many of the organizations' demands are not met. Of equal importance, migrant organizations are unhappy with German authorities' continued concern over the role of Islam in the integration of migrants from Turkey and their descendants, as indicated by the numerous reports on Islam and Muslim organizations which have been commissioned by local authorities in recent years.[17]

Kurds have repeatedly put forward their homeland political claims, Sunni organizations much less so. So why is there an atmosphere less receptive to the homeland political demands of a group demanding freedom to practice religious rights than to the demands of a group which demands freedom to practice cultural rights? Germany's attentiveness to Sunni and Kurdish homeland political claims-making does not easily lend itself to a comparison. Both agendas may be, and are increasingly being, formulated within a discourse of human rights, and both constitute controversial domestic-political issues in Turkey. More attentiveness to the Kurdish homeland political lobbying than Sunni homeland political claims-making is first and foremost because the former case is about universal problems of human rights and democracy on a completely different scale than in the latter case.

Yet, there are also less universal dynamics at play, such as Germany's relations with Turkey as well as Turks and Kurds in Germany. Turkey wants Germany to curb both radical Islamic and Kurdish activism on its territory. In turn, Germany knows that contesting the Turkish version of the principle of laicism is very controversial, and that criticism from Western partners would not be well received in Turkey. However, here the issue of Islam does not differ from the Kurdish issue. Where the two cases differ is in the way that foreign policy relations, and domestic security or integration political considerations reinforce or contradict each other.

In the case of Kurdish lobbying, both the foreign policy agenda and domestic-political concerns coincide with Kurdish claims; in the case of Islamic organizations' homeland politics, they do not. From Germany's perspective a political solution to the Kurdish issue would kill several birds with one stone. It would meet foreign policy concerns regarding Turkey' compatibility with the Copenhagen Criteria. It would stop the Kurdish issue playing itself out on German soil. At the same time, it would remove the pressure on issues concerning arms deliveries, or the right to deport asylum seekers. By contrast, Islam is far more ambiguous for the German government. Certainly, Germany wishes for Turkey to live up to the Copenhagen Criteria of human rights and democracy standards. Yet challenging Turkey's secularist laws is neither in Germany's foreign, nor domestic, policy interests. Further Islamization of Turkey is not on Germany's foreign policy agenda and Islam has become a cornerstone in debates on integration of Turks in Germany. Indeed, as one CDU foreign policy spokesperson has commented, 'Acceptance of Islam [of migrants] within a laic framework in Germany parallels European acceptance of a Kemalist Turkey' (Lamers in *Tageszeitung*, 2 February 1995). In other words, supporting those who wish to actually strengthen the role of Islam in Turkey or in Germany is by no means perceived as being in Germany's interest.

The Alevi issue

The main organizations of the Alevi community in Germany express the same aspirations as the Kurdish and the Sunni Muslim groups: recognition of their distinctiveness and the right to practice their religion in Turkey as well as in

Germany. As described in Chapter 4, Alevis (in the form of AABF) have only become mobilized on a large scale and on a federal level since the 1990s. Yet, they have received a relatively high degree of attention from German politicians, especially from the SPD and *Die Grüne* as well as the trade unions, who also have stands at the annual mass-meetings of the AABF (*Tageszeitung*, 25 June 1997). The leader of AABF finds that:

> We usually get what we want. There are no rejections. We have a good image. We are a good bridge. We are not against Christianity and we adapt well. Many do not really know about Alevis but everyone has a positive image. In particular the German press [...] Rau [the German president], invited me to Berlin a week before his visit to Turkey because he wanted to talk about the situation for Alevis in Turkey and it was reported widely in the Turkish press that he only invited us. Perhaps he wanted to give a signal that the German Alevis are accepted. And bring the issue of Alevism on the agenda.
>
> (Interview with AABF, 10 October 2000)

When the AABF held its big festival in Cologne in 2000, its information material included greetings from high-ranking politicians from all the German political parties, including the CDU and SPD. These statements praised the Alevis. For instance, one statement stressed that: 'Alevis promote human rights and equality for men and women and as such make a valuable contribution to inter-religious and cultural integration in Germany and Europe' (AABF 2000b).

The Alevis' history of discrimination and victimization in Turkey helped attract sympathy from German politicians. Moreover, German support of Alevi homeland political demands does not constitute an obstacle to German–Turkish relations as Alevi demands are no longer as controversial in Turkey as they once were (see Chapter 5). Alevis, who are strong supporters of a secular Turkish Republic, have experienced an increasing popularity with moderate Turkish political parties. Since the traditional allegiance to the CHP has been broken in recent years, Turkish political parties are fishing for the Alevi vote, and Alevi organizations have been offered substantial financial support by Turkish authorities.

Moreover, Alevis promote a moderate brand of Islam, which does not use any of those religious practices of the Sunnis (head-scarves, mosques, Ramadan) that have become almost symbolic of the 'otherness' of the Turkish communities in Germany. In this respect, Alevis have benefited from the concern with Sunni Muslim mobilization in both Germany and Turkey. As a consequence, Alevi organizations have been supported by German authorities to such an extent that one academic has suggested that German policies are contributing to a revival of Alevism (see Kaya 1998). The level of attention given to the non-violent moderate Alevi movement indicates that German politicians regard them as a safe way to enter into dialogue on homeland political issues in general and on Islam in particular. The agenda of Alevis does not go against German national interests, either in relation to Turkey or in relation to those of Turkish or Kurdish origin in Germany.

Thresholds of tolerance

In general, homeland politics is met with reluctance in Germany. Extremist activities are (obviously) not tolerated, and concern with *Ausländerextremismus* and violations of the *Gastrecht* have dominated German political debates on the homeland political activities of organizations and movements of Turkish citizens. Attempts to introduce homeland political agendas in German institutions such as trade unions and political parties are not welcomed. Such reactions on the part of German political institutions and authorities are an important part of the dynamics of institutional participation and migrants' homeland political lobbying. That is, homeland political activities test the thresholds of tolerance on issues pertaining to Turkish politics within the German polity. These thresholds again shape the agency of the homeland political actors as discussed in Chapter 5.

Within political parties, however, it is increasingly accepted that the Turkish and Kurdish minorities' homeland political interests form an integral part of their relationship with German politics. This is illustrated by the ways in which the heterogeneity of the communities of Turkish citizens is reflected in very different patterns of dialogue between certain movements and certain political institutions and parties. There are, not surprisingly, more intense relations between those political parties and movements where the political agenda *vis-à-vis* Turkey or Turkish–European are close. German political actors receive information via certain sources and seek to maintain a good relationship with some groups of Turkish citizens rather than others. Thus, when politicians talk about being sensitive towards the 2 million Turkish fellow citizens [*Mitbürger*], they are really referring to the sensitivities of a certain part of this group. Kurdish refugees and Turkish left-wing dissidents do not object when the Turkish state is criticized by German politicians. In contrast, more Kemalist-oriented Turks are offended when Turkey is depicted as non-Western and not ready for EU candidacy.

Hence, patterns of dialogue between German political institutions and Turkish and Kurdish political groups are generally determined by the compatibility of the position of the German political institution with that of the particular homeland political organization. Nonetheless, the research also shows how homeland-political organizations serve to alter the position of the German political parties in small, albeit symbolically significant ways.

Finally, the cases of Kurdish, Sunni Muslim, and Alevi demands for recognition of distinctiveness in Turkey and Germany indicate that not only universal human rights concerns, but also national foreign and domestic political concerns affect German attitudes towards both homeland-and immigrant political claims of Turkish citizens in Germany. The *Kurdish movements* have found sympathy among German left-wing opposition political parties and among the trade unions. The German government has called for Turkey to solve the Kurdish problem, although the tone has been more cautious than that demanded by Kurdish activists. Furthermore, federal and local authorities display a very cautious attitude in their dealings with Kurdish organizations in Germany, noting the controversial nature of these issues in Turkey, as well as among migrants and refugees from Turkey in Germany. *Sunni Muslim* organizations have not entered into a dialogue with German authorities on homeland political issues, most likely because they realize beforehand that there is no common ground. Germany would never challenge the principle of laicism in Turkey. Moreover, this lack of common ground is to some extent also reflected in the German response to their Sunni immigrant political claims-making regarding the practice of Islam in Germany. That only some of their demands have been met may be related to the mixed feelings with which German authorities regard the 'Muslimness' of both Turkey and the migrants from Turkey. In contrast, the demands of the Alevis are not contentious in terms of either Turkish or German politics, and so, despite their very recent mobilization, they enjoy relatively intense dialogue with German political institutions.

Thus, the link between Turkey–German relations and the relationship between Germans and Turks in Germany is increasingly being made among policy makers in Germany. In his government statement after the Helsinki Summit in December 1999, Chancellor Gerhard Schröder, of the SPD, made explicit links between Germany's support for Turkey's EU candidacy and the well-being of the Turkish minority in Germany:

> I am sure you will agree with me that the decisions in Helsinki were important for the living together of all people in Germany regardless of their heritage. In particular for the many people of Turkish descent living among us it is crucial to know if their country of origin can hope for a democratic future as a part of Europe.
>
> (Schröder in *Bulletin*, 20 December 1999)

In turn, this was welcomed by a wide range of heads of Turkish organizations in Germany all of whom stressed that the further integration of Turkey in Europe would make them feel more welcome in Germany and 'accepted in the consciousness of the German population' (ATT 1999). In other words, when the integration of Turkey in Europe becomes linked with the sensitive issue of how Germany integrates its long-term resident Turkish citizens it gains in significance. The issue of long-term resident migrant's role and place in German society is something that concerns the German public and policy makers much more than the foreign policy issue of Turkey's place in Europe.

These findings underscore the following points: first, just as homeland- and immigrant political agendas cannot be separated from the point of view of the migrants, they are also inseparable when evaluated by the political authorities of the receiving country. Second, Turkish politics is no longer only a matter of foreign policy. A situation of spatial diffusion of domestic politics between Germany and Turkey has come about. Foreign policy becomes integration policy and integration policy becomes foreign policy.

7 From 'remittance machines' to 'Euro Turks'

Turkey's changing perceptions of Turkish citizens abroad

Emigrants are often an ambiguous asset for their homeland government. They may be viewed as an economic and political resource-base, but actually tapping into these resources is sometimes easier said than done. Moreover, emigrants' political activities may be perceived as a threat when dissidence unfolds on the political stage of their receiving countries, outside the reach of the homeland state. The relationship between the Turkish State (and government) and its citizens and former citizens abroad amply illustrates this ambiguity.

There is an increasing awareness among Turkish policy makers that Turkish citizens who left for work in western Europe are not going to return. From being referred to as 'our workers abroad', they are now increasingly called 'our citizens abroad'.[1] This awareness is reflected in more than just a change of semantics. The debates, policies, and administrative efforts towards the citizens abroad have changed from offers of temporary assistance to support for their settlement abroad. However, Turkey wants its citizens abroad not to assimilate into their receiving countries, but to settle *as Turks*. Accordingly, a range of measures has been employed in order to strengthen the economic, political, and cultural ties between the Turkish citizens abroad and the homeland. Among the reasons for this is that not only does a settled Turkish community in Europe constitute an important economic resource-base, but it could also play an important role in Turkish bilateral and multilateral relations with EU member states.

However, at the same time, Turkish political authorities are also concerned with groups of Turks and, in particular, Kurds, who seek to support the opposition in Turkey from abroad and to lobby receiving country political actors with their version of domestic political conflicts in Turkey. Despite the pro-active attempts to strengthen the relationship with citizens abroad, the Turkish political authorities have taken several steps to curb such dissidence. They have put pressure on the political authorities in the receiving countries to ignore or ban such movements and organizations, and they have used their diplomatic missions and the secret service to control the dissident movements directly, sometimes bringing themselves in conflict with German authorities.

Changing perceptions and policies

Turkey did not send her workers only to European countries. Some went to the Middle East, notably Libya and Saudi Arabia, or to Australia and New Zealand.

However, while the workers going to the Middle East came back on the planned rotational basis, many of the workers in western Europe chose to stay abroad. Currently, an estimated 3.9 million Turkish citizens, that is, more than five per cent of the total Turkish citizenry, live outside the borders of Turkey (Ministry of Foreign Affairs 2001).

This post-Second World War strategy of labour export was accompanied by political and administrative measures to accommodate the citizens working abroad. Indeed, the basic principles for emigration policy are laid down in the Turkish constitution of 1982 (amended in 1995), which states:

> The State shall take the necessary measures to ensure family unity, the education of the children, the cultural needs, and the social security of Turkish nationals working abroad, and shall take the necessary measures to safeguard their ties with the motherland, and to help them on their return home.
>
> (Turkish Constitution §62)

With reference to this, a wide range of administrative measures was adopted, including the quite elaborate social security arrangements for citizens abroad via bilateral or multilateral agreements with the receiving countries. Additionally, in particular from the 1980s, minor armies of Turkish teachers and Imams were sent out from the Ministry of Education and the Directorate of Religious Affairs, respectively. More than 470 teachers teach the Turkish language and the Turkish version of Turkish history and politics to Turkish children in Germany (Ministry of Education 2001).[2] In this they are aided by the close to half a million school books on Turkish culture [*Türkiye Büyük Millet Meclisi* (TBMM) 1995a]. The Imams, paid by the Turkish state to serve around 775 mosques in Germany, are meant to accommodate the religious needs of the emigrants in general and to represent the Turkish version of secularism in particular (interview with *Diyanet*, 29 July 1998). Last, but not least, there has been a continuous introduction of measures to channel remittances back into the Turkish economy, such as investment schemes and favourable interest rates for depositing foreign currency in Turkish banks (see Abadan-Unat 1995). These measures reflected the notion of Turks abroad as temporary guest workers, whose income was, and continues to be a valued part of the Turkish national economy. Indeed, there is a widespread perception among Turkish citizens in Germany that for many years the Turkish authorities have merely regarded them as a 'döviz makinesi' (remittance machine), and have not cared for their struggle for equal rights in their new countries of residence.

These measures were mainly based on the assumption that the guest workers would want to return to Turkey and thus needed temporary aid while abroad and when settling back 'home'. However, since the late 1980s and 1990s, Turkish authorities and policy makers have become aware that their citizens are not going to return. The most important piece of legislation reflecting this awareness is the introduction of dual citizenship in 1995, as well as a range of economic and legal rights for those former citizens who have had to give up their Turkish citizenship because dual citizenship is not allowed by the receiving country.[3] Other important legislative changes include the changes in conscription of Turkish citizens resident abroad. The duration of military service has been reduced and can be further reduced in exchange for a monetary fee (see also Freeman and Ögelman 1998: 783).

In tandem with these changes, parliamentary and media debates have increasingly emphasized that Turkish authorities should begin actively working to understand and solve the problems of Turks abroad. For instance, in 1995, a special commission was set up in order to assess critically the situation of citizens abroad. The report, like the debates preceding and following it, places great emphasis on the economic and social situation of Turkish citizens abroad. In particular, there is much concern on two aspects: first, Turkish citizens in western Europe, particularly in Germany, are being treated as second-class citizens, and are the targets of general discrimination and frequent outbursts of racist attacks.[4] Second, the 'ties with the homeland' are becoming weaker, and citizens abroad are 'losing their Turkish culture'; particularly the third generation is found to be 'wavering between cultures' and 'being in an identity struggle' (TBMM 1995a).

This concern with the socio-economic, legal, and cultural plight of Turkish citizens abroad has resulted in a series of recommendations by working groups and individual parliamentarians, including that unemployment among Turks abroad be eliminated, discrimination put to an end, and local voting rights granted. Yet, there are no concrete measures on how the Turkish government should go about implementing these recommendations, reflecting the fact that these conditions relate to German rather than Turkish legislation.

More concrete measures have been suggested to make sure that Turks abroad do not lose their sense of Turkish culture and national heritage. For instance, it has been proposed that there should be more educational children's programmes on the international broadcast of Turkish state TV (TRT-INT) and that *more* teachers and religious officials should be sent to the receiving countries. It has been further suggested that the Turkish government should ensure the 'economic and moral support' of the organizations and cultural centres of Turkish citizens abroad and strengthen the resources in terms of Turkish culture. For instance, measures should be taken to make it easier for Turkish artists to perform abroad, and the TRT-INT's broadcasting schedule should be adjusted to the customs and usage of the citizens living abroad (TBMM 1995a).

However, policy recommendation is one thing, and the implementation into new policies is another. In order to ensure the implementation of and follow-up on all these recommendations, the inadequacy of the current structure for implementing policies towards citizens abroad has been scrutinized. Previously, the Turkish diplomatic representation was the main point of contact between citizens abroad and the Turkish authorities. Indeed, with an embassy and 14 consulates, the Turkish diplomatic representation in Germany constitutes one of the largest representation in the world of any one country in another. Fifty career diplomats and a total of 534 personnel from the Ministry of Foreign Affairs worked in Germany in 1996, alongside 160 officials and attaches from other ministries (TBMM 1997a).[5] Yet, there has been an uneasy feeling in Ankara about the costly and large diplomatic representation in general and the relationship between the diplomatic representatives and the Turkish citizens living abroad in particular. The report of a commission set up under Turkish National Assembly Deputy Kamuran Inan in 1996 concluded that there is a 'distance' between the consulates and the Turkish citizens (TBMM 1997a). Similarly, as formulated by another Turkish National Assembly deputy: 'The consulates do not want to touch people – they create problems rather than solve them.' (interview with National Assembly deputy for the DYP, 15 July 1998).

In order to better this situation, there have been many attempts to formulate a more convincing institutional structure for coordinating aid to citizens abroad. Several ministries have their own special department for these issues, and both right- and left-wing Turkish parties have nurtured the idea of a special ministry for Turkish citizens living abroad.[6] However, there has been more in the way of a continuing debate about the inadequacies of the administrative structures than in the way of concrete institutional changes.

In this background, it was widely welcomed when the fifty-fifth government of the DSP and ANAP (1997–9) set up the so-called Consultation Commission (Danişma Kurulu) for citizens living abroad.[7] The Consultation Commission consists of the state minister responsible for citizens abroad, three of his bureaucrats, politicians from each of the political parties represented in parliament, and, particularly important in this context, 45 Turkish citizens living abroad.[8] The aims of the Consultation Commission is to work on the administrative and legal issues and problems pertaining to the situation of Turkish citizens living abroad. The special composition is meant to facilitate a dialogue between the citizens living abroad and the Turkish state and parliament. In terms of content, the Commission hopes to help raise the education and economic standard of the citizens abroad, and to aid their integration while preserving their identity in their new countries of residence (Ministry of State 1998a).

Although the Consultation Commission includes representatives from citizens abroad, it has been criticized by the migrant organizations abroad for its top–down approach to dialogue with emigrants. The positions on the Commission were advertised on Turkish State TV and in Turkish newspapers, and the recruitment took place through the Turkish consulates. The applicants were not to be unemployed or receiving any social aid in their countries of residence, nor should they have been jailed or condemned for 'shameful acts'. Instead, they were to be well educated (preferably in law) and 'outstanding among their fellow countrymen' in their country of residence (Ministry of State 1998b).[9] Thus, migrant organizations, which for years had called for Turkish government action to better the situation of Turks abroad, were completely bypassed when the council was set up. And their reaction was, not surprisingly, very critical. A series of their press releases was reprinted in Turkish newspapers, questioning the 'authority and representation' of the Commission and encouraging everyone to boycott it:

> This commission does not have the authority or the right to represent our citizens who live abroad ... the commission will not manage to find solutions

for our problems. We greet all democratic people and organizations that refuse to get a position on this commission.

(HDF in *Hürriyet*, 20 June 1998)

Moreover, critical voices argue that most of the concerns of the citizens living abroad relate to the political and legal structures of their receiving country. On these matters, the Turkish government has little power to change anything. Nonetheless, the gesture of inviting Turkish citizens living abroad to Ankara for consultations on their situation is of significant symbolic value. The speeches and press releases surrounding the first meeting of the Consultation Commission included assurances from the then Deputy Prime Minister Bülent Ecevit, Foreign Minister Ismail Cem and State Minister Refat Serdaroğlu, such as: 'Ankara will not forget it's Turkish citizens of Europe'; 'The Turkish citizens abroad are the pupil of our eyes and we will watch over them with great care'; 'We will teach Europe a lesson on racism' (*Hürriyet*, 17 July 1998; *Sabah*, 17 July 1998; own observations at inaugural meeting 16 July 1998).

Thus, in recent years, the overall line of the various administrative agencies, government, and all political parties is becoming clearer: Turkish citizens abroad should integrate and be good citizens abroad, but they should not assimilate and forget their Turkish cultural and religious roots.

Transnational participation in Turkish elections

Another recent political measure aimed at reinforcing the ties between the citizens abroad and their homeland is the attempt to include citizens abroad in the electoral process. The Turkish electorate in Germany alone is approximately 1,400,000 and hence constitutes approximately four per cent of the total Turkish electorate, capable of electing between 20 and 25 Turkish parliamentarians.[10] However, Turkish citizens living in Germany cannot participate in elections in Turkey from afar. Only by returning to the homeland may they vote at the border crossings. Accordingly, the participation in elections of Turkish citizens living outside of Turkey has been low – approximately 50,000 in 1987 and 1991, approximately 85,000 in 1995, and 65,254 in 1999 (State Statistical Institute 1996, 1999).[11]

Turkish migrant organizations abroad have demanded such rights for decades. In Turkey, one of the first long parliamentary debates on this issue appeared in 1986, and demands for voting rights for citizens abroad have frequently appeared in parliamentary debates and party political programmes since then (see especially, TBMM 1986, 1995b). Yet, any efforts to improve the situation were stalled by the fact that it was not constitutionally possible to allow voting from abroad because of the technically complicated judicial requirements in Turkish election laws. This was rectified with the amendments to the constitution in 1995, which now state, that 'necessary measures should be taken to facilitate the voting of citizens living abroad' (Turkish Constitution §67).

Still, more than six years later, this constitutional change has not resulted in the implementation of the appropriate legislation.[12] This is because of the complexity involved in having such a large number of citizens vote from abroad. Most of the obstacles are technical in nature. For instance, should the citizens abroad vote by mail, in ballot boxes at the consulates, or through representatives? How is it possible to uphold the particular Turkish system, in which an independent judge presides over each constituency, in elections abroad? In this respect, the electorate in Germany constitutes the main problem because of its size. With only 14 consulates, it is not possible for everyone to vote in ballot boxes at the consulates, and German authorities are not willing to make alternative facilities available for Turkish elections in Germany. Indeed, there is a general reservation from German political authorities regarding the potential wider effects of Turkish elections in Germany. This is based on a supposition that if Turkish citizens in Germany are going to have voting rights in Turkey, but not in Germany, this will most likely reinforce the resurgent interest in homeland political issues among the Turkish citizens in Germany. Among the more particular reservations of the German authorities are security concerns during the election. Hence, in terms of technical solutions, Germany prefers voting by mail (*Deutscher Bundestag* 1995c). Turkish authorities, on the contrary, have reservations regarding the reliability of voting by mail because pressure from family, peers, or even political or religious organizations may make independent voting difficult (see also Kiliç 1996: 212). Thus, transnational voting rights have remained an electoral promise, as it is easier said than done to implement them.

Transnational party-politics

One side effect of the necessary constitutional changes to allow voting rights for citizens abroad was the legitimization of Turkish political parties' transnational links with organizations abroad. Until 1995 it was forbidden for Turkish political parties to have any formal party-political branches abroad. With the amendment of the constitution in 1995, the first step was taken towards legalizing such transnational links, but no political party has yet formally engaged in such activity. Yet, as described in Chapters 4 and 5, there is an intricate transnational network of 'informal' contacts between political actors in the homeland and Turkish citizens abroad along party-political, ethnic, and religious lines.

Turkish political parties have different levels of interest in and engagement with the emigrants in western Europe. Among the parties most active in Germany are those with a religious or nationalist political agenda such the *Fazilet Partisi* and MHP. Both of these parties make explicit reference to citizens abroad in their political programmes. Leading politicians from these parties attend mass meetings of the Sunni Muslim *Milli Görüş* or the nationalist *Türk Federasyon* in order to attract economic and political support. In turn, and in some cases in exchange, leaders of the European-based organizations run as candidates in Turkish elections. Most famously, the long-standing leader of *Milli Görüş*, Osman Yumakoğullari, was elected for the *Fazilet Partisi* (then *Refah Partisi*) in a safe seat in Istanbul in 1995. In addition, a number of other high-ranking supporters from Europe have stood as candidates in Turkish elections, but only a few have been elected.

By contrast, the transnational dialogue of more mainstream parties has mainly been initiated and conducted through individuals with a particular background in the communities abroad. It has been these individuals, such as Ercan Karakaş from CHP or Bülent Arkacali from ANAP, who attend meetings organized by like-minded organizations in Germany and who raise questions or initiate debates regarding 'our citizens abroad' in the Turkish grand National Assembly. These more sporadic practices have only lately been replaced by more comprehensive measures, such as expressing support for citizens abroad in the party programmes, or assigning special deputies with the task of communicating with citizens abroad. The more reserved attitude of the mainstream parties is also related to their perception of where the party-political preferences of Turks abroad lie. General surveys show that the large majority of Turks abroad would actually vote for the mainstream Social Democrats and Conservative Liberal parties (ZfT 2000c). Yet, those who turn up for political rallies in Germany or, indeed, go to the borders to vote, are rumoured to support the religious or nationalist parties. However, the discrepancy between general surveys and voting patterns at the border may also reflect 'long distance' voting patterns. That is, those willing to drive or fly to Turkey to vote are not ordinary voters, but those with a stronger homeland political commitment, which in this case is evoked by the nationalist or religious parties. In any case, this has reinforced the perception of Turkish citizens abroad as supporters of these parties only.

Turks abroad as good representatives for Turkey

The processes of administrative and political integration of Turkish citizens abroad with the homeland are generally justified as the duty of any emigration country. However, there are many incentives for Ankara to strengthen the ties with citizens in EU member states, to listen to their problems, and to re-include them as part of the electorate. Like most sending countries, Turkey welcomes the continued flow of remittances and investments from citizens abroad, who, despite their high unemployment rates, are still much more affluent than those in the homeland.

Moreover, it is not against Turkey's interests if Turks abroad become good and loyal representatives of their country of origin. Already, citizens abroad constitute an integral part of the foreign relations with western Europe, in particular the EU. As expressed by one Turkish National Assembly deputy: 'Their presence is a lobby in and of itself' (interview with National Assembly deputy for ANAP, 23 October 2000). Within this line of reasoning, there is a keen interest to support the 'social capital upgrading' of citizens abroad. Hitherto, the Turkish workers abroad have been regarded as giving western European countries the wrong image of Turks and Turkey. Although this is a sensitive issue, there is a widespread concern in Ankara that Turkish citizens in western Europe do not represent the modern secular Turkey of Ankara, but rather the more traditional rural life of

Anatolian villages.[13] Therefore, Ankara places great emphasis on the social mobility of the communities abroad, especially the growth of private enterprises owned by Turkish citizens in Germany, and the increase in Turkish citizens attending German universities. As one Turkish National Assembly deputy pointed out, Turkish citizens living in western Europe could serve as exemplary representatives of Turkey, and that they should:

> Help us promote relations between Germany and Turkey and also with the EU. Until now the Turkish citizens, and with them the Turks in general, carry the image of workers that are rough and rude and from a village. But this image will change day by day. There are many successful Turkish citizens – take Öker Tour, the textile companies, and the scientists. They can be our spokesmen and that will change the image of Turkey.[14]
> (Interview with National Assembly deputy for the DYP, 15 July 1998)

Thus, the foreign ministry has posted on its website that: 'Turkey encourages its citizens to do their best for enhancing their social, economical, cultural and political status' (Ministry of Foreign Affairs 2001). This they should do first and foremost for their own sake, but it is clearly also in Turkey's interest.

Beyond the issue of emigrants as 'good representatives' is the more contentious question of Turks abroad as a foreign policy lobby for Ankara. 'Everybody wants a Jewish lobby', one National Assembly deputy commented during an interview. He then continued to outline how Turks abroad could serve to counter the information campaigns of dissident Turkish and Kurdish movements abroad as well as other 'anti-Turkish' groups including the Armenian and Greek lobbies in Europe and the US (interview with National Assembly deputy for DSP, 20 October 2000).[15] Another National Assembly deputy outlined how Turkish citizens abroad should mobilize, first, to defend their own rights and, second, to:

> Be a kind of public relations for Turkey, and if possible a lobby for their own country. This should be one of the tasks of a more efficient diplomacy – to mobilize the people abroad. If you look at anti-Turkish activities by Turks in western Europe these are developed on a large scale and also sponsored by local forces [...] political activity on behalf of Turkey – as usual it is very quiet and not well organized. And so this is one of the major issues, which should be on the agenda of any government and parliament in this country.
> (Interview with National Assembly deputy for ANAP, 6 December 1996)

However, the notion of a Turkish lobby in Europe – the conscious instrumental use of Turkish citizens abroad – is also treated with much caution in Ankara. Turkish citizens abroad are not viewed as very powerful in Germany because of their lack of political rights and economic power. Similarly, the migrant organizations are viewed as weak in terms of political influence in German politics. It is rather the *potential* of Turkish citizens that is estimated to be of great value to Turkey. The more established and influential the 'Euro Turks' in Germany (and other EU-countries) get, the more they may represent Turkey and Turkish interests abroad.

Several measures originating from Turkey can be interpreted as intentions to mobilize citizens abroad: diplomatic representations organize and fund the celebration of national days abroad. They meet with migrant organizations to encourage them to counter 'anti-Turkish' activities. More importantly, the Turkish media in Germany does not just serve to report events in Turkey. Since the early 1980s, major Turkish dailies with a large distribution within the communities in Europe have run fax-campaigns urging citizens abroad to fax their protests against local and national politicians who have criticized Turkey regarding the Kurdish issue, human rights deficiencies, or Turkish relations with the EU. One columnist in the European pages of the Turkish daily *Hürriyet* has been named one of the most important opinion makers in Europe (*Süddeutsche Zeitung*, 17 October 1998). In particular, the Turkish media has scrutinized Turkish descent representatives in local and national parliaments to determine whether they are too critical of their homeland. The first Turkish representative in a European national assembly, Cem Özdemir, has thus engaged in a year-long argument with the Turkish press, which has depicted him as 'The dagger in our back' (*Hürriyet*, 16 December 1994). Özdemir in turn has stated that he wants 'to free Turks from the reigns of Ankara' (*Süddeutsche Zeitung*, 17 October 1998).[16]

Similarly, the TRT-INT, the Turkish state television channel, which, via cable, is widely available throughout Europe, seeks to convey the ideology of the Turkish state and the Turkish state's version of 'Turkishness'. In the mornings there are stories of Atatürk, and in children's programmes the viewers are encouraged to sing along when the national hymn is played. Many programmes encourage listeners in Germany to call the studio in Istanbul or Ankara to contribute to discussions on Turkish politics and society. Most famous is the campaign 'Hand in hand with Turkish soldiers', a 56-hour live programme that encouraged the 'Turkish nation' to donate 'moral and economic support' for the Turkish army in 1995. The broadcast provoked an outcry from human rights groups and German media authorities, which probably explains why this sort of propaganda was not repeated at such a level.

In one final example, leading Turkish policy makers voiced their opinion on the way Turkish descent voters should vote in the 1998 Federal election in Germany. Several party leaders, such as the leader of the social democratic CHP, told Turks to vote for the SPD because this party would implement citizenship reforms including dual citizenship and in general improve German integration policies. More famously, the then Prime Minister, Mesut Yilmaz stated, 'I am sure that Turks in Germany will vote in favour of those who favour Turkish membership of the EU'. He then proceeded to hold then Chancellor Kohl of the CDU responsible for the EU failure to grant Turkey the status of candidate to EU membership at the Luxembourg Summit in 1997 (*Süddeutsche Zeitung*, 19 August 1998).

That Ankara wishes to have a lobby in EU member states in general and in Germany in particular is the firm conviction of most leaders of migrant organizations in Germany. It is also noted by German policy makers and authorities as counter-productive to the political integration of Turks in Germany. For those against dual citizenship, interventions by Turkish media and politicians in German elections confirm their fear of Turkey's influence on German politics through the Turkish minority in Germany. For others, Turkey's intervention is regretted as stigmatizing Turks in the eye of German public and hence damaging their general and political integration.

However, the influence of Ankara on its citizens abroad should not be overestimated. Indeed, more often than not, Turkey is criticized by migrant organizations for asking for something for nothing. As one leader of a migrant organization formulates it:

> [Ankara wants us to be] like the Armenians in the United States, but Turkey is very poor at this. They say: 'go and settle and get influence and lobby for us.' Like the Jews in the United States, and as Greeks do it in the US. But what they do not see is that Turks will have a pro-Turkish attitude everywhere they are. You do not have to push them from the state level. And they forget another point. You have to take care of your people if you want their support, and Turkey never did. People here were faced with a lot of Turkish government and state discrimination [...] Even here when they go to the consular departments [...] And this creates an atmosphere where Turkey cannot say: 'So I did this for you and now you do something for me.'
> (Interview with *Milli Görüş*, 13 October 2000)

As argued in Chapter 4, Turks and Kurds in Germany engage themselves in the political developments in Turkey and in Turkish–European relations. Yet, Turkish migrant organizations continuously emphasize that they are not the 'tool of Ankara'. When Prime Minister Yilmaz told Turkish descent voters not to vote for the CDU, this intervention was immediately decried by leaders of migrant organizations in Germany, in particular those organizations working more closely with the CDU. 'We are not a 5th column', stated one head of a migrant organization. 'We are not remote-controlled by Ankara', stated another (*Welt*, 21 August).

Long-distance dissidence

Political dissidence abroad constitutes another reason for Turkey to seek to strengthen the ties with the communities abroad. The less opposition is tolerated in a country, the more it is likely to unfold within the diaspora. From the point of view of the Turkish state, governments, and main political parties represented in parliament, there has been much concern with the activities of dissident movements among Turks and in particular Kurds living abroad. Since the 1980s, western Europe has received not only economic migrants seeking work, but also political refugees seeking asylum. The height of the number of asylum seekers was around the 1980 military coup in Turkey, and then again in the early 1990s, with the escalation of the Kurdish conflict in south east Anatolia. Turkey finds it awkward that Turkish citizens arriving in western Europe claim to be politically persecuted and in need of asylum. Indeed, Turkey criticizes EU countries accepting asylum seekers from Turkey for hosting anti-Turkish State forces, tolerating Kurdish separatism, and disregarding Turkish territorial and political integrity.

Political dissidence is furthermore not just a matter of asylum seekers. Political identity within the communities abroad is constantly renegotiated. Some Turkish migrants become more defensive about their homeland not least because of the very critical media coverage of Turkey in western European media. Others become more sceptical towards the Turkish political regime from afar. There is much awareness among Turkish politicians that one of the main obstacles to creating a Turkish lobby abroad are these differing homeland-oriented agendas within the community. The Parliamentary report of 1995 on citizens abroad phrases the problem diplomatically, suggesting that the 'dialogue between the various organizations is weak' (TBMM 1995a).

While most receiving country politicians ascribe this intra-communal strife to the influence of Turkish politics, Turkish politicians blame the receiving country's political authorities for the lack of unity. Indeed, there is a consensus among the representatives from Turkish political parties interviewed for this research: in particular, German authorities are said to have realized that the community is easier to handle if it is divided, and hence, they are 'playing with the ethnic and religious feelings of the community'. Importantly, Turkish politicians suggest that not enough is done to curb anti-Turkish terrorist organizations. Despite Germany's ban of the PKK, and the legal prosecution of its leaders, Turkey has repeatedly complained about the tolerance of the PKK by German authorities. Similarly, the financial support (in western Europe) to religious migrant organizations is viewed with much annoyance, even suspicion, among Turkish politicians. It is, for instance, pointed out that constitutional provisions in Holland ensure state aid to religious groups, forcing the Turks to organize along religious lines. One quote may illustrate this line of reasoning:

> Germany feels that the Turkish community is a threat [...] Germany has discovered the weaknesses of the Turkish society. Oh, they have been very tolerant. Just behind the main station in Köln there is a street with three mosques, one from *Milli Görüş*, one from Kaplan [ICCB], and one from DITIB. Now, Germans do not give permission to have three McDonalds on the same street. If there is one then another cannot get a permit – but three mosques! This is because they want to divide and rule. They support the religious tendencies indirectly. Just like they support the PKK.
> (Interview with National Assembly deputy for the DSP, 14 July 1998)

As described in Chapter 6, Sunni Muslim or Kurdish organizations are by no means actively supported by German authorities. Their immigrant political demands are often not met. Still, Turkish perception that Germany wishes to 'divide and rule' is also replicated in the argument against the 'multicultural strategies' of German local authorities. Multiculturalism, is in other words, only acceptable in so far as it does not question Turkish minority policies. The fact that

Kurdish, Alevi, various Sunni Muslim, and party-political organizations are being funded through local or federal authorities is seen by Turkey as a means to compartmentalize the Turkish community.

Long-distance policing

Turkish or Kurdish political activists in Germany may find themselves withheld for questioning and sometimes arrested when returning to Turkey if their activities are perceived as sufficiently subversive by Turkish authorities. This is one of many indications that Turkish authorities try to monitor political dissidence abroad. Yet, the case of Turkey illustrates how it is not so straightforward to exert control abroad as it is at home.

In order to curb political dissidence abroad, Turkish political authorities have repeatedly urged western European governments to control the activities of opposition groups such as the Maoist New Left, the radical Sunni Muslim groups such as the ICCB/Kaplancilar, and, in particular, the Kurdish organizations such as the PKK. Such pressure has been exerted on every single level of governance. Turkey voices its opinion on these issues in international meetings, meetings with heads of state, or communication with national and local German governments who are urged not to publish separate material on Kurdish migrants. Besides seeking to influence the receiving state authorities, one of the means by which the homeland may seek to curb opposition movements abroad is through diplomatic representations. Embassies and consulates have attempted to influence the pattern of organizations and events organized by the movements in the diaspora. For instance, in 1982 the Turkish General Consul for Cologne tried to change the programme of the Cultural Week 'Turkey in Cologne' because it was being organized by 'Kurdish and left-wing separatists'. He also tried to use the Turkish teachers in the area to obtain information on all local organizations and mosques (*Deutscher Bundestag* 1982c).[17] However, beginning in the early 1980s, and during the early 1990s, the consulates started mobilizing the Turkish citizens living abroad in a more systematic way. Most importantly, they have sought to establish the so-called 'coordination councils', initiated and financed via the consulates. Only organizations not in opposition to the Turkish state may be included in these coordination councils, and the consulates financially support only pro-Turkish organizations, such as the organizations to promote Atatürk's ideas. However, most of the organizations of the diasporas have wanted to stay independent of the consulates, and one Turkish parliamentary report concludes that the dialogue among the various organizations in the diaspora, as well as between the organizations and the Turkish consulates, is weak. Hence, the recommendation is that:

> It is necessary to strengthen the relations and common agency among the organizations, associations, and federations founded among and by our citizens and to assist in great importance on establishing tight dialogue with our consulates.
>
> (TBMM 1995a)[18]

Another means by which Turkey has sought to control the citizens living abroad has been through the umbilical cord between its citizens abroad and the state: the passport.[19] Particularly in the beginning of the 1980s (and before), there were numerous cases of Turkish citizens, who, because of their political activities in Germany, lost their passport – becoming illegal aliens and sometimes being forced to apply for asylum although they had been living on German territory for many years. The method was to refuse to renew passports, compelling dissidents either to return to Turkey to resolve the problem or to become illegal aliens in Germany and by necessity apply for the sparsely granted 'Fremden Pass'. People suffering from 'passport harassment' were mainly trade union activists and other 'unpleasant Turkish compatriots' and those whom the Turkish authorities wanted to force to return to Turkey to complete their military service.[20]

Although the 'passport harassment' did not take place on a large scale, it reinforced the hostility between the consulates and the left-wing movements in Germany. Often, Turkish citizens with these problems would turn to their trade union (e.g. IGMetall), which would contact the SPD, which in turn raised these issues several times in the *Bundestag*. In response, the German government would contact the Turkish government on these issues, but they were met with an unsympathetic attitude and, given that this is a matter of Turkish internal affairs, there was nothing that could be done from the German side (see *Deutscher Bundestag* 1986a, 1987).

The suspicion with which the consulates were regarded was confirmed by the frequent rumours concerning the work of the Turkish Secret Service [Milli Ishhbarat Teşkilatı (MIT)] through the consulates as well as the branches of the Turkish Directorate of Religious Affairs. For instance, in 1990, a diplomatic crisis was triggered after a claim on the German television channel *ARD*'s programme 'Panorama' that 30 MIT agents were working undercover in Germany as officials at the consulates. According to Panorama, two such agents had tried to force a young man in a pub in Hamburg to be an informer (*Tageszeitung*, 4 April 1990). It suggested further that MIT generally worked to include members of religious, nationalist, or political groups in their ranks (*Tageszeitung*, 21 April 1990). Fifteen Turkish diplomats were expelled from Bonn, and later Ankara retaliated by expelling eight German diplomats on the grounds that they 'were tied up in activities not related to their mission' – that is, they were accused of being intelligence officers as well (*Tageszeitung*, 21 April 1990).

Thus, while Turkey views the work of dissident movements in western Europe as strengthening dissident forces inside Turkey, and damaging Turkey's image in western Europe, the instruments and leverage with which Turkey may control political dissidence abroad are relatively limited.

Help from abroad: political opposition's assessment of transnational political campaigns from abroad

How are transnational political efforts of communities abroad assessed by non-state, dissident political counterparts in Turkey? If Turkish authorities want to promote transnational loyalty and control transnational dissidence, then it is easily supposed that opposition movements in Turkey would want to tap into the resources of transnational dissident movements and organizations. However, while migrant organizations abroad stress their contribution to democratization at home, interviewees in Turkey from Kurdish or human rights organizations usually bypass these efforts or only mention them in the vaguest of terms. The exception to prove the rule is the Alevi Haci Bektas Veli, which praises the work of European-based Alevis and offers a range of concrete examples of cooperation on cultural events and information campaigns. For instance, the support of organizations in Germany in the beginning of the 1990s is recognized as important for the Alevi organization in Turkey. As the leader of one Alevi organization in Ankara explains:

> In Europe there is freedom of association. But in our country we were not able to express all our wishes and as you know we experienced difficulties because of this. But in Europe it was different. In the beginning, these [Alevi] organizations supported us from there. We followed their examples of organization. Whether it is because of this or of other things our government is now beginning to look at us more positively. Lots of things are now happening for us.
> (Interview with *Haci Bektas Veli*, 19 October 2000)

By contrast, specific to the political parties to the left of the social democrats, such as *Işci Partisi*, is a sense of disappointment with transnational political connections. This party has a past in the more revolutionary communist movements, which were hard hit by the military coup in 1980. The efforts of the comrades, who continued the struggle from a more comfortable position abroad, is acknowledged but not overestimated. One former left-wing activist imprisoned for work in unions in the early 1980s expressed it most directly:

> We know that some of our countrymen in the West were concerned, but did they contribute to anything? It was important for them and we appreciate that – they had their conscience to soothe, but it added up to nothing. Today it is all a touristic exchange of delegations.
> (Interview with *Türk-İş*, 31 July 1998)

Similarly, the Kurdish movements and parties are cautious in their appreciation of the aid of organizations and individuals abroad. One of the main problems that Kurdish political movements and parties face in Turkey is the right to participate in the democratic political process without fear of persecution. As has also been observed in the case of other human rights issues (Keck and Sikkink 1998), outside support not only secures the economic basis for local organizations but also lends legitimacy to their work within a restricted and censured political environment. As such, the political support from the outside could be thought to be of great value to Kurdish political movements and human rights organizations in Turkey.

Certainly, the information campaigns organized by migrant and refugee organizations abroad are generally valued as they are thought to bring the Kurdish issue to the attention of central political actors in western Europe, who can then put pressure on the Turkish authorities. However, Kurdish political movements in Turkey do not want to publicize their relations to organizations abroad. The Turkish authorities already scrutinize the relatively radical rhetoric and claims of Kurdish political organizations abroad. Therefore, interviewees from Kurdish political groups in Turkey are very careful not to point to particular links between them and diaspora political Kurdish groups. Close ties may serve to damage and further marginalize Kurdish political movements or parties in Turkey. Instead, legal political Kurdish activists in Turkey, such as those from the political party Hadep, welcome support from foreign human rights organizations or government institutions rather than specific Kurdish political organizations.

Turkey's conceptions of a de-territorialized nation and state

The Turkish citizens living in western Europe are not the only 'Turks' living outside the borders of Turkey. Indeed, it has always been an integral part of Turkish national identity that the Turkish nation reached beyond the steppes of Anatolia to include the 'outside Turks' (*dış Türkler*), that is, the Turkic people in Caucasia, Central Asia, Iran, and parts of eastern Europe. Atatürk, the founder of Turkey, was initially against pan-Turkism or Turanism, the idea that all Turkic people, inside and outside of Turkey, should be united in one political unit.[21] Nonetheless, in the attempt to propagate a stronger Turkish national identity, Central Asia, in particular, was heralded as original fatherland of the Turks in Turkey and the Central Asian Turks were referred to as close ethnic kin. These 'kin outside' also include the Muslim population in the Balkans, which identifies with Turkey, the Muslim minority in western Thrace, and the Cypriot Turks (Poulton 1997). These lines of identification have been strengthened in the post-Cold War era. After the demise of the Soviet Union and the independence of the former Soviet Republics of Central Asia and the Caucasus, there were new possibilities for cooperation with the Turkish speaking world. Also, on a less positive note, ethnic conflicts, notably in the former Yugoslavia, have reinforced the bonds of solidarity between Turkey and the Muslim populations dispersed throughout the Balkans.

The main difference between the Turks living in the Balkans, Central Asia, and Caucasia and the Turkish citizens in western Europe is the fact that the latter are actually citizens of Turkey residing abroad while the former are regarded as 'co-ethnics' in a broader sense. Thus, while the notion of a de-territorialized Turkish *nation* is not new, the process towards a de-territorialized Turkish *state* is. Another important difference between the 'outside Turks' and the 3.5 million Turkish citizens living in western Europe is that the latter reside in a region with which Turkey has a different and highly coveted relationship. A Turkish lobby, particularly, in Germany may constitute a powerful advocate for Turkey's interests in western Europe. Combined, these two factors provide a crucial background to explain why the Turkish citizens in western Europe (and the US and Canada) are being urged to integrate and obtain the citizenship of their receiving country, but, at the same time, are being admonished never to forget their homeland. Turkish citizens in Germany add an important new dimension to the conceptualization of a de-territorialized Turkish nation. This conceptualization is qualitatively different from the notion of pan-Turkism, in the sense that it builds on the notion of 'transnational relations' rather than on a quest for one political unit.

The gradual accommodation of the Turkish administration and electoral system to include Turkish citizens residing outside of Turkey follows Ankara's realization that these citizens are no longer 'remittance machines' but 'Euro Turks', who are unlikely to return. The largely economic project of labour export on a rotational basis has been followed by a largely political project of tying these citizens back in with the state.

Nevertheless, while Ankara's changing *perceptions* of its citizens abroad are interesting in and of themselves, it is important not to over-state the effectiveness of the *policies* directed at these citizens. First, these perceptions are not easily translated into political agency. Indeed, the case of Turkey illustrates that the relationship between sending states and emigrants is often ambiguous. Turkish bureaucratic practices are not easily coordinated or streamlined, and the complexities of transnational electoral law are difficult to implement to the satisfaction of both German and Turkish authorities. Second, these processes are further complicated by the fact that 'Turkey' is not a unitary actor. Different political parties have their own perceptions, links, and agendas *vis-à-vis* Turkish citizens abroad. While some policy-makers promote their party-political agendas abroad, others take note of the fact that Germany regards Turkey's political relations with its citizens abroad as highly counter-productive to their integration.

At the level of the state and government institutions, the mobilizing measures seem reactionary rather than pro-active. They are about controlling rather than mobilizing emigrants' and refugees' engagement in Turkish politics. Pro-Turkish sentiment is promoted through media and diplomatic representations, but actual calls for lobbying are met with scepticism among migrant organizational leaders abroad. And for those already critical of the Turkish political regime, the image of the controlling state casts a long shadow of mistrust on the image of the mobilizing state.

8 Conclusions

Migrants' and refugees' transnational political engagement is likely to become increasingly important in the coming years, given the scale of current migration and the ease with which migrants may stay in touch with their country of origin. This book has placed immigrants' and refugees' political participation within a transnational framework in order to highlight the scope, forms, and outcomes of their homeland political engagement. Preceding chapters have dealt with subjects as diverse as German–Turkish relations, Kurdish refugees' campaigns in Germany for Kurdish rights in Germany and Turkey, and Turkish migrants' defence of Turkey's EU candidacy. It is necessary to include such diverse issues so as to reflect the political universe of migrants and refugees engaged in transnational practices as well as the factors which German and Turkish political actors have to consider when interacting with migrants' or refugees' political movements. When Turkish and Kurdish migrants and refugees engage in politics of their homeland, they are both outsiders on the inside of German politics and insiders on the outside of Turkish politics. They become a linking pin between the domestic and foreign politics of their homeland and receiving country. Thus, framing Turks and Kurds as transnational actors complements studies of Turkish and Kurdish 'immigrant political participation', since it demonstrates how homeland political mobilization constitutes an integral part of immigrant political mobilization and participation.

Concepts such as 'diaspora' or 'transnational community' have been invoked as part of an approach to explore transnational and homeland political practices. Migration research increasingly draws on these concepts to describe the experience and engagement of migrants and refugees (Cohen 1997; van Hear 1998; Portes et al. 1999). It is, however, important to apply concepts of diaspora or transnational community with care in the case of Turks and Kurds. Certainly, their political mobilization and organization has a transnational dimension in the sense that migrants and refugees are informed by events or are in contact with actors in Turkey. They are transnational in their orientation and work but not necessarily in the sense of physical movement. The term diaspora, in its more narrow and traditional sense, is more easily applied to the Kurds in Germany, who clearly perceive themselves as exiles dispersed in many countries. In its broader meaning of a sense of 'congregation', the term 'diaspora' may capture the trend towards

124 Conclusions

Turkish migrants' sense of being a community distinct from the polity in Turkey, which increasingly manifests itself in the speeches and writing of Turkish migrant organizations. However, a unifying sense of community is only evoked with the lowest common denominator such as 'Euro Turks'. Otherwise, Turks and Kurds in Germany are divided into religious, ethnic, and even party-political groups who sometimes have more contacts within their separate transnational networks than with other migrant organizations living in the same country.

Similarly, it is must be emphasized that not all Kurds and Turks are engaged in transnational political activities. When viewing political practices through migrant organizations, one is automatically in a field of more consistent political engagement than is the case among the general population of migrants and refugees. Those engaged in 'core' or 'narrow' transnational activities are few and far between. So too are those engaged in migrant political activities. Moreover, among migrant organizations, homeland political engagement and transnationalism vary a great deal. A Muslim organization is not homeland political by definition, but only in so far as it works for changes in the homeland. A Kurdish organization is not transnational by definition, but only in so far as it has consistent links with counterparts in Turkey or among counterparts in other countries.

In academic and policy-making circles, it is increasingly accepted that assimilation is no longer the inevitable outcome of long-term residence of immigrants and refugees. Interestingly, in this case study, a historical perspective highlights the fact that homeland politics and transnational engagement come and go among Turkish and Kurdish migrant organizations in Germany. In the 1970s and 1980s, there was a tendency towards less homeland politics and more immigrant politics. Indeed, immigrant political agendas have been introduced in most of the organizations of Turkish citizens since the mid-1980s, and today homeland political aspirations are usually presented as a thing of the past within Turkish migrant organizations. Yet, from the late 1980s, homeland politics have re-entered the work of some of these organizations. The continuously failing attempts to form all-inclusive common platforms for immigrant political lobbying relate to the persistence of different homeland political 'profiles' and engagement of the various organizations.

At present, Kurdish and Turkish organizations in Germany engage in all types of transnational, migrant political, homeland- and emigrant-political activities. While Kurdish, Sunni, and Alevi organizations are more consistently engaged in homeland politics and draw on transnational networks, the homeland political dimension of Turkish organizations has taken a backseat to immigrant political concerns. Yet, the homeland political dimension persists and the way that it plays into the political agency of these organizations has been of overriding interest in the preceding chapters. Indeed, in many cases, one agenda does not exclude the other. Migrant politics and homeland politics overlap and feed into each other, reflecting the political diffusion of politics in Turkey and Germany.

These overlaps are reflected in both of the two overall sets of homeland political engagement. One set of homeland political agendas pertains to Turkish domestic politics. Pro-Turkey groups, while usually critical of Turkey's political instability and inadequate governance, defend the more general principles on which the Republic of Turkey was founded. By contrast, leftist movements advocate radical transformation of the Turkish political regime. Kurdish and Alevi organizations challenge Turkey's minority politics. Kurds demand ethnic equality and various degrees of autonomous rule. Alevis demand equal state acknowledgement and support for their different religious practices and needs. Sunni groups criticize Turkey's Kemalist principles of secularism by demanding more freedom for religious expression and practices. In all cases, calls for further rights at home are paralleled by, or formulated as, demands for further ethnic or religious rights in Germany as well. These agendas are tied in with national projects, but are also increasingly formulated within the language of universal rights. As such, it is not straightforward to disentangle the nationalist elements from the more cosmopolitan calls for democratization and respect for human rights.

The other set of homeland politics addresses EU–Turkish relations, including Germany's stance towards Turkey's EU candidacy. In the past, dissident groups urged European governments to keep Turkey at a distance until its human rights record had improved. In recent years, however, all Turkish and Kurdish groups call for closer Turkey–EU relations. Dissidents take this stance because it gives German institutions more European leverage on Turkish political affairs. Pro-Turkey groups take the same stance because Turkey's EU candidacy is a key part of Ankara's foreign policy agenda. In both it is recognized that recognition of Turkey as part of the EU also changes the status of Turkish migrants from 'third country nationals' to EU citizens.

Thus, one important finding is that homeland political agendas often cannot be separated from immigrant political agendas. Within homeland politics is immigrant politics and within immigrant politics is homeland politics. When an organization advocates recognition of distinctiveness in Germany (such as mother-tongue teaching or religious education), this also sends a strong signal to the political authorities in Turkey if such distinctiveness is not tolerated there. Indeed, the very existence of a range of migrant organizations that would not be allowed to exist in the homeland serves such a purpose. Similarly, organizations may focus on homeland political issues for immigrant political reasons. The above-mentioned case of Turkey's EU membership is one case in point. Moreover, migrant organizations may organize events on a Turkish political issue with the purpose of countering the factionalism related to Turkish politics in Germany through raising greater awareness of common ground. Notably, Turkish organizations' activities pertaining to the Kurdish issue have been justified in this way. The fact that homeland political agendas are formulated in immigrant political terms indicates an increased awareness within the communities that this is a better issue for cooperation with German authorities.

Determinants of homeland political engagement

There are several routes to homeland political engagement of Turks and Kurds in Germany. Clearly, the refugee experience is a strong incentive to work for democratization in the homeland. Kashmiris, Eritreans, or Bosnians, among many others, have used their exile as an arena for voicing their discontent with events in their respective homelands (see Ellis and Khan 2002; Frykman 2002; Koser 2002). Similarly, organizations representing Kurdish refugees are more consistently engaged in Turkish politics than organizations representing Turkish migrants. However, it is worth noting that the categories of Kurdish refugees and Turkish migrants are not clear-cut. There are Turkish dissidents and refugees and Kurdish migrants, although in recent years the vast majority of asylum seekers are of Kurdish descent. Moreover, migrants also engage in defending or opposing Turkish domestic and foreign policies. Such engagement does not necessarily pale the longer migrants stay abroad. Organizational leaders of the so-called 'first generation' are more directly plugged into Turkish politics than those who have grown up, or were born, in Germany. The latter group is more engaged in immigrant political concerns, although they do join organizations with homeland political engagements and endorse, or even part-take in, information campaigns relating to Turkish politics or Turkey–EU relations.

In particular, this type of engagement has been linked to the socio-economic position of migrants in their receiving country. Studies of Turkish youth in Germany argue that Turkish nationalism or 'fundamentalism' is a result of the exclusive and unreceptive German context (Heitmeyer et al. 1997; Schiffauer 1999). This study does not contradict this. There are certainly elements of 'reactive identity' among Turks and Kurds – in particular, youth – in Germany. However, the descriptions of migrant political organizations demonstrate how the multitude of political movements – most of which are *not* radical – questions the reductionist notion of political identity as a function of integration in the receiving society. For instance, members of the DTU are more often than not well educated and integrated in the German labour-market and society. Yet, their homeland political affiliation is reflected in their support for a defensive and 'sensitive' German stance to Turkish domestic politics, including the rejection of asylum seekers from Turkey, and protection from Kurdish and left-wing intra-communal violence on German soil. Another example is the Alevi AABF, which has been able to mobilize the community in Germany on account of the massacres in Turkey and the mobilization of Sunni Islamists in Germany. The AABF is by no means radical or against integration into German society. It is, in other words, not enough to try to infer homeland political engagement from the relationship between migrants and their country of settlement.

In terms of the country of origin, political developments in Turkey have, in and of themselves, given plenty of occasions for migrants and refugees to mobilize. With the widespread availability of Turkish media, these events have been easier to follow. Turkish and Kurdish homeland politics is, however, not just a result of 'bottom up' reactions to developments in Turkey. A range of Turkish political actors, including vote catchers, missionaries, opinion makers, and state representatives, seek to extract political and economic support. From Turkey, human rights organizations or Kurdish political parties barred from democratic participation ask for outside support in the form of information campaigns and public debates on issues closed to public discussion in Turkey. Thus, some migrant organizations in Germany have actually been set up by political parties or religious movements in Turkey. While such organizations may continue to cultivate links to Turkish political counterparts, many have developed a more independent and critical outlook. The landscape of Turkish, and Kurdish organizations in Germany is thus not a mere microcosm of politics in Turkey; Turkish, and Kurdish organizations pursuing their own agendas in a different political institutional environment.

Even the Turkish government, a late comer to this type of transnational mobilization, has reached out to its citizens abroad with legislation on dual citizenship and promises of voting rights from afar. The case of Turkey, however, highlights that it is not straightforward to re-include citizens abroad in the polity at home. Policy reforms are halted by constitutional constraints, bureaucratic inefficiency, and the diverging interests of domestic actors. Certain political parties are cautious and ambivalent about the voting potential of migrants abroad as their political leanings are (mis)interpreted as mainly motivated by strong religious or nationalist sentiments. Moreover, Turkish migrant organizations usually oppose being associated with the Turkish government and state. In particular, they do not want to be perceived as a 'fifth column' or 'foreign policy tool' by German political counterparts. In this book, the role of the homeland is, therefore, presented last, based on the premise that the transnational mobilization of the Turks and Kurds in Germany is not merely the result of successful remote control from the Turkish government or state, or various parties and organizations.

Last, but not least, an important source of mobilization lies in the dynamics among the different organizations in Germany. When different groups stand up to represent Turks or Kurds, Sunnis or Alevis, others will immediately dispute their legitimacy as overall spokespersons. Similarly, the information campaign or claims-making of one organization is rarely left uncommented upon by others. One suggestion for changes in Turkey or Germany releases a chain reaction of counter-suggestion by opposing groups.

Thus, the plurality of different ethnic, religious, and party-political groups among Turks and Kurds abroad is central to the way in which this empirical study may aid the conceptual work on immigrants' transnational political engagement and practices. This study highlights the significance of inter-communal dynamics among migrants, the fragmented interaction with the receiving state political institutions, and the ambiguity with which the homeland government and state view citizens abroad. It is this plurality that shows that migrants' political loyalties and practices are not only a function of the political developments in the country of origin or of the migrants' integration into the receiving country, but also a result of the complex interplay between the two, combined with interaction and counter-action among migrant organizations in Germany.

Multi-level institutional channelling

One of the main questions dealt with in preceding chapters is how migrants' political practices are articulated and received within the political institutional context in the countries of origin and settlement. Turkish and Kurdish migrant organizations not only interact with but also accommodate to local power structures. When migrant organizations are analysed as migrant political participants only, the role of the receiving country's political opportunity structure is used as the main explanatory factor accounting for their degree of participation. Yet, migrants' transnational political practices, in particular their homeland political claims-making, are not only a function of the local political structures of opportunities available to them.

The empirical findings of the analysis of different Turkish and Kurdish groups within one political system add to the theory of institutional channelling. First, the analysis demonstrates that 'homeland oriented participation' is not a separate form of participation contingent on the work of consulates or dissident movements, as stated by Ireland (1994). Increasingly, most migrant organizations in Germany do not try to exert influence in Turkey directly, but rather seek to introduce homeland political agendas into German political institutions. To that end, they use multi-layered strategies. These strategies fall into the two main categories of confrontational activities and institutional participation. This categorization structures the analysis of forms of participation, and demonstrates that some groups are more confrontational (utilizing demonstrations, mass meetings, and even illegal activities) while others have chosen to cooperate with, or work within, German political institutions, such as trade unions and political parties.

These political practices are transnational in the sense that they draw on personal or institutionalized links with Turkey or other organizations outside Turkey and Germany. Nonetheless, at the same time, most Turkish and Kurdish homeland political engagement is not transnational in the sense of entailing movement back and forth between Turkey and Germany. It is also not transnational in that it does not entail direct participation in Turkish politics such as voting or candidacy within Turkish political parties. Rather, it is transnational from afar as Turks and Kurds engage themselves in Turkish politics in Germany. Thus, political relations between the Turks abroad and Turkey have undergone a qualitative transformation whereby most organizations have added a set of indirect transnational practices to their more direct participation in homeland politics.

The differences among Turkish and Kurdish homeland political information campaigns are one of the indicators that there is another process of institutional channelling at play than that which may apply to migrant political participation. Homeland political claims-making is channelled differently because those channels and fora open to dialogue on migrant political issues are only sometimes also open to dialogue on homeland political issues. German political actors find themselves at a two-way junction between Turkey and its citizens abroad. Like other receiving states, they lay down various rules for homeland political participation.

Obviously, organizations that turn to violent confrontational means are banned and prosecuted. Although only a small set of organizations engage in this kind of activity, it has a high profile in the public eye and has served to stigmatize other homeland political organizations. More generally, German authorities shape activities by ignoring them. There are quite consistent normative criteria determining with which migrant organizations German authorities and policy makers engage in dialogue. The comparison of the different use of strategies for participation among organizations shows that the main variable determining the extent to which an organization cooperates with German political institutions is the content of the homeland political agenda of the movement or organization: the more radical the agenda of the organization compared to the stance of German political institutions, the less institutional participation. Indeed, there is a mirror effect between affiliation with German and Turkish political systems. Most of those organizations that have an explicit affiliation with a Turkish political party find it more difficult to gain access to German political institutions, unless, of course, there is a close relationship between the particular German and Turkish political party. In turn, the more radically an organizations' agenda diverges from German domestic or foreign policy agendas, the less it seeks German interlocutors to promote its case. In some cases, radicalization feeds on marginalization, and a continuing exclusion of homeland political lobbying is not conducive to curbing developments among some of the nationalist and religious movements.

Yet, this book has demonstrated that migrants' transnational political networks are not synonymous with terrorism or radical movements. Homeland political claims-making is not only a matter of molotov cocktails or demonstrations, but also the politics of school curricula and mother-tongue teaching. Homeland political affiliation of immigrants and refugees covers the whole span of the political spectrum with a large majority of moderate left- and right-wing groups working on immigrant issues while taking a continued interest in how Turkey is viewed by German politicians. It is hoped that drawing a more complex picture does justice to the phenomenon of migrants' transnational politics.

German political institutions seek to limit the extent to which homeland-political debates unfold within their realm. 'Gatekeepers' such as trade unions or political parties play a crucial role in filtering out homeland politics. Interestingly, such political parties may engage themselves in Turkish politics and highlight these policies if it attracts support from the Turkish or Kurdish descent constituency. Yet, such parties are also aware that there are both German and Turkish votes to be lost if a party is identified too closely with a particular stance towards Turkey and Turkey–EU relations. In any case, thresholds of tolerance for homeland politics constitute a major barrier for Turkish and Kurdish information campaigns and claims-making. The reactions of German political institutions and authorities are an integral part of the dynamics of political participation of Turkish citizens in Germany.

However, the story does not end here. The field of transnational practices is more complex than migrant–receiving country dynamics. Migrant organizations' continuous use of different sites to promote homeland political agendas is the result of a process of multi-level institutional channelling, relating to their local and national context in both the sending and receiving countries, their international institutional and normative environment, and their networks with kin organizations in other countries.

Some of these sites are physical. Migrant organizations may move away from direct participation in Turkish politics towards indirect homeland politics in the form of information campaigns in Germany. Some make this move because their dissident agenda bars them from constructive dialogue with Turkish authorities. Others move in this direction because Turkish political actors are not attentive to emigrants' needs or lack the policy tools to improve the situation of emigrants abroad. If and when German authorities and policy makers turn a blind eye to migrant organizations' information campaigns, these organizations may draw on their networks with kin organizations in other countries to coordinate and strengthen their campaigns, and, importantly, to have a European constituency behind them when they approach European institutions.

Other sites are discursive. In order to overcome local constraints, homeland political information campaigns draw on two discourses that are more readily acceptable to German authorities. On the one hand, the language of universal human rights and democratization provides a common platform for dialogue. On the other hand, migrant organizations emphasize the link between their role and place in German society and Turkish domestic politics. The trends in migrants' claims-making based on universal human rights norms has been interpreted by 'post-nationalist' scholars as a strong indication of how citizenship increasingly is legitimized beyond the realm of the nation state (see Bauböck 1994; Soysal 1994, 2000; Jacobson 1996). The discursive and physical sites feed on one another as migrants increasingly approach European and international institutions and adopt universalist language.

This book does not contradict such trends but points to how migrant politics, certainly a discourse legitimated within the nation state, may serve as a discursive site for dialogue and negotiation with policy makers. It is when Turks and Kurds merge their homeland political concerns with migrant-political issues that they gain more attention. German authorities are primarily concerned with the peaceful co-existence of different ethnic minorities in Germany; after this comes the concern with minority rights in Turkey. The presence and activities of a certain national, ethnic, or religious minority help to 'scale up' the issue of their homeland- and immigrant political concerns as German authorities and policy makers may see the link between the two. They may consider the minority rights (mother-tongue teaching, Alevi religious practice) in Germany rather than Turkey while becoming aware that their current practice may be a continuation of, rather than a challenge to, Turkey's minority policies.

Again, this points to the fact that the 'legitimacy' of a homeland political agenda constitutes an integral part of the 'political structures of opportunity' available to a transnational political network. Just as migrant political participation is located within a transnational perspective of Turkish politics, homeland political claims-making is likewise embedded in a German discourse on how migrant-political participation should occur. Some organizations are more successful than others in negotiating their way through this multi-level institutional environment. Yet, generally, there is a process of institutional channelling at work whereby organizations' homeland political activities test the thresholds of tolerance of host country political actors, and these thresholds again shape the agency of the migrants and refugees.

Transnational politics and democratization

The homeland political engagement of Turks and Kurds in Germany poses a challenge to both German and Turkish authorities and political institutions. Yet, the effectiveness of migrants' transnational political activities cannot be appreciated by only looking at the extent to which they change state behaviour. Turkish and Kurdish homeland political lobbying, if evaluated only in terms of the extent to which it impacts domestic or foreign policy behaviour, is negligible. Rather, it is necessary to have a differentiated understanding of 'effectiveness', which includes the extent to which the migrants are able to establish channels of communication with central political institutions of the receiving country. Such analysis highlights how migrants' transnational politics enter the relationship between both homeland and receiving countries and their minorities, testing the boundaries between different countries' domestic politics as well as between the domestic and the international.

Homeland politics is increasingly being recognized as an integral part of the relationship between German political institutions and Turkish citizens living in Germany, as various groups are able to establish channels of communication with German political institutions. A complex pattern of dialogue emerges: organizations in opposition to Turkey's political regime have mainly linked up with the trade unions and left-wing German political parties. Turkish organizations that defend the homeland are mainly linked up with more conservative organizations such as the CDU or FDP. Moreover, a comparison of German tolerance of Kurdish, Sunni Muslim, and Alevi claims, indicates that German national interests, such as domestic security or good bilateral relations with Turkey, matter in terms of German attitudes to both the homeland- and immigrant political claims of Turkish citizens. In particular, it is in the interests of German authorities to not support homeland political movements, which may fuel intra-communal strife among the diasporas in Germany. Kurds, Sunni Muslims, and Alevis formulate their demands for recognition of ethnic and/or religious distinctiveness in Turkey, as well as in Germany, in compliance with international norms of human rights. Yet, the response of host country political institutions demonstrates that just as homeland- and immigrant political agendas cannot be separated from the point of view of the migrants, they are also inseparable when evaluated by political institutions of the receiving country. All three cases highlight the spatial diffusion of domestic politics between Germany and Turkey. Foreign policy becomes integration policy and integration policy becomes foreign policy.

It has been argued that migrants' transnational political practices contribute to the development of multicultural democracy in their country of settlement (Faist 2000a). However, Turkish and Kurdish homeland political engagement also serves as a stumbling block to political participation. Homeland political factionalism hinders the formation of common platforms from which immigrant political concerns can be voiced. Mutual slandering limits the access of certain Turkish or Kurdish groups. German politicians, wary of being associated with the 'wrong' Islamic or Kurdish organizations, are reluctant to accept invitations to festivals, seminars, and panel discussions. More generally, homeland political engagement, be it a high-profile Kurdish demonstration or the attempt of Turkish politicians to tell Turkish-descent Germans how to vote in German elections, provides a welcome argument for those German political actors who are against dual citizenship. Such instances, in their opinion, illustrate the problems that dual allegiance will impose on the German polity.

By contrast, the preceding chapters also show how organizations, including those founded on homeland political grounds, serve as platforms from which Turks and Kurds may orient themselves in German politics. They serve as fora for discussions of migrant political issues and as meeting points for extended contact with German policy makers. Moreover, homeland political campaigns of Kurds, Alevis, and Sunnis challenge migrant incorporation regimes based on national rather than ethnic or religious minorities. They prompt the question of whether German minority policies should be based on – or even mirror – Turkey's minority policies or take heed of the claims for minority rights by the migrants or refugees themselves.

The challenges and contributions of Turkish and Kurdish transnational practices to Turkey are more difficult to assess. Turkish political parties and NGOs are interested in support from the outside, but one rarely hears that they welcome contributions other than funding and votes. That is, there is little recognition of how Turks and Kurds abroad can contribute to democratization at home. Even those political actors who are marginalized by Turkey's strict criteria for democratic representation are wary of being linked with dissident movements abroad, as this would serve to stigmatize rather than legitimate them in the eyes of Turkish authorities. Yet, these actors do welcome political information campaigns abroad, including public discussion of issues on which it is more difficult to voice an opinion within Turkey.

These Turkish political actors notwithstanding, the debate in Turkey is, perhaps not surprisingly, more on what Turkey can do for its citizens abroad, and how its citizens, in turn, can represent Turkey's interests abroad, than on how Turks abroad can contribute to democratization at home. Turkey takes a keen interest in the social capital upgrading of its citizens abroad, because these citizens are considered a potentially important lobby, which may represent Turkey's interests in western Europe. However, at the same time, the homeland political authorities are concerned with the political dissidence unfolding among the Kurdish, extreme left-wing, and Sunni Muslim movements in particular. This, it is felt, damages Turkey's image in the receiving country and strengthens the opposition to the state within Turkey; hence, a wide range of measures is taken to curb such activities. Both dimensions illustrate the de-territorialization of the Turkish state, as Ankara is seeking to accommodate the fact that both pro-state and anti-state parts of the Turkish polity have settled in Germany.

Migration and the spatial diffusion of domestic politics

International migration has clearly affected the relationship between Germany and Turkey. It has tied the two countries closer together, although issues such as the (lack of) integration of Turkish citizens settled in Germany or German fears of further immigration and asylum seekers from Turkey have damaged relations between the two countries. Migrants and refugees engage themselves in these relations, but this agency is far from always welcomed, particularly if it goes against domestic or foreign policy concerns. Thus, not surprisingly, Germany and Turkey have different views on the causes of homeland political allegiance of the Turkish citizens in Germany. Germany points to the role of Turkish media and political institutions as the main reason for the homeland political division in the Turkish and Kurdish communities. Turkey blames German policies of integration for being the main factor contributing to polarization of Turks and Kurds. Germany wishes that Turkey would 'let go' of its citizens, while Turkey wishes that Germany would start welcoming, albeit not assimilating its citizens in Germany. Thus, a curious asymmetrical pattern emerges in the triadic relationship among the migrants, the government of their country of settlement, and the government of their country of origin. Issues pertaining to Turkish politics feature in the relationship between the migrants and German political institutions, while German immigration and integration policies play a prominent role in the relationship between the migrants and Turkish political institutions.

However, migrants and refugees are not pawns but players in transnational politics. The phenomenon of homeland politics of Turkish citizens in Germany is as complex as the multitude of the interests of the political actors involved. But common to all the various instances and forms of transnational politics is that the migrants from Turkey have become a linkage group between their receiving country and their country of origin. The distinctive forms of transnational politics introduce the politics of Turkey to Germany, and provide an external dimension to the politics of Turkey, acting as a resource for political counterparts. In this way, migrants' transnational politics entails the spatial diffusion of domestic politics between their homeland and their receiving country.

The overall conclusion of the empirical case study is that transnational politics of Turkish citizens in Germany is a phenomenon in the making, as political authorities in both the country of origin and settlement are realizing the potential of, and threat posed by, transnational political activities. Germany is not known for its inclusive policies towards migrants. Similarly, its stance towards homeland political claims-making is exclusive compared to other European countries and the US. Still, the case study does share parallels with other cases of the interaction between migrant transnationalism and state responses, such as the case of Mexicans in the US. However, what stands out is how the case of Turks and Kurds is far less institutionalized. There are no extensive transnational Turkish election campaigns in Germany. The phenomenon of homeland political 'block'-voting is not known in Germany to the extent that it is in the US. One can even speculate on the extent to which transnational engagement among Turks may be reduced now that their low rates of naturalization have been reversed with German citizenship reforms. Certainly, this was the expectation of those German political parties opposing the inclusion of dual citizenship in these reforms. Their argument against dual citizenship was that it would serve to institutionalize migrants' 'dual loyalties' and transnational political engagement. By contrast, allowing for only one German passport would encourage amongst migrants a commitment to participate in German politics only. Yet, the case of several ethnic minorities in the US does not point in this direction only. There is no zero-sum relationship between homeland political engagement and political integration in the receiving country.

Importantly, the case of Turks and Kurds in Germany puts a note of caution to the current enthusiasm with the growing de-territorializing strength of transnational movements in domestic and world politics. The study shows how such activities are constrained by the national boundedness of the political sphere. As migrants' transnational political networks push for the de-territorialization of the political, the case of Turkish citizens in Germany demonstrates how receiving country political actors limit the scope and effectiveness of homeland politics. Yet, homeland politics does not simply delimit the thresholds of tolerance towards homeland political claims. The homeland political movements have managed to get a foot in the door, as their presence and activities do challenge and provoke the very notion of these boundaries. Through their homeland political claims-making, migrants raise the issues of the legitimacy of dual political allegiance, and the unboundedness of domestic politics in both Turkey and Germany. By introducing the politics of Turkey to German political institutions, the migrants further break down the distinction between domestic and international politics and force German policy makers to combine, albeit reluctantly, foreign policy with domestic integration policy in their dealings with Turkey – and the Turkey that exists in Germany.

Appendix A: Table and figures

Table A1 Number of applications for asylum by Turkish citizens in Germany, refusal rates, and protection from deportation, 1979–2000

Year	Application	Acceptance	Protection from deportation
1979	18,192		
1980	57,913		
1981	6,337		
1982	3,719		
1983	1,563		
1984	4,180	244	
1985	7,528	500	
1986	8,693	254	
1987	11,426	978	
1988	14,873	1,098	
1989	20,020	664	
1990	22,082	1,283	
1991	23,877	1,669	
1992	28,327	1,421	
1993	19,104	3,577	
1994	19,118	8,771	
1995	25,518	7,426	817
1996	23,814	5,120	704
1997	16,840	3,086	658
1998	20,286	2,659	575
1999	16,231	1,886	676
2000	14,355	1,477	672
Total	383,996	42,113	4,101

Sources: Federal Department for Statistics (1980–98); personal correspondence with Federal Department for the Recognition of Refugees, 2 February 2002.

Notes: The figure for 1979 are for western Europe, but when comparing the figures for 1980 for both western Europe and Germany there is little difference (57,913 of the 58,073 asylum seekers in western Europe in 1980 were from Germany). The figures for acceptance and deportation only became available in 1984 and 1995, respectively.

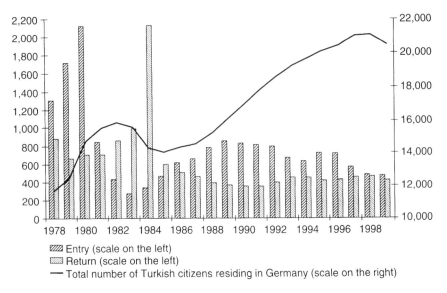

Figure A1 Migration and return migration from Turkey to Germany, and total number of resident Turkish citizens (in thousands), 1978–2000.

Source: Federal Department for Statistics (1978–2000).

Note: The figures are based on the obligatory notification of new residence.

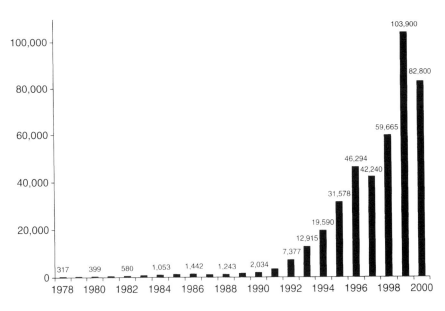

Figure A2 Turkish citizens obtaining German citizenship, 1978–2000.

Source: Federal Department for Statistics (1979–2001).

Appendix B: Methodology

In 1995, I conducted a minor survey of local politicians of Turkish descent in Denmark and was perplexed and intrigued by the complex political universe of Turkish immigrants there. For instance, one Turkish-descent member of the city council of Copenhagen told me how his Danish social democratic colleagues had offered to fetch social democrats from Turkey to aid his election campaign. He, then, had to explain to them that standing next to a Turkish social democrat would reduce his chances of getting elected. This is because a majority of the Turkish citizens in Copenhagen are conservative in terms of Turkish politics and only vote for the Danish social democratic party because of its relatively liberal attitude towards issues of immigration and integration.

Determined to discover more about these issues, I have ended up researching transnational political practices in Germany and Turkey. Findings in this book are based on fieldwork in Germany and Turkey undertaken in several rounds between 1996 and 2000. The data collection concentrated on the following two sets of actors: (a) the political activities of the immigrant groups; and (b) the reactions to these activities by selected political institutions and actors in the host country and the homeland.

When I undertook my fieldwork in Germany, there was relatively little available information on Turkish and Kurdish migrant organizations compared to the situation today. Presently, information is much easier to acquire through the Internet and the widely available official and academic publications on these matters. Only five years ago, there was quite a bit of hearsay information floating around, in particular, regarding the more extremist associations. Distinguishing migrant organizations from one another in terms of homeland political orientation became an integral part of the snowballing method I used to identify relevant organizations and community leaders for interviews.

There were three main dimensions in my research on migrant organizations. First, I carried out more than 50 qualitative interviews with Turkish and Kurdish migrant organizations in Germany, mainly those working at the federal level, but also a range of local associations. Most of the federations are based in the *Länder* of Nordrhein-Westfalen (Cologne, Bonn, and Düsseldorf) and Berlin. I mainly interviewed leading members of Turkish and Kurdish associations. In this research, *in-depth interviewing* proves the best tool to probe into political commitment and levels of intervention by different organizations and movements. Hence, the use of qualitative methods of data gathering in this exercise has been supported by the need to address sensitive questions of political affiliation and loyalty of immigrants towards their country of origin. The emphasis in the empirical investigation is on how the leaders of migrant associations perceive their role and scope of agency in promoting their homeland political agendas. This includes their reservations, their agency, and their expectations of change and non-change brought about by their activities.

Second, besides the more formal interviewing, I also participated in more than 25 board meetings, seminars and panel discussions, festivals, and demonstrations. Here, I listened to speeches and spoke to members and supporters at a more informal level. This provided a good perspective on the information gathered among the organizations' executives. Many times it was also at these events that the transnational political dimension of an organization's network and activities stood out, because members from organizations in other western European countries and policy makers from Turkey were among the participants. In addition to participating in political events, I enjoyed the hospitality of a Kurdish family, a Turkish left-wing family active in several Turkish left-wing organizations, and a Turkish Sunni Muslim family active in *Milli Görüş*. These families not only facilitated my research through their respective social and political networks but also provided a highly interesting 'sounding board' to the more formal parts of the research.

Third, I collected a vast pile of publications, membership journals, press releases, copies of letters of opinion to German and Turkish newspapers, as well as correspondence between the organizations and German and Turkish authorities. This material has proved particularly useful in triangulating as well as supplementing the information in the interviews.

The other main line of research concentrated on how host state and homeland policy makers and NGOs perceive Turkish and Kurdish organizations' political engagement. I carried out 22 interviews with German policy makers at local, national, and federal levels and with representatives of German NGOs and trade unions, and 45 interviews with Turkish actors occupying similar positions in Turkey. Some of these interviews were of a more formal and factual character, while others evolved into lengthier sessions during which the interviewee gave a more personal account of his or her opinion on these issues. All of the interviews with German and Turkish policy makers were conducted with representatives who had a well-known engagement in either German–Turkish relations or the Turkish and Kurdish migrant associations in Germany. Seven of the interviews with German policy makers were conducted with representatives of Turkish or Kurdish descent. Five of the interviews in Turkey were with policy makers with a past in migrant organizations in Germany. In Turkey, I interviewed representatives not only from the more established parties but also from those parties that have never made it past the 10 per cent threshold to Turkey's Grand National Assembly. In addition, I interviewed representatives from human rights organizations and Kurdish parties standing in stark opposition to the Turkish authorities. Only some of these interviews are mentioned or listed in this book.

Appendix B: Methodology

The information collected in interviews with policy makers and state agencies were triangulated and contextualized with detailed archival research of German and Turkish parliamentary proceedings from 1980 to 2000. Other official documents included party political reports, policy statements, and press releases. I also went through newspaper databases, through the courtesy of Turkish and German parliamentary libraries, in order to collect opinions and news coverage of central events and issues.

Almost all of the interviews with migrant associations, policies makers, NGOs, and state agencies have been conducted in either German or Turkish, and all quotes in this book are my own translation. Approximately 80 per cent of the interviews were taped, although the interviewees who were taped sometimes asked me to turn off the tape recorder when they wanted to speak about particularly sensitive issues. I have respected this as well as individual wishes for anonymity throughout the text. Interested readers may consult Østergaard-Nielsen (1998) for more details on interviewees and material collected from 1996 to 1998.

During my research, the necessity of a historical perspective became increasingly clear. Therefore, the research concentrates on developments in transnational political activities since 1980. This cutting date has been chosen for the following reasons. First, the military coup in Turkey in September 1980, with the ensuing ban of all political parties followed by the (re)establishment of some of these parties, provides a significant 'cutoff point'. Second, in Germany, Turkish citizens gradually realized that they had come to stay after 1980, and the process of settlement began. It is from 1980 that the interface between immigrant politics and homeland politics becomes more interesting. Third, the past decade has entailed the arrival of political dissidents and activists, affecting some political mobilization of, in particular, the Kurdish communities. Fourth, the current migrant organizations of significance have mainly been formed since 1980. Most of the organizations that were of significance in the 1970s no longer exist, and those archives that existed have been lost. Thus, a 20 year time frame enables a dynamic view of the shifting patterns of mobilization and degrees of cooperation with German and Turkish political institutions dealt with in Chapters 4–7. Moreover, it provides a highly relevant sounding board to the host state and homeland reactions to the transnational political activities of Turkish citizens living in Germany.

Appendix C: Migrant associations, political parties, and state agencies with whom interviews were conducted

Migrant associations

Leftist organizations

Demokratik Işçi Dernekleri Federasyonu (DIDF) (Federation of Democratic Workers Associations)

Migrant organization founded in 1980 through a merger of two new left communist organizations. The federation currently has 25 membership organizations in Germany as well as in several other European countries.

Interviews with the same member of executive committee, 14 July 1997 and 12 October 2000, Cologne.

Türkiyeli Göçmen Dernekleri Federasyonu (GDF) (Federation of Turkish Migrants' Associations)

Migrant organization founded in 1988 by supporters of the Turkish communist parties. The federation currently has 25 membership organizations in Germany.

Interviews with members of the executive committee, 21 July 1997, Cologne; 28 November 1997, Cologne; the chairman, 16 December 1997, Düsseldorf.

Social Democratic and Kemalist organizations

Social Demokrat Halk Dernekleri (HDF) (Social Democratic Peoples Associations)

Organization of the Turkish Social Democrats founded by migrants, as well as members of the Turkish party, Cumhuriyet Halk Partisi (CHP), in 1977. The federation currently has 43 membership organizations.

Interviews with the chairman, 11 November 1996, Berlin; a member of the executive committee, 3 December 1997, Cologne; the (new) chairman, 5 August 1998, Duisburg.

Almanya Atatürkçu Düşünce Derneği (AADD) (German Association for Kemalist Ideas)

Founded in 1998 by a previous member of HDF. The association has five membership organizations.

Interviews with the founder and chairman, 16 July 1997 and 10 October 2000, Cologne.

Nationalist organizations

Avrupa Demokratik Ülkücü Türk Dernekleri Federasyonu (*Türk Federasyon*) (*Federation of European Democratic Idealist Turkish Associations*)
Founded in 1978. The federation has strong links to the nationalist Turkish party, Milli Hareket Partisi (MHP), and has 200 membership organizations in Germany and other European countries.
Interview with the chairman, 13 February 1998, Frankfurt.

Moderate right-wing organizations

Hürriyetçi Türk-Alman Dostluk Dernekleri (*Hür-Türk*) (*Liberal Turkish–German Friendship Associations*)
Conservative liberal federation set up by migrants and members of the Turkish conservative liberal Adalet Partisi (AP) in 1979. The federation has 55 membership organizations in Germany and nine in Turkey.
Interviews with a member of the executive committee, 16 February 1998, Düsseldorf, and the deputy chairman, 22 May 1998, Bonn.

Sunni Muslim organizations

Diyanet İşleri Türk İslâm Birliği (*DITIB*) (*Turkish Islamic Union for Religious Affairs*)
Sunni Muslim federation set up by the Turkish Directorate for Religious Affairs Diyanet İşleri Başkanlığı in 1982. By far the largest Sunni Muslim federation in Germany with more than 775 organizations.
Interview with a local branch chairman, 22 October 1996, Berlin; and the manager, 15 July 1997, Cologne.

Verband der Islamischen Kulturzentren e.V. (*VIKZ/Süleymancıs*) (*Association of Islamic Cultural Centres*)
Founded in 1973 in Cologne by the Sufi Süleymancılars, followers of Süleyman Hilmi Tunahan Efendi (1888–1959). The religious order was outlawed in Turkey in 1925, but has since been tolerated and even supported by various Turkish governments. The organization puts great emphasis on religious education through Koran courses and has a world-wide network of followers. In Germany, there are an estimated 275 organizations.
Interview with the general secretary, 15 July 1997, Cologne.

Jama'at Un-Nur (*Congregation of Light – 'Nurcus'*)
Founded in 1979 in Cologne by the Sufi Nurcular, followers of the writings of Bediuzzaman Said Nursi (1873–1960). The Nurculuk movment has been regarded with much suspicion by the Turkish authorities. Today, the movement has a world-wide network of followers. The Nurcus has 50,000 followers in Germany and run an estimated 200 'schools', where the work of Said Nursi is studied and disseminated. These figures are difficult to verify because the Nurcus work through more informal structures than the other Sunni organizations.
Interview with the chairman, 29 May 1998, Cologne.

Islamische Gemeinschaft Milli Görüş V. (IGMG) (Islamic Community of National Vision)

Founded in 1976 by supporters and members of the Turkish party, Milli Selamet Partisi, later Fazilet Partisi. There are still strong links between Milli Görüş and Fazilet Partisi. Today Milli Görüş, which is monitored by the Verfassungsschutz, claims to have 274 organizations in Germany and 463 in Europe.

Interviews with the general secretary, 25 July 1997, and 11 October 2000, Cologne.

Islam Cemaatleri ve Cemiyetleri Birliği (ICCB) (Union of Islamic Congregations and Associations)

Founded in 1984 in Cologne by a splinter group from Milli Görüş, headed by the late Cemaleddin Kaplan who was in favour of the Iranian revolution. The organization is estimated to have around 70 associations in Germany but only an estimated 1,100 members.

No interview was granted with leaders of ICCB, who instead sent a big box of material on their ideology and activities.

Avrupa Türk Islam Birliği (ATIB) (Turkish Islamic Union in Europe)

Founded in 1987 by a splinter group from Türk Federasyon. Claims to be apolitical and working on migrant related issues only.

Interviews with the higher education commissioner, 24 July 1997, Cologne; the chairman and the deputy general secretary, 11 October 2000, Cologne.

Zentralrat der Muslime in Deutchland e.V. (ZMD) (Central Council for Muslims in Germany)

Platform for Sunni Muslim organizations formed in 1994 in order to voice Sunni Muslim concerns to German authorities. Includes VIKZ and ATIB.

Interview with the deputy chairman, 15 July 1997, Cologne.

Alevi organizations

Almanya Alevi Birlik Federasyonu (AABF) (Alevi Unity Federation in Germany)

Main federation of Alevis in Germany, founded in 1989, with presently 130 membership organizations.

Interviews with a former member of executive committee, 3 December 1997; the chairman, 13 December 1997, Cologne; the (new) chairman, 10 October 2000, Cologne.

Cumhuriyet Eğitim Vakfı (C.E.M. Vakfı) (Republican Education Foundation)

Alevi organization founded in 1997, which has a more conservative and educational emphasis on the Turkish politics and Alevi organizations abroad than AABF.

Interview with the chairman, 12 October 2000, Essen.

Kurdish organizations

YEK-KOM, Föderation Kurdischer Vereine in Deutchland e.V. (Federation for Kurdish Associations in Germany)

Founded in 1994 and works on Kurdish migrant issues, but is also sympathetic to the PKK. Currently, the federation has around 70–80 membership organizations in Germany.

Interviews with the same member of the executive committee, Bochum, 19 July 1997 and 12 October, Düsseldorf.

Yekitiya Komelen Kurdistan (KOMKAR) (The Union of Associations from Kurdistan)

Founded in 1979, works on Kurdish migrant issues but also supports the Kurdistan Socialist Party, PSK, which is illegal in Turkey. Has around 30 membership organizations in Germany.

Interviews with member of the executive committee, 23 July 1997, Cologne; the founder of KOMKAR, 19 February 1998, Bonn.

Civata li Kurd (The Kurdish Associations)

The federation was founded in 1992. It works on Kurdish migrant issues but is also sympathetic to the Kurdistan Socialist Unity Party in Turkey, PSYIK.

Interview with the manager, 16 July 1997, Cologne.

Kurdish Exile Parliament

Parliament of exiled Kurdish politicians founded in 1995, which convenes in parliamentary buildings throughout Europe.

Interview with representative, July 1996, London.

MEDYA-TV

Kurdish TV Station founded in 1993. Has been re-locating offices and satellite transmitters continuously throughout the 1990s because of its alleged sympathies for the PKK.

Interviews with the manager and staff at the office in London, July 1996, London.

Joint platforms

Almanya Türk Toplumu (ATT) (The Turkish Community in Germany)

Platform for migrant federations and organizations, founded in 1985 by former members of HDF and other social democratically oriented Turkish migrant organizations. Currently has around 100 membership organizations and federations.

Interviews with the federal chairman, 10 November 1996, Berlin and 19 November 1997, Hamburg; the deputy federal chairman, 11 October 1996 and 19 November 1997, Berlin.

Rat der Türkische Staatsbürger (RTS) (Council for Turkish Citizens)

Platform for migrant federations founded in 1990 to promote migrant political interests. Represents right-wing and Sunni Muslim organizations only.

Interview with the chairman, 9 December 1997, Bonn.

Organizations set up in co-operation with German political parties

Deutsch–Türkische Union (DTU) (German–Turkish Union)

Organization set up by Turkish-descent supporters of the CDU in Berlin in 1996.

Interview with the chairman, 9 October 1996, Berlin.

Deutsch–Türkische Forum (DTF) (German–Turkish Forum)
 Organization set up by Turkish-descent supporters of the CDU in 1997 in Bonn.
 Interview with member of executive committee, 16 February 1998, Düsseldorf.

Employers associations

Türk-Alman İşadamları Dernekleri Almanya Federasyonu (TIDAF) (Federation of Turkish–German Businessmen Associations in Germany)
 Organization that promotes the interests of Turkish employers and industrialists in Germany.
 Interview with the general secretary, 11 October 2000, Cologne.

Avrupa Türk İşadamları ve Sanayicileri Derneği (ATIAD) (Association of Turkish Businessmen and Industrialists in Europe)
 Association that promotes the interests of larger Turkish industrialists in Europe.
 Interview with the manager, 25 May 1998, Düsseldorf.

German political parties

Christlich Demokratische Union (CDU) (Christian Democratic Union)
 Interviews with member of *Bundestag* and leader of the German–Turkish Joint Parliamentarian Group (1994–8), 11 December 1997, Bonn, and 27 September 2000, Berlin.

Sozialdemokratische Partei Deutschland (SPD) (Social Democratic Party of Germany)
 Interviews with same member of *Bundestag*, 11 December 1997, Bonn, and 28 September 2000, Berlin; member of *Bundestag* and leader of the SPD Parliamentarian Group on Turkey, 12 December 1997, Bonn.

Partei des Demokratischen Sozialismus (PDS) (Party of Democratic Socialism)
 Interview with same member of *Bundestag*, 9 December 1997, Bonn, and 28 September 2000, Berlin; member of Berlin Senate, 20 October 1996 and 29 September 2000, Berlin; representative in Cologne local council, 10 October 2000, Cologne.

Bündnis 90/Grüne (Die Grüne) (The Greens)
 Interviews with three members of the Berlin Senate, 9 October 1996, 3 October 1996, and 29 September 2000, Berlin; interviews with two members of *Bundestag*, 11 February 1998.

German organizations and state agencies

Deutscher Gewerkschaftsbund (DGB) (German Federation of Trade Unions)
 Interview with Department for Foreign Workers, Federal Executive Committee, 10 August 1998, Düsseldorf.

IGMetall (Trade Union for Metal Workers)
Interviews with two former representatives of IGMetall, 16 October 1996, Berlin, and 27 May 1998, Cologne; with former member of federal board of IGMetall, 17 December 1998 and 13 October 2000, Frankfurt.

Die Ausländerbeauftragte des Berlin Senats (Foreigners Commission of Berlin Senate)
Interview 25 September 1996, Berlin.

Die Beauftragte der Bundesregierung für die Belange der Ausländer, Berliner Referat (Foreigners Commission for the Federal Government, Berlin Office)
Interview 25 October 1996, Berlin.

Turkish political parties

Refah Partisi (RP) (The Welfare Party) later reconvened as Fazilet Partisi (FP) (The Virtue Party)
Interviews with same member of the Turkish Grand National Assembly, who is also former head of Milli Görüş in Germany, 27 November 1996, and 18 October 2000, Ankara; with member of the Turkish Grand National Assembly who is a FP representative on the Coordination Committee for the Turkish citizens living abroad, 16 December 1996, Ankara; with member of the Turkish Grand National Assembly, 23 October 2000, Ankara.

Anavatan Partisi (ANAP) (The Motherland Party)
Interviews with same member of the Turkish Grand National Assembly who is deputy chairman for the German–Turkish Joint Parliamentarian Group, 9 December 1996 and 25 October 2000, Ankara; with same member of the Turkish Grand National Assembly who is chairman of Foreign Relations Commission, 6 December 1996 and 23 October 2000, Ankara; with member and president of the Turkish Grand National Assembly, 25 June 1998, Ankara.

Doğru Yol Partisi (DYP) (The True Path Party)
Interviews with same member of the Turkish Grand National Assembly, who is a member of the Coordination Committee for Turkish Citizens living abroad, 15 July 1998 and 23 October 2000, Ankara.

Demokratik Sol Partisi (DSP) (The Democratic Left Party)
Interviews with same member of the Turkish Grand National Assembly, 27 November 1996 and 20 October 2000, Ankara; with member of the Turkish Grand National Assembly who is a member of the Foreign Relations Commission, 14 July 1998 and 20 October 2000, Ankara; with member of the Turkish Grand National Assembly who is a DSP representative on the Coordination Committee for Turkish citizens living abroad, 23 October 2000, Ankara.

Cumhuriyet Halk Partisi (CHP) (The Republican Peoples Party)
Interviews with same member of the Turkish Grand National Assembly, 5 December 1996 and 22 July 1998, Ankara.

146 *Appendix C: Associations, parties and agencies*

Milli Hareket Partisi (MHP) (The National Action Party)
Interviews with deputy chairman, 30 June 1998, Ankara; with member of Grand National Assembly who is MHP representative on the Coordination Committee for Turkish citizens living abroad, 23 October 2000, Ankara.

Turkish political parties outside of Turkey's Grand National Assembly

Buyük Birlik Partisi (BBP) (The Great Unity Party)
Interview with deputy general secretary, 29 July 1998, Ankara.

Işci Partisi (IP) (The Workers Party)
Interview with general secretary, 13 July 1998, Ankara.

Halk ve Demokrasi Partisi (HADEP) (The People and Democracy Party)
Interviews with two deputy general secretaries, 1 July 1998, Ankara; with the chairman, 24 October 2000, Ankara.

Barış Partisi (BP) (The Peace Party)
Interview with the general secretary, 17 July 1998, Ankara.

Özgürlük and Dayanışma Partisi (ÖDP) (The Freedom and Solidarity Party)
Interview with the information officer, 20 July 1998, Ankara.

Organizations in Turkey

Türkiye İşçi Sendikaları Konfederasyonu (Türk-İş) (Confederation of Trade Unions of Turkey)
Interview with general advisor to the president, 31 July 1998, Ankara.

İnsan Hakları Derneği (IHD) (Human Rights Association)
Interviews with the president, 13 December 1996, Ankara; with a member of the executive committee, 24 October 2000, Ankara.

Hacı Bektaş Derneği (Hacı Bektaş Association)
Interview with the chairman, 10 December 1996, Ankara.

Alevi Cem Vakfı (The Alevi Cem Foundation)
Interview with the chairman, 9 October 2000, Ankara.

Turkish state agencies

Dışişleri Bakanlığı (Ministry of Foreign Affairs)
Interview with general director of the Department of Turks living abroad, 21 November 1996, Ankara. Interview with general director of the Department of Intelligence and Research, 21 November 1996, Ankara.

Turkish General Consulate, Berlin
Interview with the general consul, 6 November 1996, Berlin.

Turkish Embassy, Bonn
Interview with the Turkish ambassador to Germany, 17 February 1998, Bonn.

Appendix C: Associations, parties, and agencies 147

Çalışma ve Sosyal Güvenlik Bakanlığı (Ministry for Labour and Social Security, Department for Workers Living Abroad)
Interview with general director, 16 December 1996, Ankara.

Devlet Bakanlığı (State Ministry, Department for Citizens Living Abroad)
Interview with advisor to the minister of state, 6 July 1998, Ankara. Interview with secretary to the Coordination Committee for Turkish citizens living abroad, 20 October 2000, Ankara.

Türkiye Büyük Millet Meclisi (Turkish Grand National Assembly, Department for Laws and Decisions)
Interviews with law expert, 2 July 1998, Ankara; with advisor to the president of the National Grand Assembly, 2 July 1998, Ankara; with expert for the Constitution Commission, 25 June 1996, Ankara.

Diyanet İşleri Başkanlığı (Turkish Directorate for Religious Affairs)
Interview with general director, Department of Foreign Relations, 29 July 1998, Ankara.

Turkish, German, and English newspapers cited

Cumhurriyet
Evrensel
Financial Times
Frankfurter Allgemeine Zeitung
Frankfurter Rundschau
Hürriyet
Milliyet
Özgür Politika
Sabah
Spiegel, Der
Tagesspiegel, Die
Tageszeitung, Die
Türkiye
Welt, Die
Zeit, Die

Notes

1 Introduction

1 The various meanings of the concepts of 'transnational communities' and 'diasporas' will be discussed at greater length in Chapter 2.
2 The concept of 'spatial diffusion of domestic politics' comes from Miller (1981) who argues that 'foreign workers' increase the permeability of both the political systems of the receiving country and the homeland to exogenous political influences (Miller 1981: 23).
3 Almost all interviews were conducted in German or Turkish. The translations of these, as well as all written sources in Turkish and German are by this author. The interviews, largely kept anonymous, are briefly referenced in the main text, and the reader can consult Appendix C for more detail. Closure, re-organization, or re-naming of German or Turkish political parties or migrant organizations taking place after the end of the research in 2000 have not been included.

2 Migrants' transnational claims-making: rethinking concepts and theories

1 Shain, in his study of exile governments, makes a distinction between 'home nation' and 'home regime', since exiles identify with the former and seek to overthrow the latter (Shain 1989: 25). Otherwise, it has been suggested that the existence of a political centre in the homeland as a defining criterion is a contested issue in the literature because of the legacy of the Jewish diaspora in the understanding of modern diasporas. For instance, it has been argued that the creation of the state of Israel makes the Jewish diaspora less 'archetypal' (see Armstrong 1976; Marienstras 1989: 120; Cohen 1997: 198, fn 11).
2 This reformulation of the relationship between the homeland and its emigrants has a historical parallel in the Italian policies towards the Italian citizens living abroad under Mussolini. Here, the term 'emigrant' was replaced by 'citizen' as part of Fascist policies to 'redeem the emigration from the political ineptitude and social irresponsibility of the liberal state' and to achieve 'the spiritual recovery of all Italian communities abroad by strengthening material and moral contacts between Italy and the citizens abroad' (Shain 1989: 51).
3 So far, there are only few comparative studies that have tested these suppositions about the relationship between political opportunity structures and the scope of transnational political orientation. Research on transnational 'claims-making', understood as the frequency with which it is reported in the media in Germany, Great Britain, and the Netherlands, concludes that in particular Germany's exclusive treatment of immigrants makes for transnational political mobilization. In the Netherlands, there was only a third of the transnational political activity found in Germany (Koopmans and Statham 2001).
4 Ireland's category of 'confrontational participation' resembles the concept of 'contentious politics', which includes strategies of mass demonstrations and large-scale protests, civil disobedience, or political violence (Tarrow 1998; see also Adamson 2002).

5 Ireland also includes the category of 'homeland-oriented participation' as a third type of participation. Homeland political participation is encouraged from homeland governments via their consular services, or consists of the presence of homeland opposition parties and movements (Ireland 1994: 25). This form of participation is, however, included in a less systematic fashion in Ireland's study.
6 See Geddes (2000) for an analysis of how migrant politics is conducted also at transnational level in Europe.
7 Similarly, in their study of advocacy networks of NGOs in areas such as human rights, environment, and womens' issues, Keck and Sikkink (1998: 25) suggest five criteria of effectiveness ranging from agenda setting to influence on state behaviour.
8 Kaiser stresses how transnational politics have been set in motion by interaction within a transnational society, transnational society being 'a system of interaction in a specific issue area between societal actors in different national systems' (Kaiser 1971: 802, 804).

3 Migration, transnational spaces, and German–Turkish relations

1 According to a recent survey, more than 60 per cent of Turks in Germany do not want return to Turkey (ZfT 2000a).
2 There are several interesting anthropological analyses of the transformations of Turkish consumption and popular culture in urban Germany (see Çaglar, 1995, 1998). See also Mandel (1996) for an analysis of the experiences of 'space' among Turks in Berlin.
3 This figure is the percentage of naturalizations of both Turkish citizens and Turkish descent Germans. This means that those with dual citizenship are counted twice. As a per cent of Turkish citizens alone, the figure is 21.5 per cent (ZfT 2000a).
4 Indeed, ATIAD distributes copies of the book *En Üstekiler*, meaning 'those at the top'. The title is a conscious play on the famous book of Günther Wallraff: *Ganz Unten* meaning 'Those at the bottom' (Koçak and Kilinç 1997: 13). In Wallraff's book, the author describes his experiences of discrimination and abuse while he was disguised as illegal immigrant from Turkey (Wallraff 1988). By contrast, *En Üstekiler* is a collection of biographies of the most successful and wealthiest Turkish origin industrialists in Europe (ATIAD 1997).
5 This is also the case with official publications on Turkish citizens living in Germany. For instance, the most recent booklet on Turks in Berlin opens with a very lengthy article by the Turkologist and Historian Klaus Schwarz on German–Turkish relations, with the main emphasis on warm pre-First World War relations, followed by a section on the German refugees in Turkey during the Nazi regime by the journalist Alfred Joachim Fischer (see Greve and Çinar 1998: 7–12).
6 A number of accounts of European–Turkish relations do not emphasize the scope and significance of the German–Turkish relationship except for the military cooperation and the alliance during First World War (see Zürcher 1993). Pettifier (1997) only stresses the role of immigrants in German–Turkish relations but does not consider the trade or arms relations. Pope and Pope (1997: 189) however, do acknowledge that it is Germany that 'by far has the closest and broadest relationship with Turkey'. By contrast, German accounts such as those by Steinbach (1996) or Kramer (1996) value the German–Turkish relationship in and of itself as well as its significance for European–Turkish relations.
7 Within academic circles, the role of the Turkish minority in Germany has only very recently been recognized as an important factor in German–Turkish, or for that matter European–Turkish relations. Rather than being confined to the disciplines of sociology or anthropology, volumes on European–Turkish relations increasingly include a chapter on the Turkish citizens in Europe in general, and in Germany in particular (see Kadioğlu 1993: 157; Şen 1996: 233–66; Pettifier 1997). Barchard's analysis of Turkey and the West is one of the first to consider the role of Turkish immigrants in Germany for German–Turkish relations (Barchard 1985: 72–5). Further, the role of the

150 *Notes*

Turkish minorities in Germany has in a very recent work by German Middle Eastern experts such as Heinz Kramer and Udo Steinbach been given a prominent place in the analysis of German foreign policy towards Turkey (see Steinbach 1996; Kramer 1998: 411–31).
8 See Art. 12, based on Arts. 48–50 of the EEC Treaty.
9 For a very comprehensive discussion of EU–Turkish relations see Kramer (1996), who stresses the significance of economic and trade relations in his analysis (see also Balkir and Williams 1993).
10 Policies of granting formal citizenship are often depicted as closely connected with national traditions, and most observers link the German exclusiveness to its historical ethnic form of national identity (see among others Brubaker 1992; Klusmeyer 1992; Heckmann 1994). Until 2000, the rules governing the acquisition of German citizenship largely derived from the Reichs- and Staatsbürgergesetz (Basic Law) of 23 July 1913. The Imperial Naturalization Law of 1913 had been designed to make the attainment of German citizenship difficult for aliens out of fear that the Reich was being inundated with immigrants from the East, especially Poles and Jews. At the same time, the law sharply reduced the barriers to the immigration of ethnic Germans, the *Aussiedler*, from outside the Reich (Klusmeyer 1992: 84). By singling out the shared racial inheritance of the German 'stock' as a criterion for repatriation, the framers invoked a distinctly biological conception of Germanness (Klusmeyer 1992: 85).
11 Application procedures were made easier with the modifications of German citizenship laws in 1991 (see Halfmann 1997).
12 The granting of dual citizenship is, however, at the discretion of the various *Länder*, and in recent years the local authorities have become more forthcoming on the issue of dual citizenship, with some local variations. For instance, in Bayern dual citizenship is hardly ever granted, whereas Berlin has been less strict on this issue (Halfmann 1997: 272). At federal level, dual nationality was allowed in 34 per cent of the naturalizations granted in 1995 (Federal Commissioner for Foreigners 1997: 24). This high percentage is explained by the fact that many of these are temporarily dual citizens for procedural reasons, and hence, the real figure is significantly lower (Federal Commissioner for Foreigners 1997).
13 Cem Özdemir describes how, when he tried to give up his Turkish citizenship in order to obtain the German one, the consulate staff demanded he bring his father who was then told off for not bringing his child up properly (Özdemir 1997).
14 In the early 1990s, a number of hostels for foreigners in Hoyerswerda, Rostock, and other cities in former eastern Germany were firebombed by right-wing extremist groups. In November 1992, three Turkish citizens died when their house was firebombed in Mölln, a small town in former western Germany. Six months later another five Turkish citizens were killed in a similar attack in Solingen. Hundreds of thousands of Germans participated in the numerous large-scale demonstrations protesting against these expressions of extreme right-wing xenophobia (*Deutscher Bundestag* 1993a; Braunthal 1995: 214).
15 The *Verfassungsschutz* watches organizations which: (a) are opposed to the free democratic constitutional order of Germany – for instance, if they are working hand in hand with German extremists; (b) endanger the security at Federal or *Länder* level by fighting out their political disputes on German soil; and (c) carry out or prepare violent actions in other countries and thereby endanger the foreign interests of Germany (*Verfassungsschutz* 1992: 43).
16 Asylum laws in Germany were once among the most liberal in Europe (and in the world). The policies were based on the Basic Law Article 16(2) which stated: 'Persons persecuted on political grounds shall enjoy the right of asylum' United Nations High Commissioner for Refugees [(UNHCR) 1995: 199]. This article in the Basic Law was not least due to a wish to distance the Bonn Republic from the racist policies of the Third Reich. However, during the 1980s, the asylum laws were gradually tightened,

culminating in the amendment of 1 July 1993. Article 16 was amended with the support of a reluctant SPD, who was worried about the anti-foreigner sentiment stirred up by, and strengthening, the Republicans (Braunthal 1996: 158).
17 On the one hand, the recent changes of 1 July 1993 in German asylum regulations restrict access of asylum seekers and facilitate deportation of rejected applicants. On the other hand, the inflow of asylum seekers from Turkey has increased, not least because of the exodus of Kurdish refugees in the aftermath of the Gulf War and the escalation of the conflict in southeastern Anatolia.
18 EU–Turkish relations have been widely analysed. For a discussion on Turkey's role in European enlargement (see, among others, Michalski and Wallace 1992; Balkir and Williams 1993; Kramer 1996; Müftüler-Baç 1997). For an analysis of Turkish views on cooperation with Europe see, among others, Atancanli's analysis of Turkey's role in European security political cooperation (Atacanli 1992), and Eralp's analysis of the position of the various political actors in Turkey regarding Turkey's membership of the EU (Eralp 1993).
19 A number of studies discuss the Ottoman Empire or Turkey as the 'other' for Europe (see Said 1978: 59; Naff 1984).
20 The Cascade Programme is NATO's Equipment Transfer and Equipment Rationalization Programme, which transfers Treaty-limited equipment under the Conventional Armed Forces in Europe (SIPRI 1997).
21 Before this, on 7 November 1991, there was a parliamentary ban of further deliveries of Leopard Tanks to Turkey supplied under a 1988 agreement.
22 Yet the day after, it was revealed that 15 Leopard-I main battle tanks had been supplied illegally to Turkey in late 1991 due to a 'bureaucratic' error and in contravention of a parliamentary ban of 7 November. As a consequence, Gerhard Stoltenberg, CDU's longest-serving Cabinet member at the time, resigned as Defence Minister on March 31 (*Financial Times*, 1 April 1992).

4 Between homeland political and immigrant political mobilization

1 For a more detailed description of the situation before the 1980s, see Özcan (1992).
2 The list of organizations chosen for closer scrutiny in this chapter is not exhaustive but still represent main trends in migrant mobilization and relations with German and Turkish authorities. For a more detailed description of these and other organizations see Ozcan (1992) and Østergaard-Nielsen (1998).
3 Similar issues are discussed in an edited volume on *Immigrant Associations in Europe*, which includes studies of Asians and Cypriots in Britain, Turks in Berlin, Portuguese and Italians in France, Finns in Sweden, and Spaniards in the Netherlands and Switzerland (see Rex *et al.* 1987).
4 Complementary to this argument, in their study of Turkish associations in Berlin, Gitmez and Wilpert suggest that associations may play a much larger role than indicated by their formal membership. They involve more persons through their programme and activities (Gitmez and Wilpert 1987: 111).
5 No doubt due to its political heritage, the DIDF was reported on in the *Verfassungsschutz* until 1987. The reports, however, only mentioned immigrant political activities that the DIDF continuously undertakes, such as collecting signatures, or comparing German immigration policies to the persecution of the Jews in the 1930s (*Verfassungsschutz* 1981–7).
6 The ideology of pan-Turkism, the idea that all Turkic people, inside and outside of Turkey should unite in one political unit, is the main exponent of irridentism in Turkey (Landau 1981). The *Türk Federasyon* could also be mentioned as a Sunni Muslim organization since it increasingly emphasizes Islamic elements, such as organizing *hac*, that is, pilgrimage to Mecca, and having Imams recite the Koran at mass meetings (own observation and interview with *Türk Federasyon*, 13 February 1998).

152 Notes

7 Because of its extremist character the *Türk Federasyon*, as is the case with the Sunni Muslim movements, has attracted more academic attention than more moderate groups. Furthermore, due to its increasingly religious character the organization is mentioned in most publications on Muslims in Germany (see Özcan 1992: 180–91; Feindt-Riggers and Steinbach 1997: 25–6; Heitmeyer *et al.* 1997: 132–42; NRW 1997: 150–4; Spuler-Stegemann 1998: 77, 104, 123, 125).
8 See *Türk Federasyon Bülteni*, Avrupa Demokratik Ülkücü Türk Dernekleri Federasyonu'nun Aylık Yayınıdır, December 1996–Juni 1998.
9 There are several such organizations and they have tried to found a federation, but not all AADD organizations are members herein.
10 Also, the AADD is behind the 1994 campaign requesting major German companies to penalize German newspapers by not placing advertisements in them, because of their 'campaign' against Turkey (*Hürriyet*, 17 August 1994).
11 The two main Turkish employers associations are *the Avrupa Türk Işadamları ve Sanaycileri Derneği* (ATIAD) and the *Türk Isadamlari Dernekleri Avrupa Federasyonu* (TIDAF). While the former represents small- and medium-sized companies, the latter represents larger entrepreneurs and industrialists (see www.tidaf.de and www.atiad.de).
12 There is a fast-growing literature on Sunni Muslims in Germany, although the majority is in German language (see among others, Heine 1997; Spuler-Stegeman 1998 and NRW 1997; Trautner 2000). Some analysis of Sunni Muslim organizations in Germany try to identify more radical elements within the organizations (see Nirumand 1990; Gür 1993; Feindt-Riggers and Steinbach 1997). In English, the article by Karakaşoğlu and Nonneman (1996) neatly sums up the main differences and changes among Turkish Sunni Muslim organizations (see also Faist 2000a: 229–31).
13 This list is not exhaustive, but serves to illustrate some of the main trends and differences among Sunni migrant organizations. Among the other Sunni Muslim organizations, in particular the *Avrupa Türk Islam Dernekleri* (ATIB) deserves mentioning. The outlook of the ATIB follows the so-called Turkish–Islamic synthesis, which combines Turkish nationalism with Islam. In that respect, it is not far from the aforementioned nationalist *Türk Federasyon* of which it is also a splinter group formed in 1987. The ATIB has made great efforts to distance itself from the followers of Türkeş and claims to have no political links with parties in Turkey. Indeed, no such links are identifiable in the written material or in interviews with leading members of ATIB.
14 To identify the relationship between the Sufi-tariquats and the political parties is a complex matter even in Turkey because of the secrecy which surrounds it (Ayata 1994: 224).
15 The literature on Alevism, in general, is growing. For a more detailed description of Alevi history and religious practices see Vorhoff (1995). For an interesting account of the dynamics between the Alevi and Sunni at the level of an Anatolian village, and how these groups deal with modernization and the relationship with the state see Shankland (1993). For an analysis of Alevi communities in Turkey including the political relationship with the various political parties, see Poulton (1997: 252–85). Also, the developments of the Alevi communities in Germany are increasingly the object of inquiry (see Mandel 1996; Kaya 1998; Kehl-Bodrogi 1998).
16 There are a large number of Kurdish resistance movements inside and outside of Turkey and the landscape of political organizations and parties has fluctuated greatly. For the sake of clarity, this section will only focus on a selection of the more influential groups. For detailed descriptions of other political movements see, among others, Gürbey (1996), McDowall (1996), and Barkey and Fuller (1998).
17 For information on the PKK and PKK-related organizations in Europe, see www.kurdstruggle.org/index, www.kurdishobserver.com/, and www.serxwebun.com.
18 There is a long list of other significant organizations working on a European and wider international level. Among these is the 'Kurdish Exile Parliament', established in Haag

in 1995, with 65 parliamentarians from the *Demokrasi Partisi* (DEP), mayors of cities in Kurdistan, and the like (Steinbach 1996: 372–3). The Exile Parliament has held meetings in a range of parliamentarian buildings in Europe.

19 Only four years after the KOMKAR, the *Civata li Kurd* was founded with six membership organizations. Initially, this organization, then known as the KKDK, supported the PKK, but after a congress in November 1991, the name was changed to the *Civata li Kurd* and its political goals shifted in the aftermath of the Gulf War. The *Civata li Kurd* is the smallest of the main Kurdish federations in Germany with approximately 30 membership organizations and committees and an estimated 1,500 members (interview with *Civata li Kurd*, 16 July 1997).

5 From confrontational to multi-layered strategies

1 Further, although the activities of Turkish extremists intensified after the 1980 coup, the Turkish extremists constituted a relatively small part of the community (3.5 per cent). In comparison, the Greek extremists were considered to constitute 11 per cent of the Greek community in Germany in 1981 (*Verfassungschutz* 1981: 149).
2 There was, however, a repeated refusal to discuss the ban of specific groups, since it was feared that discussing the ban of group x and not group y could be misinterpreted by these groups (*Deutscher Bundestag* 1981b).
3 To which the answer was that the right of association, also for political purposes, is the same for Germans and foreigners and also the right to use symbols and banners unless these are explicitly banned (*Deutscher Bundestag* 1983).
4 Kurdish movements cooperate with both German NGOs which are specifically working on Turkish affairs including organizations such as the Solidaritätsverein für Demokratie und Menschenrechte in der Türkei (TÜDAY) or Dialog-Kreis 'Krieg in der Türkei'. They also cooperate with international NGOs with a wider human rights agenda such as Amnesty International.
5 Mother-tongue teaching is the discretion of the individual *Länder*. Bremen, Hamburg, and Niedersachsen offered mother-tongue teaching in Kurdish in 1999 (The Federal Commisioner for Foreigners 2000: 133).
6 On a smaller scale, the ICCB produces a TV programme 'Hakk-TV', explaining its ideas of the Kalifate state which are beamed straight into Turkey (*Verfassungschutz* 2000: 205).
7 To illustrate: the ATIAD sent letters to Minister-President Papandreou of Greece explaining that the Customs Union would be the right tool to soothe the conflict between Turkey and Greece. The ATIAD executive committee visited the European Parliament twice and conducted talks with the leaders of all parties, it sent letters to the President of the European Council, French Prime Minister Balladur as well as his successor Gonzales. ATIAD members spoke with the President of Turkey, Demirel, the Prime Minister Çiller, other members of the Turkish government and parliamentarians. EU parliamentarians were invited to Antalya to meet with the leading business people of Turkey. Finally, one month before the vote in the European Parliament, ATIAD arranged a 'Turkey evening' with the title: 'Market Place Turkey' to which all EU parliamentarians and important European politicians were invited. The ATIAD works with its 'sister organization' from Turkey, the TÜSIAD, when dealing with Brussels (interview with ATIAD, 25 May 1998).

6 Thresholds of tolerance

1 A third political institution is the immigrant consultative platforms, the *Ausländerbeirate*. These have been nicknamed '*Türkenbeirate*' or '*Muslimenbeirate*' because they have been used by Turks more than other migrant groups. These consultative institutions have also had their share of competition among various Turkish and

154 *Notes*

   Kurdish homeland political groups, and have, in particular, been approached by more conservative Islamic organizations (see Østergaard-Nielsen 1998).
 2 Yet, in the literature on Turkish immigrants in Germany, there has been little academic attention paid to the role of Turkish citizens in German trade unions. Vranken's comparative discussion of 'industrial rights', that is, the rights of immigrants and unions in western Europe, includes foreigners in Germany, but does not deal with the case of Turkish citizens in particular (Vranken, 1990).
 3 Due to the large-scale recruitment of guest workers, the *Deutsche Gewerkshaftsbund* (DGB) had established special 'Italian', 'Greek', 'Turkish', etc. offices dealing with issues relating to the working situation of these workers in Germany in 1972. These offices were closed down in 1996 and replaced by an office for migration and foreign workers in general. Because of the existence of what are perceived to be very sensitive documents, the archives of the Turkish (and Greek, but not Italian) offices are closed down for a period of 20 years, hence excluding my time-period of study. Instead the descriptions of DGB are based on interviews, as well as the press-releases, annual reports and protocols from the general federal congresses in 1982, 1986, 1990, and 1994, the extraordinary congress in 1996, and written material from the main office in Düsseldorf.
 4 This information stems from written communication with DGB Federal Executive, Department for Migration, December 1998.
 5 These figures are based on written communication with DGB Federal Executive, Department for Migration, December 1998.
 6 These views are stated in the IGMetall's membership journal *Metall* (IGMetall 1995: 7), as well as in numerous DGB's press releases. Also, at the twelfth and thirteenth Ordentliche Bundeskongress in 1982 and 1986, motions were approved, which protested against military rule in Turkey (DGB 1982: motions 70–3; DGB 1986: motions, nos 62 and 63).
 7 However, formally DGB mainly dealt with the pro-Turkish state confederation of trade unions, Türk-Iş. In contrast, the IGMetall continued to have close links with the more anti-establishment confederation of socialist trade unions, DISK.
 8 Tellingly, after Baştürk was released, he first appeared outside Turkey in June 1987 as a speaker at a mass event in Cologne sport stadium, held under the patronage of DGB with the aim of criticizing human rights and trade union rights in Turkey (DBG, press release, 3 June 1987).
 9 The sharp criticism of the right-wing nationalist movements among Turkish workers was shown by the resolutions from the DGB Bundeskongresses in 1982 and 1986 as well as in several press releases.
10 It is also linked to the role of the *Arbeiter Wohlfahrt* (Workers Welfare), a charity organization founded as part of the SPD who took care of the Turkish guest workers. Basically the task of informing guest workers about social welfare was divided between the three big welfare associations in Germany. The Catholic Caritas charity got the Italian, Spanish, Portuguese, and Catholic Yugoslavian guest workers; the Diakon charity took care of the Greek guest workes and the *Arbeiter Wohlfart* took care of all the non-Christian guest workers including the Turks (Heckmann 2001: 8).
11 Alongside the letter from the Turkish social democrats, the *Tageszeitung* also printed a letter from a Kurdish organization including the request that if Turks wanted to leave the SPD then they should not be held back. 'This would be a great bonus for the German social democrats in Germany – and for a democratic development in Turkey and Kurdistan.' (Letter reprinted in *Tageszeitung*, 13 April 1994.)
12 The rest of this section relies on this interview and written sources from the SPD.
13 Similarly, the FDP began to show an active interest in Turkish descent voters up through the 1990s. The party had high expectations of its support among Turkish descent voters and carried out a ten-day election campaign by placing advertisements for FDP in all major Turkish dailies before the German federal election in 1994 [*Liberale Türkische–Deutsche Vereinigung* (LTD) 1997]. Its Turkish membership

organization, Liberal Türk-Alman Derneği (LTD) estimates that 15 per cent of the 'Turkish population in Germany' could be FDP voters (*Frankfurter Allgemeine Zeitung*, 6 November 1996). The LTD itself, however, only has 'more than 200 members'. According to its spokesman, the FDP is attractive to Turkish descent voters because admittedly the SPD and the *Bundnis 90/Die Grüne* do what they can for the rights of Turks in Germany, but they are critical of Turkey. The CDU is for a good relationship to Turkey but does less for the Turks in Germany. The FDP achieves both. (*Frankfurter Allgemeine Zeitung*, 11 April 1996).

14 On 19 August 1996, there was a debate on this in the CDU Landescommittee. One fraction wanted the CDU to distance itself from the DTU. Another wanted for the DTU to be accepted as a membership organization within the CDU. A compromise was made, whereby the CDU welcomed the initiative of the DTU but did not accept it as an organization *within* the CDU, only as an organization *close* to the CDU.

15 The lobbying included sending a report entitled 'German institutions as the extension of Turkish minority policies' to all relevant ministries at the Länder and federal levels on these issues (see Hermes 1990: 67).

16 The *Deutsche Muslimische Gesellschaft* applied as early as in 1957 for the recognition of their religion as a public corporation (körperschaft des öffentliches Rechts), but in vain. Since then, Muslim organizations have tried again and again, especially in the 1970s, to obtain this right (Heine 1997: 114). This has so far been denied because in order to be officially recognized in Germany, a religion must meet the following criteria: (a) it must concern a sufficiently large group of believers; (b) it must be established that the religious community will be existing in Germany for a long period of time; and (c) the religious community must be represented by *one* person or one committee vis-à-vis the German authorities (Heine 1997). While the first two criteria are met by the large, settled Muslim community in Germany, the last criterion currently poses an insurmountable challenge as various Muslim migrant organizations find it difficult to come together under one umbrella organization (see Chapter 4).

17 Of these, the Heitmeyer study, *Verlockender Fundamentalismus*, which claims widespread fundamentalist beliefs among second and third generation Turks in Germany, reflected beliefs that Islam may constitute an obstacle to the coexistence of Germans and Turks in Germany (Heitmeier *et al.* 1997, see also reports on debates of the Heitmeier study in *Hürriyet*, 3 November 1996; *Frankfurter Rundschau*, 3 May 1997).

7 From 'remittance machines' to 'Euro Turks'

1 The change in semantics from 'our workers living abroad' [*yurtdışında yaşayan işçilerimiz*] to 'our citizens living abroad' [*yurtdışında yaşayan vatandaşlarımız*] is not entirely consistent when looking at parliamentary debates and newspaper articles between 1980 and 1998. However, there is a trend towards mainly referring to them as 'citizens'. Another much used term is 'gurbetçi', meaning those who live in foreign countries.

2 Concern in the homeland with the education of its citizens living abroad does not pertain to Turkey alone. Of the other migrant communities originating in labour migration, notably the Greek, national schools have been surrounded with controversy concerning the nationalist content of the teaching there. Among the Italian community there has been disputes between the representatives of the Catholic church and the Christian democrats who demand bilingual and bicultural education and the communist and social democratic parties who demand that Italian children in Germany receive only German education (see Schönberg 1992: 127).

3 Those who have given up their Turkish citizenship with the permission of Turkish authorities can live and work in Turkey without further permission (law 4112). They can obtain the so-called 'Pink Card', a type of identification card introduced in 1995, which also allows for certain rights to import without duty, facilitates recognition of

marriages abroad, and exemption of military service. This type of quasi-dual citizenship has been questioned by, in particular, the CHP, which advocates to put pressure on the German government to introduce dual citizenship instead (TBMM 1998).
4 In particular, the incidents in Mölln and Solingen led to suggestions to form parliamentary commissions to look into the scope of German discrimination against Turkish citizens in Germany (TBMM 1992; TBMM 1993; TBMM 1997b). More frequently, National Assembly deputies urged the Turkish government to engage in helping citizens abroad or criticized the governments' lack of effective intervention in these matters (TBMM 1989; TBMM 1990).
5 Indeed, a Turkish consulate in Germany is a microcosm of the Turkish administration with attachés from the ministries of Finance, National Education, Labour, Treasurer, Foreign Trade, Defence, and the Directorate of Religious Affairs, among others (TBMM, 26 February 1997).
6 This idea is also mentioned in the political programmes of MHP, CHP, and DSP.
7 Part of this construction was a 'High Commission' (*Yurtdışında yaşayan vatandaşlar üst kurulu*), consisting of the Prime Minister, the Foreign Minister, and State Minister responsible for citizens living abroad. This construction is intended to allow for swift legislative changes if the citizens abroad have a certain pressing need.
8 The Turkish citizens come from every country where they have settled, and the amount of representatives correspond to the size of the community in the country. Hence, the Turkish citizens from Germany comprise more than half of the commission. There are 26 from Germany, three each from France, Holland, and the US, two each from Australia and the UK, and one each from Canada, Belgium, Sweden, Switzerland, Austria, and Denmark (interview with the State Ministry, 6 July 1998).
9 Indeed, the process of choosing Turkish citizens living abroad curiously indicates what a Turkish citizen living abroad should aspire to be. Of the 3.5 million citizens living abroad, only 468 applied to be on the Consulation Commission (interview with the State Ministry, 6 July 1998).
10 This figure is based on the number of Turkish citizens above 18 years of age in Germany by the end of 1999, the electorate in Turkey in the general elections in April 1999 (ZfT 2001), and the fact that the Turkish parliament consists of 550 parliamentarians.
11 The reason for the high number of the voters from the diasporas in 1995 is popularly ascribed to the efforts of *Milli Görüş*, which were said to fly potential voters home in chartered air planes. Similarly, the Alevi *Barış Partisi* was rumoured to transport voters home in buses and planes from Europe. However, a less exciting, but more plausible, explanation is that the timing of the election on the 24 December meant that a large number of Turkish citizens living in western Europe went home during the Christmas holidays.
12 On 28 October 1995, the High Election Council (*Üst Seçim Kurulu*) unanimously decided that Turkish citizens abroad could not participate in the coming election of 24 December 1995 since there were too many legal and practical conditions that were not met. Further, the permission from the receiving countries had not been obtained (Kılıç 1996: 209). A very heated debate on this issue in Parliament preceded this discussion (see TBMM 1995b). This debate was not repeated before the 1999 elections, but Turkish National Assembly deputies continuously raise the issue in parliamentary proceedings.
13 Similarly, in a recent volume on Turkish–European relations, one Turkish academic argues that 'one unexpected development arising from Turkish migration into western Europe has been the enhancement of European perceptions that Turkey is indeed very different from Europe in cultural terms' (Müftüler-Bac 1997: 21).
14 Such views are also expressed in material such as introductions to books on Turkish citizens living abroad. Ismet Binurgh, General Director of the State Archives, writes in his introduction to a bibliography on Turkish citizens abroad that '[...] The Turkish

citizens abroad compose a great potential to publicize Turkey'. And that they can 'play a positive role in the interest of their country' (State Archive, 1993: xiii).
15 Armenian and Greek lobbies pertain to two historically rooted conflicts that manifest themselves in the diaspora. The Greek lobby, in particular in the US, has tried to influence US policy against Turkey because of the historical territorial disputes (Cyprus and the Aegean islands) between Greece and Turkey. This was particularly the case in the 1980s, but persists until this day (see Constas and Platias 1993). The Armenian lobby, notably in the US and France, wants government and international institutions (like the European Parliament) to recognize and condemn that a 'genocide' took place against Armenians in the Ottoman Empire in 1915–16. The work of both lobbies is the concern of Turkish authorities who try to publicize and promote their version of these events to both western governments and Turkish communities abroad.
16 Some Turkish newspapers in Germany has local correspondents and journalists and publishes separate 'European pages' covering events throughout Europe which are only distributed outside of Turkey. Besides *Hürriyet* there are many more moderate newspapers as well as critical newspapers such as *Evrensel* or indeed newspapers such as the pro-Kurdish *Özgür Politika* that is only published outside Turkey. *Hürriyet*, however, dominates the European market with as many daily copies as all other newspapers together.
17 Such activities are made legitimate via the Vienna Agreement on Consular Relations of 1963, which states that it is the task of the consular representation to represent the interests of the homeland in the receiving country within public law, as well as to obtain information on the citizens and their organizations (*Deutscher Bundestag* 1982c). This means that although these issues were repeatedly raised in the *Bundestag* by the SPD, the position of the German government was that of adhering to the principle of non-interference in Turkish affairs.
18 Here, there is here a curious parallel to the Italian policies toward its emigrant communities before Second World War. In 1927, Mussolini, in order to curb dissidence among Italian emigrants in notably western Europe, established the General Bureau of Italians Abroad, which was a special agency designed to organize and 'protect' Italian communities abroad. Similarly, a number of historical examples such as Korea, Iran under the Shah, Stalin's Soviet Union, have tried to curb dissidence abroad (Shain 1989: 51).
19 The following is based on documents from the German *Bundestag* and not from the Turkish side. Information on such issues is not available from Turkish sources.
20 While the archive on correspondence and statements of DGB on these cases is closed down (see Chapter 6), the membership journal of IGMetall reported these cases in some detail. See, for instance, the case of Aysan Uçta in IGMetall (1985: 5). At some point the number of cases was so high that IGMetall claimed that there were suspicions that the Turkish government was conducting a veritable campaign to punish Turkish members of trade unions in Germany by withholding their passports (IGMetall 1987: 5).
21 The ideology of pan-Turkism is the main exponent of irridentism in Turkey. Turanism refers to all people considered to be Turanic, including the Hungarians, Finns, and Estonians, but by the 1920s the term had become interchangeable with pan-Turkism and referred to all Turkic people only (Landau 1981).

References

AABF (Almanya Alevi Birlik Federasyonu) (1997). *Das Alevitentum: Eine Handreichung über die religiösen und kulturellen Grundlagen der Aleveiten aus der Türkei*, Köln: AABF.
—— (2000a). *Alevilerin Sesi*, February, Köln: AABF.
—— (2000b). *Bin Yılın Türküsü*, Saga of the Millenium, Köln: AABF.
Abadan-Unat, N. (1995). Turkish migration to Europe, in: R. Cohen (ed.), *The Cambridge Survey of World of Migration*. Cambridge: Cambridge University Press, pp. 279–284.
Abadan-Unat, N. (1997). Ethnic business, ethnic communities, and ethnopolitics among Turks in Europa, in: E. M. Ucarer and D. J. Puchala (eds), *Migration into Western Societies: Problems and Policies*. London and Washington: Pinter, pp. 229–251.
Adamson, F. B. (2002). Mobilizing for the transformation of home: politicized identities and transnational practices, in: N. Al-Ali and K. Koser (eds), *New Approaches to Migration? Transnational Communities and the transformation of Home*. London: Routledge, pp. 155–168.
Adler, S. (1977). *International Migration and Dependence*. Farnborough: Saxton House.
Aksoy, A. and Robins, K. (2000). Thinking across spaces: transnational television from Turkey, *European Journal of Cultural Studies*, 3, 3: 343–365.
Al-Ali, N., Black, R. and Koser, K. (2001). The limits to 'transnationalism': Bosnian and Eritrean refugees in Europe as emerging transnational communities, *Ethnic and Racial Studies*, 24, 4: 578–600.
Al-Ali, N. and Koser, K. (2002). Transnationalism, international migration and home, in: N. Al-Ali and K. Koser (eds), *New Approaches to Migration? Transnational Communities and the Transformation of Home*. London: Routledge, pp. 1–14.
Anderson, B. (1992). The new world disorder, *New Left Review*, 32, 193: 3–13.
Armstrong, J. A. (1976). Mobilized and proletarian diasporas, *The American Political Science Review*, LXX, 2: 393–408.
Armruster, H. (2002). Homes in crisis. Syrian orthodox christians in Turkey and Germany, in: N. Al-Ali and K. Koser (eds), *New Approaches to Migration? Transnational Communities and the Transformation of Home*. London: Routledge, pp. 17–33.
Aslantepe, C. (1990). Federal Almanya'da Sendikalarin Yabanci Iscilere ve Turk işçilerinin sendikalara yaklasımları. Unpublished Doctoral Thesis, Ankara University.
Atacanlı, S. (1992). Views from Turkey: political union as a contribution to the new Europe, in: R. Rummel (ed.), *Towards Political Union: Planning a Common Foreign and Security Policy in the European Union*. Boulder, Co: Westview Press, pp. 259–263.
ATIAD (Avrupa Türk Işadamları ve Sanayıcıleri Derneği) (1996). *Die Aktivitäten und Thesen des ATIAD zur Zollunion und ihre Resonans in den Medien*. Düsseldorf: ATIAD.

ATIAD (1997). *Türkisches Untrenehmertum in Deutschland – Die Unsichtbare Kraft*. Düsseldorf: ATIAD.
ATT (Almanya Türk Toplumu) (1996). *Gründung, Ziele,Arbeitsprogramm, Vorstand, Satzung, Pressespiegel*. Hamburg: ATT.
—— (1999). *Press Release on Turkey's EU Candidacy*, 16 December. Hamburg: ATT.
Ayata, S. (1994). Traditional Sufi orders on the periphery: Kadiri and Nakşibendi Islam in Konya and Trabzon, in: R. Tapper (ed.), *Islam in Modern Turkey: Religion, Politics and Literature in a Secular State*. London: I.B. Tauris, pp. 223–253.
Balkir, C. and Williams, A. M. (eds) (1993). *Turkey and Europe*. London: Pinter Publishers.
Barchard, D. (1985). *Turkey and the West*. London: Royal Institute of International Affairs.
Barkey, H. J. and Fuller, G. E. (1998). *Turkey's Kurdish Question*. Oxford: Rowman and Littlefield Publishers.
Bauböck, R. (1994). *Transnational Citizenship: Membership and Rights in International Migration*. Aldershot: Edward Elgar.
—— (2001). Towards a political theory of migrant transnationalism. Unpublished comments, Workshop on Transnational Migration: Comparative Perspectives, 30 June–1 July, Princeton University.
Bell, J. B. (1981). Contemporary revolutionary organizations, in: R. O. Keohane and J. S. Nye, Jr. (eds), *Transnational Relations and World Politics*. Cambridge, MA: Harvard University Press, pp. 153–171.
Berlin Senate's Administration for Health and Social Issues (1996). (Senatsverwaltung für Gesundheit und Soziale, Berlin) *AulBB2 19 September 1996*. Berlin: Berlin Senate.
Braunthal, G. (1995). Civil liberties: migrants, in: P. H. Merkl (ed.), *The Federal Republic of Germany at Forty-Five: Union without Unity*. London: Macmillan Press, pp. 206–218.
—— (1996). *Parties and Politics in Modern Germany*. Oxford: Westview Press.
Brieden, T. (1996). Die Bedeutung von Konflikten im Herkunftsland für Ethnisierungsprozesse von Immigranten aus der Türkei und Ex-Joguslawien, in Fiedrich-Ebert Stiftung. *Ethnisierung gesellschaflicher Konflikte*, Gesprächskreis Arbeit und Soziales, nr. 62, pp. 31–54.
Brubaker, R. (1992). *Citizenship and Nationhood in France and Germany*. Cambridge, MA: Harvard University Press.
Bruinessen, M. v. (1991). *Agha, Shaikh and State*. London: Zed Books.
Bulletin (1999). *Regierungserklärung des deutschen Bundeskanzlers, Gerhard Schöder,zu den ERgebnissen des Europäischen Rates von Helsinkin vor dem Deutschen Bundestag am 16 Dezember*. Berlin: Presse und Informationsamt der Bundesregierung.
Çaglar, A. S. (1995). McDöner: Döner kebab and the social positioning struggle of German Turks, in: J. A. Costa and G. J. Bamossy (eds), *Marketing in a Multicultural World: Ethnicity, Nationalism and Cultural Identity*. London: Sage, pp. 209–230.
Çaglar, A. S. (1998). Popular culture, marginality and institutional incorporation: German–Turkish Rap and Turkish pop in Berlin, *Cultural Dynamics*, 10, 3: 243–261.
Cema'at Un-Nur (1995). Nur, Das Licht, Eine Zeitschift der Islamischen Gemeinschaft Jama'at Un Nur e.V., (April), Köln: Cema'at Un-Nur.
Clifford, J. (1994). Diasporas, *Cultural Anthropology*, 9, 3: 302–338.
Cohen, R. (1997). *Global Diasporas: An Introduction*. London: UCL Press.
Collinson, S. (1996). *Shore to Shore: The Politics of Migration in Euro–Mahgreb Relations*. London: The Royal Institute of International Affairs.
Constas, D. C. and Platias A. G. (1993). Diasporas in world politics: an introduction, in: D. C. Constas and A. G. Platias (eds), *Diasporas in World Politics: The Greeks in*

References

Comparative Perspective. Athens: Macmillan Press in Association with the Institute of International Relations, pp. 3–28.

Demetriou, M. (forthcoming). Politicizing the diaspora: the Cypriot diaspora and 'its' home government, in: E. Østergaard-Nielsen (ed.), *International Migration and Sending Countries: Perceptions, Policies and Transnational Relations*. London: Palgrave.

Deutsch, K. *et al*. (1957). *Political Community and the North Atlantic Area*. Princeton, NJ: Princeton University Press.

Deutscher Bundestag (1981a). *Reaktion der türkischen Öffentlichkeit auf die Einführung des Visumszwangs für türkische Staatsangehörige*, Drs 9/143, 6 February, Bonn.

—— (1981b). *Auswirkungen der Machtübernahme der Militärs in der Türkei auf in der Bundesrepublick Deutschland lebende Türken*, PlPr09/21, 12 February, Bonn.

—— (1981c). *Vorfürfe der Anklagevertretung im Prozess gegen den Führer der MHP, Alparslan Türkeş*, PlPr 09/45, 24 June, Bonn.

—— (1981d). *Aktivitäten türkischer Rechtsextremisten, insbesonderere gegen Mitglieder von Amnesty International in Bingen*, Drs 9/672, 17 July Bonn.

—— (1981e). *Uberwachung von Vereinigungen extremistischer Türken*, PlPr 09/51, 16 September, Bonn.

—— (1982a). *Ausweisung von Vorstandsmitgliedern verbotener Ausländerorganisationen*, Drs 09/1701, 1 June, Bonn.

—— (1982b). *Enstellungspraxis der Arbeiterwohlfahrt bei Türken; Zahl der Mitglieder in linksextremistischen türkischen Organisationen*, Drs 09/1929, 20 August, Bonn.

—— (1982c). *Einflussnahme des türkischen Generalkonsuls auf das Veranstaltungsprgramm der Kulturwoche 'Türkei in Köln' und auf andere türkische Aktivitäten*, PlPr 9/128, 12 November, Bonn.

—— (1983). *Zulassung türkischer Demonstrationen in der Bundesrepublik Deutschland*, Drs 10/224, 1 July, Bonn.

—— (1986a). *Einhaltung von Pässen türkischer Arbeitnehmer duch da türkische Konsulat in Essen*, Drs 10/5908, 1 August, Bonn.

—— (1986b). *Verweigerung kurdisher Namensgebung bei Neugeborenen türkischer Nationalität durch deutsche Standesämter*, Drs 6030, 19 September 1986, Bonn.

—— (1987). *Nichtverlängerung der Reisepässe türkischer Gewerkschafler in der Bundesrepublik Deutschland durch die türkische Regierung*, Drs 11/934, 9 October, Bonn.

—— (1993a). *Deutsch–türkische Beziehungen vor dem Hintergrund der Brandanschläge in Deutschland*, PlPr, 12/162, 16 June, Bonn.

—— (1993b). *Aktuelle Stunde: Haltung der Bundesregierung zur Lage der Kurden in der Türkei im Rahmen ihrer Gespräche mit der türkischen Minister präsidentin Çiller*, PlPr 12/177, 24 September, Bonn.

—— (1994). *Bericht der Bundesregierung zu den deutsch–türkische Beziehungen*, PlPr 12/218, 13 April, Bonn.

—— (1995a). *Fundamentalismus in der arabischen Welt*, PlPr 13/31, 30 March, Bonn.

—— (1995b). *Behinderung der kommunalen Integrationsarbeit kurdischer Vereine*, Drs 13/2066, 25 July, Bonn.

—— (1995c). *Briefwahl des in Deutschland lebenden Türken bei der geplanten türkischen Parlamentswahl am 24 December*, Drs 13/3352, 11 December 1995, Bonn.

—— (1996). *Vermittlungsinitative der Bundesregierung für eine politische Lösung in Kurdistan/Türkei*, PlPr 13/98, 18 April, Bonn.

—— (1999). *Erklärung der Bundesregierung zu den gewalttätigen Aktionen aus Anlass der Verfagtung des PKK-Vorsitzenden Abdullah Öcalan*, PlPr 14/20, 23 February, Bonn.

Deutscher Bundestag (2000). *Islam in Deutschland*, Drs 14/4530, 8 November, Berlin.
DGB (Deutscher Gewerkschaftsbund) (1980). *Hintergründe türkischer extremstischer islamischer Aktivitäten in der Bundesrepublik Deutshland (Sekten und Organisationen)*. Düsseldorf: DGB.
—— (1982). *12. Ordentlicher Bundeskongress Berlin, 16–22 Mai 1982*. Frankfurt am Main: Union-Druckerie und Verlagsanstalt.
—— (1983). *DGB für Verbot von Ausländerorganisationen in der extremistischen Rechten.* 9 February. Düsseldorf: Bundespressestelle des DGB.
—— (1986). *13. Ordentlicher Bundeskongress Berlin, 25–30 Mai 1986*. Frankfurt am Main: Union-Druckerie und Verlagsanstalt.
—— (1992). *Stoppt die Massaker unter der kurdischen Bevölkerung*, 25 March. Düsseldorf: Bundespressestelle des DGB.
DGB Federal Executive, Department for Migration (1998). *Written Communication Concerning Election of Turkish Workers within German Trade-Unions*. Düsseldorf: DGB.
Deutsch-Kurdischer Freundschaftsverein (German–Kurdish Friendship Association) 2000. *Kurdinnn und Kurden in Deutschland foerden ihr recht.* Berlin: Deutsch–Kurdischer Freundschaftsverein.
DIDF (Demokratik Işci Dernekleri Federasyonu (1993). *Wer wir sind, Was wir wollen, Was wir Machen*. Köln: DIDF.
—— (1995). *Fest der Internationalen Solidarität 9 May, Kölner Sporthalle*. Köln: DIDF.
—— (1998). Erste Kongres der Emegin Partisi, in: *Tatsache*, nr. 1. Köln: DIDF.
—— (2000). 'Eine Klasse Eine Front, in: *Tatsache*, nr. 1. Köln: DIDF.
Doomernik, J. (1995). The institutionalization of Turkish Islam in Germany and The Netherlands: a comparison, *Ethnic and Racial Studies*, 18, 1: 46–63.
DTF (Deutsch–Türkische Forum) (1997). *Gründungsaufrufes für das Deutsch–Türkische Forum*. Bonn: DTF.
DTU (Deutsch–Türkische Union) (1996). *Statuten und Inhaltliche Anliegen der Deutsch–Türkischen Union*. Berlin: DTU.
Ellis, P. and Khan, Z. (2002). The Kashmiri diaspora: influences in Kashmir, in: N. Al-Ali and K. Koser (eds), *New Approaches to Migration? Transnational Communities and the Transformation of Home*. London: Routledge, pp. 169–185.
Eralp, A. (1993). Turkey and the European community: prospects for a new relationship, in: A. Eralp, M. Tünay and B. Yeşilada (eds), *The Political and Socioeconomic Transformation of Turkey*. New York: Praeger.
Esman, M. J. (1986). Diasporas and international relations, in: G. Sheffer (ed.), *Modern Diasporas in International Politics*. Kent: Croom Helm, pp. 333–349.
—— (1992). The political fallout of international migration, *Diaspora: A Journal of Transnational Studies*, 2, 1: 3–41.
—— (1994). *Ethnic Politics*. London: Cornell University Press.
European Commission (1989). *The Statement Relating to Turkey's Application for Membership of the European Community*, 18/12, pp. 1–10.
Faist, T. (2000a). *The Volume and Dynamics of International Migration and Transnational Social Spaces*. Oxford: Oxford University Press.
Faist, T. (ed.) (2000b). *Transstaatliche Räume: Politik, Wirtschaft und Kultur in und zwischen Deutschland und der Türkei*. Bielefeld: Transcript Verlag.
Federal Commissioner for Foreigners (Beauftragte der Bundesregierung für Ausländer) (1997). *Bericht der Beauftragte der Bundesregierung für Ausländer in der Bundesrepublik Deutschland*. Bonn: Bonner Universitäts-Buchdruckerei.

162 References

Federal Commissioner for Foreigners (Beauftragte der Bundesregierung für Ausländer) (2000). *4. Bericht zur Lage der Ausländer in der Bundesrepublik Deutchland.* Berlin: Federal Commissioner for Foreigners.

—— (2001). *In Deutschland geborende Ausländische Bevölkerung am 31 December 2000.* Berlin: Federal Commissioner for Foreigners. Online, available at: http://www.bundesausländerbeauftragte.de/daten/tab5.pdf.

Federal Department for the Recognition of Refugees (Bundesamt für die Anerkennung Ausländischer Flüchtlinge) (2002). *Asylum-Seekers from Turkey.* Online, e-mail: info@bafl.de (2 February 2002).

—— (2002). *Statistics on Asylum-Seekers from Turkey*, 1998–2001. Online, available at: http://www.bafl.de (January 2002).

Federal Department for Statistics (Statistisches Bundesamt) (1960–2001). *Statistisches Jahrbuch für die Bundesrepublik Deutschland.* Stuttgart: Metzler-Poescel.

Federal Ministry for Labour and Social Security (Bundesministerium für Arbeit und Sozialordnung) (1996). *Representativuntersuchung '95: Situation der ausländischen Arbeitnehmer und ihrer Familienangehörigen in der Bundesrepublik Deutschland*, Forschungsbericht nr. 263.

Feindt-Riggers, N. and Steinbach, U. (1997). *Islamische Organisationen in Deutschland: Eine aktuelle Bestandsaufnahme und Analyse.* Hamburg: Deutsches Orient-Institut.

Fennema, M. and Tillie, J. (2001). Civic community, political participation and political trust of ethnic groups, *Connections*, 23, 2: 44–59.

Freeman, G. and Ögelman, N. (1998). Homeland citizenship policies and the status of third country nationals in the European Union, *Journal of Ethnic and Migration Studies*, 24, 4: 769–788.

Frykman, M. P. (2002). Homeland lost and gained: Croatian diaspora and refugees in Sweden, in: N. Al-Ali and K. Koser (eds), *New Approaches to Migration? Transnational Communities and the Transformation of Home.* London: Routledge, pp. 118–137.

Garbaye, R. (2000). Ethnic minorities, cities, and institutions: a comparison of the modes of management of ethnic diversity of a French and a British city, in: R. Koopmans and P. Statham (eds), *Challenging Immigration and Ethnic Relations Policies.* Oxford: Oxford University Press, pp. 283–311.

GDF (Türkiyeli Göçmen Dernekleri Federasyonu) (1994). *Satzung.* Düsseldorf: GDF.

—— (1997). *GDF Aktuell, Informationsdienst des GDF-Bundesvorstandes*, April. Düsseldorf: GDF.

—— (1998). *GDF Aktuell, Informationsdienst des GDF-Bundesvorstandes*, April. Düsseldorf: GDF.

Geddes, A. (2000). Lobbying for migrant inclusion in the European Union: new opportunities for transnational advocacy?, *Journal of European Public Policy*, 7, 4: 632–649.

Gitmez, A. and Wilpert, C. (1987). A micro-society or an ethnic community? Social organization amongst Turkish migrants in Berlin, in: J. Rex, D. Joly, and C. Wilpert (eds), *Immigrant Associations in: Europe.* Aldershot: Gower, pp. 86–125.

Glick Schiller, N., Basch, L. and Blanc-Szanton, C. (1995). From immigrant to transmigrant: theorizing transnational migration, *Anthropological Quarterly*, 68, 1: 48–63.

Glick Schiller, N. G. and Fouron, G. E. (1999). Terrains of blood and nation: Haitian transnational social fields, *Ethnic and Racial Studies*, 22, 2: 340–366.

Goldring, L. (1997). Power and status in transnational social spaces, *Soziale Welt: Sonderband*, 12, pp. 179–195.

Greve, M. and Çinar, T. (1998). *Das Türkische Berlin.* Berlin: Die Ausländerbeauftragte des Senats.

References

Guarnizo, L. E. (2000). Notes on transnationalism. Unpublished paper for Workshop on Transnational Migration: Comparative Conceptual and Research Perspectives, Transnational Communities Programme and the Social Science Research Council, Oxford University, July 7–9.

Guarnizo, L. E. and Portes, A. (2001). From assimilation to transnationalism: determinants of transnational political action among contemporary migrants. Working paper 01–07, Center for Migration and Development, Princeton University.

Guarnizo, L. E. and Smith, M. P. (1998). The locations of transnationalism, in: M. P. Smith and L. E. Guarnizo (eds), *Transnationalism from Below*. New Brunswick, NJ: Transaction Publishers, pp. 196–238.

Gür, M. (1993). *Türkisch–islamische Vereinigungen in der Bundesrepublik Deutschland*. Frankfurt am M: Brandes und Apsel.

Gürbey, G. (1996). The Kurdish nationalist movement in Turkey since the 1980s, in: R. Olson (ed.), *The Kurdish Nationalist Movement in the 1990s*. Kentucky: The University Press of Kentucky, pp. 9–37.

Halfmann, J. (1997). Immigration and citizenship in Germany: contemporary dilemmas, *Political Studies*, 45, 2: 260–274.

Hammar, T. (1985). Citizenship, aliens' political rights, and politicians' concern for migrants: the case of Sweden, in: R. Rogers (ed.), *Guests come to Stay: The Effect of European Labor Migration on Sending and Receiving Countries*. Boulder, Co: Westview Press, pp. 85–107.

—— (1990). The civil rights of aliens, in: Z. Layton-Henry (ed.), *The Political Rights of Migrant Workers in Western Europe*. London: Sage Publications, pp. 74–93.

Heckmann, F. (1994). Nation, nation-state, and policy towards ethnic minorities, in: B. Lewis and D. Schnapper (eds), *Muslims in Europe*. London: Pinter Publishers, pp. 116–129.

—— (2001). *Integrationsmassnahmen der Wohlfartsverbände*. Bamberg: Europäische Forum für Migrationsstudien.

Heine, P. (1997). *Halbmond über Deutschen Dächern: Muslimisches Leben in Unserem Land*. München: List Verlag.

Heitmeyer, W., Schröder, H. and Müller, J. (1997). *Verlockender Fundamentalismus: Türkische Jugendliche in Deutschland*. Frankfurt am Main: Suhrkamp Verlag.

Hermes, A. (1990). Deutsche Institutionen als verlängerter Arm türkischer Minderheitspolitik? Armenier, Assyrer und Kurden im bundesdeutschen Exil diskriminiert. *Pogrom*, 155, September: 66–67.

Huntington, S. P. (1997). The erosion of American national interests, *Foreign Affairs*, 76, 5: 28–49.

—— (1993). The clash of civilizations, *Foreign Affairs*, Summer: 22–49.

Hür-Türk (Hürriyetçi Türk Alman Dostluk Cemiyeti) (1990). *10 Yil, Hür-Türk, 1979–1989*. Bonn: Hür-Türk.

IGMG (Islamische Gemeinschaft Milli Görüş) (2000). *Glaubens – und Gewissensfreiheit in der Türkei*. IGMG Bericht, Kerpen: IGMG. Online, available at: http://www.igmg.de/deu/

IGMetall (1985, 1987, 1994, 1995). *Metall: Das Monatmagazin*, 12/85; 11/87; 13/94; 8/95. Frankfurt: IGMetall.

IMF (International Monetary Fund) (2001). *Balance of Payments Statistics Yearbook 2001*. Washington, DC: International Monetary Fund.

Irbec, Y. Z. (1993). Professional education and employment opportunities of the Turkish immigrants in Western Europe since the oil-shock 1973/74 with a special reference to

Germany. Unpublished paper for the International Seminar on Skilled and Highly Skilled Migration, 28–29 October, Rome.

Ireland, P. R. (1994). *The Policy Challenge of Ethnic Diversity: Immigrant Politics in France and Switzerland*. Cambridge, MA: Harvard University Press.

Ismet, E. (1990). The problem of freedom of movement of Turkish workers in the European Community, in: A. Evin and G. Denton (eds), *Turkey and the European Community*. Opladen: Leske and Budrich, Schriften des Deutschen Orient-Institut, pp. 183–194.

Itzigsohn, J. (2000). 'Immigration and the boundaries of citizenship, *International Migration Review*, 34, 4: 1126–1154.

Itzigsohn, J., Carlos, D. C., Medina, E. H. and Vazquez, O. (1999). Mapping Dominican transnationalism: narrow and broad transnational practices, *Ethnic and Racial Studies*, 22, 2: 316–339.

Jacobson, D. (1996). *Rights across Borders. Immigration and the Decline of Citizenship*. Baltimore: The Johns Hopkins University Press.

Jama'at Un-Nur (1995). *Nur, Das Licht*, April, Köln: Jama'at Un-Nur.

Josselin, D. and Wallace, E. (2001). The state and other actors, in: D. Josselin and W. Wallace (eds), *Non-State Actors in Global Politics*. London: Palgrave, pp. 1–20.

Kadioğlu, A. (1993). The human tie: international labour migration, in: C. Balkir and A. M. Williams (eds), *Turkey and Europe*. London: Pinter Publishers, pp. 140–157.

Kaiser, K. (1971). Transnational politics: toward a theory of multinational politics, *International Organization*, 25, 4: 790–818.

Karakaşoğlu, Y. and Nonneman, G. (1996). Muslims in Germany, with special reference to the Turkish-Islamic community, in: G. Nonneman, T. Niblock and B. Szajkowski (eds), *Muslim Communities in the New Europe*. Reading: Ithaca Press, pp. 241–267.

Kaya, A. (1998). Multicultural clientilism and Alevi resurgence in the Turkish diaspora: Berlin Alevis. *New Perspectives on Turkey*, 18: 23–49.

Keck, M. E. and Sikkink, K. (1998). *Activists Beyond Borders: Advocacy Networks in International Politics*. London: Cornell University Press.

Keesing (1985–1995). *Record of World Events*. Washington: Keesings Worldnews.

Kehl-Bodrogi, K. (1998). 'Wir sind ein Volk!' Identitätspolitiken under den Zaza (Türkei), *Sociologus*, 48, 2: 111–135.

Keohane, R. O. and Nye, J. S. (1971). Transnational relations and world politics: an introduction, in: R. O. Keohane and J. S. Nye (eds), *Transnational Politics and World Politics*. Cambridge, MA: Harvard University Press, pp. ix–xxiv.

Kılıç, M. (1996). Das Wahlrecht der Auslandstürken. *Zeitschift für Türkeistudien*, 2: 207–225.

Kirisci, K. (1991). *Contemporary Turkish Refugee Problems: A Research Outline*. Unpublished paper for the Meeting of the European Association of Development Institutes, Working Group on Refugees, 14–16 February, Webster University, Geneva, Switzerland.

Klusmeyer, D. B. (1992). Aliens, immigrants, and citizens: the politics of inclusion in the Federal Republic of Germany, *Dædalus*, 38: 81–115.

Kocak, B. and Kilinç, K. (1997). *En Üstekiler: Avrupa'nın Türk Patronları* (Those at the Top: Europe's Turkish Leaders). Istanbul: Ekonomi Vitrini Basın Yayın.

Koopmans, R. and Statham, P. (2000). Challenging the liberal nation-state? Postnationalism, multiculturalism and the collective claims-making of migrants and ethnic minorities in Britain and Germany, in: R. Koopmans and P. Statham (eds), *Challenging Immigration and Ethnic Relations Policies*. Oxford: Oxford University Press, pp. 189–232.

—— (2001). How national citizenship shapes transnationalism. A comparative analysis of migrant claims-making in Germany, Great Britain and The Netherlands. Working paper WPTC–01-01, Transnational Communities Programme, Oxford University. Online, available at: http://www.transcomm.ox.ac.uk.
Koser, K. (2002). From refugees to transnational communities? in: N. Al-Ali and K. Koser (eds), *New Approaches to Migration? Transnational Communities and the Transformation of Home*. London: Routledge, pp. 138–152.
Koser, K. (forthcoming). Long-distance nationalism and the responsible state: the case of Eritrea, in: E. Østergaard-Nielsen (ed.), *International Migration and Sending Countries: Perceptions, Policies and Transnational Relations*. London: Palgrave.
Kramer, H. (1996). Turkey and the European Union: a multi-dimensional relationship with hazy perspectives, in: V. Masteney and R. Craig Nation (eds), *Turkey Between East and West: New Challenges for a Rising Regional Power*. Boulder, Co: Westview Press, pp. 203–232.
Kramer, H. (1998). *The Institutional Framework of German–Turkish Relations*. Washington, DC: American Institute for Contemporary German Studies of Johns Hopkins University.
Kundu, A. (1994). The Ayodha aftermath: Hindu vs. Muslim violence in Britain, *Immigrants and Minorities*, 13, 1: 26–47.
Landau, J. M. (1981). *Pan-Turkism in Turkey: A Study in Irrendentism*. London: C. Hurst and Company.
Landolt, P., Autler, L. and Baires, S. (1999). From hermano lejano to hermano mayor: the dialectics of Salvadoran transnationalism, *Ethnic and Racial Studies*, 22, 2: 290–315.
Layton-Henry, Z. (1990). Immigrant associations, in: Z. Layton-Henry (ed.), *The Political Rights of Migrant Workers in Western Europe*. London: Sage Publications, pp. 94–112.
Levitt, P. (2001). Transnational migration: taking stock and future directions, *Global Networks*, 1, 3: 195–216.
Louie, A. (2000). Re-territorializing transnationalism: Chinese Americans and the Chinese motherland, *American Ethnologist*, 27, 3: 645–669.
McDowall, D. (1996). *A Modern History of the Kurds*. London: I.B. Tauris.
Mahler, S. J. (1998). Theoretical and empirical contributions toward a research agenda for transnationalism, in: M. P. Smith and L. E. Guarnizo (eds), *Transnationalism from Below*. New Brunswick, NJ: Transaction Publishers, pp. 64–100.
—— (2000). Constructing international relations: the role of transnational migrants and other non-state actors, *Identities*, 7, 2: 197–232.
Mandel, R. (1996). A place of their own: contesting spaces and defining places in Berlin's migrant community, in: B. D. Metcalf (ed.), *Making Muslim Space in North America and Europe*. Berkeley, CA: University of California Press, pp. 147–166.
Maney, G. M. (2000). Transnational mobilization and civil rights in Northern Ireland, *Social Problems*, 47, 2: 153–179.
Marienstras, R. (1989). On the notion of Diaspora, in: G. Chaliand (ed.), *Minority Peoples in the Age of Nation-States*. London: Pluto Press, pp. 119–125.
Marshall, B. (2000). *The New Germany and Migration in Europe*. Manchester: Manchester University Press.
Martin, P. (1991). *The Unfinished Story: Turkish Labour Migration to Western Europe with a Special Reference to the Republic of Germany*. Geneva: International Labour Office.
Meier-Braun, K. (1995). 40 Jahre 'Gastarbeiter' und Ausländerpolitik in Deutschland, *Aus Politik und Zeitgeschicte*, 35, 45: 14–22.

Mertens, I. (2000). Von einer 'Inneren Angelegenheit', die auszog, Europa das Fürchten zu lehren. Transstaatliche politische Mobilisierung und das 'Kurdenproblem', in: T. Faist (ed.), *Traansstaatliche Räume: Politisk, Wirtschaft und Kultur in und zwischen Dutschland und der Türkei*. Bielefeld: Transcript.

Michalski, A. and Wallace, H. (1992). *The European Community: The Challenge of Enlargement*. London: Royal Institute of International Affairs.

Miller, M. J. (1981). *Foreign Workers in Western Europe: An Emerging Political Force*. New York: Praeger Publishers.

Ministry of Education, Republic of Turkey (T.C. Millet Eğitim Bakanlığı) (2001). *Information on Teachers Abroad* (in Turkish). Online, available at: http://www.meb.org.tr (30 November 2001).

Ministry of Foreign Affairs, Republic of Turkey (2001). *Turks Living Abroad*. Online, available at http://www.mfa.org.tr (30 November 2001).

Ministry of State, Republic of Turkey (T.C. Devlet Bakanlığı) (1998a). *Yurtdışında Yaşayan vatandaşlar üst kurulu ve koordinasyon kurulu hakkında bilgi notu* (Information about High Commission and Consultation Commission for Citizens living abroad) 17 July, Ankara.

Ministry of State, Republic of Turkey (T.C. Devlet Bakanlığı) (1998b). *Yurtdışında Yaşayan vatandaşlar koordinasyon kurulu, personel ve prencipler* (Personnel and principles for Consulation Commission for citizens living abroad), Ankara.

Müftüler-Bac, M. (ed.) (1997). *Turkey's Relations with a Changing Europe*. Manchester: Manchester University Press.

Naff, T. (1984). The Ottoman Empire and the European States System, in: H. Bull and A. Watson (eds), *The Expansion of International Society*. Oxford: Clarendon Press, pp. 143–170.

Neumann, I. B. and Welsh, J. M. (1991). The other in European self-definition: an addendum to the literature on international society, *Review of International Studies*, 17, 4: 327–348.

Nirumand, B. (ed.) (1990). *Im Namen Allahs: Islamische Gruppen und der Fundamentalismus in der Bundesrepublik Deutschland*. Köln: Dreisam-Verlag.

NRW (Ministerium für Arbeit, Gesundheit und Soziales des Landes Nordrhein-Westfalen (1997). *Türkische Muslime in Nordrhein-Westfalen*. Duisburg: Waz-Druck.

Olson, R. (ed.) (1996). *The Kurdish Nationalist Movement in the 1990s: Its impact on Turkey and the Middle East*. Kentucky: The University Press of Kentucky.

Østergaard-Nielsen, E. K. (1998). Diaspora politics: the case of immigrants and refugees from Turkey residing in Germany since 1980. Thesis, Oxford University.

—— (2000). Trans-state loyalties and politics of Turks and Kurds in Western Europe, *SAIS Review*, 20, 1: 23–38.

—— (2001a). Diasporas in global politics, in: W. Wallace and D. Josselin (eds), *Non-State Actors in Global Politics*. London: Palgrave, pp. 218–234.

—— (2001b). Transnational political practices and the receiving state: Turks and Kurds in Germany and The Netherlands. *Global Networks: A Journal of Transnational Affairs*. Oxford: Blackwell.

—— (2002a). Working for a solution through Europe: Kurdish lobbying in Germany, in: N. Al-Ali and K. Koser (eds), *New Approaches to Migration? Transnational Communities and the Transformation of Home*. London: Routledge, pp. 186–201.

—— (2002b). *Politik over graenser, Magtudredningens skriftserie*. Aarhus Universitet: Magtudredningen.

Özcan, E. (1992). *Türkische Immigrantenorganisationen in der Bundesrepublik Deutschland: Die Entwicklung Politischer Organisationen und Politischer Orientierung unter Türkischen Arbeitsimmigranten in der Bundesrepublik Deutschland und Berlin West.* Berlin: Hitit Verlag.

Özdemir, C. (1997). *Ich bin Inländer: Ein anatolischer Schwabe im Bundestag.* München: Deutcher Taschenbuch Verlag.

Pannosean, R. (forthcoming). Old mentalities, new policies: the first Armenia-Diaspora conference as a turning point?, in: E. Østergaard-Nielsen (ed.), *International Migration and Sending Countries: Perceptions, Policies and Transnational Relations.* London: Palgrave.

Pettifer, J. (1997). *The Turkish Labyrinth: Atatürk and the New Islam.* London: Penguin Books.

Pope, N. and Pope, H. (1997). *Turkey Unveiled: Atatürk and After.* London: John Murray.

Popkin, E. (1999). Guatamalan Mayan migration to Los Angeles: constructing transnational linkages in the context of the settlement process, *Ethnic and Racial Studies*, 22, 2: 267–289.

Portes, A. (1999). Conclusion: towards a new world – the origins and effects of transnational activities, *Ethnic and Racial Studies*, 22, 2: 463–477

Portes, A. (2001). Introduction: the debates and significance of immigrant transnationalism, *Global Networks*, 1, 3: 181–193.

Portes, A., Guarnizo, L. E. and Landolt, P. (1999) The study of transnationalism: pitfalls and promise of an emergent research field, *Ethnic and Racial Studies*, 22, 2: 217–237.

Poulton, H. (1997). *Top Hat, Grey Wolf and Crescent: Turkish Nationalism and the Turkish Republic.* London: Hurst and Company.

Rex, J., Joly, D. and C. Wilpert (eds) (1987). *Immigrant Associations in Europe.* Aldershot: Gower.

Risse-Kappen, T. (1995). *Bringing Transnational Relations back in.* Cambridge: Cambridge University Press.

Rivera-Salgado, G. (2000). In search of the Mexican communities abroad: transnational immigrant politics across the US Mexican border. Unpublished paper, Workshop on Perceptions and Policies of Sending Countries. London: London School of Economics.

Roberts, B. R., Frank, R. and Lozano-Ascencio, F. (1999). Transnational migrant communities and Mexican migration to the US, *Ethnic and Racial Studies*, 22, 2: 238–265.

Robins, P. (1996). More apparent than real? The impact of the Kurdish issue on Euro–Turkish relations, in: R. Olson (ed.), *The Kurdish Nationalist Movement in the 1990s: Its Impact on Turkey and the Middle East.* Kentucky: The University Press of Kentucky, pp. 114–132.

Rogers, A. (1999). *Traces*, 5 January–March. Online, available at: http://www.transcomm.ox.ac.uk/traces.htm.

—— (1999). *Traces*, 8 October–December. Online, available at: http://www.transcomm.ox.ac.uk/traces.htm.

—— (2000). A European space for transnationalism. Working paper WPTC 2K-07, Transnational Communities Programme. Online, available at: http://www.transcomm.ox.ac.uk.

Rosenau, J. (1993). Foreword, in: D. C. Constas and A. G. Platias (eds), *Diasporas in World Politics: The Greeks in Comparative Perspective.* Athens: Macmillan Press in Association with the Institute of International Relations, pp. xv–xxi.

Ruggie, J. G. (1997). The past as prologue? Interests, identity and American foreign policy, *International Security*, 21, 4: 89–125.

Safran, W. (1991). Diasporas in modern societies: myth of homeland and return, *Diaspora: A Journal of Transnational Studies*, 1, 1: 83–99.

References

Said, E. W. (1978). *Orientalism*. New York: Vintage Books.

Schiffauer, W. (1999). Islamism in the Diaspora. The fascination of political Islam among second generation German Turks. Working paper, WPTC-99-06, Transnational Communities Programme, Oxford University.

Schöneberg, U. (1992). *Gestern Gastarbeiter, Morgen Minderheit: Zur Sozialen Integration von Einwanderern in einem 'Unerklärten' Einwanderungsland*. Frankfurt am Main: Verlag Peter Lang.

Seifert, W. (1996). Occupational and social integration of immigrant groups in Germany, *New Community*, 22, 3: 417–436.

Şen, F. (1996). Turkish communities in Western Europe, in: V. Mastney and R. C. Nation (eds), *Turkey between East and West: New Challenges for a Rising Regional Power*. Boulder, CO: Westview Press, pp. 233–266.

Şen, F. and Karakaşoğlu, Y. (1994). Ausländer und Politische Partizipation, Einstellungen zum Kommunalen Wahlrecht, zu Parteien und zu der doppelten Staatsangehörigkeit, in: *ZfT – Aktuell*, 30. Essen: ZfT.

Shain, Y. (1989). *The Frontier of Loyalty: Political Exiles in the Age of the Nation-State*. Connecticut: Weslayan University Press.

—— (ed.) (1991). *Governments-in-Exile in Contemporary World Politics*. New York: Routledge.

—— (1999). *Marketing the American Creed Abroad, Diasporas in the U.S. and their Homelands*. Cambridge: Cambridge University Press.

Shankland, D. (1993). Alevi and Sunni in rural Anatolia: diverse paths of change, in: P. Stirling (ed.), *Culture and Economy: Changes in Turkish Villages*. Cambridgeshire: The Eothen Press, pp. 46–64.

Sheffer, G. (ed.) (1986). *Modern Diasporas in International Politics*. Kent: Croom Helm.

SIPRI (Stockholm International Peace Research Institute). *Yearbook 1993, 1995, 1997, 1998, 2001*. Oxford: Oxford University Press.

Skrbis, Z. (1999). *Long-distance Nationalism, Diasporas, Homelands and Identities*. Aldershot: Ashgate.

Smith, G. (1999). Transnational politics and the politics of the Russian diaspora, *Ethnic and Racial Studies*, 22, 3: 500–523.

Smith, M. P. (1999). New approaches to migration and transnationalism: locating transnational practices. Paper for Conference on New Approaches to Migration: Transnational Communities and the Transformation of Home, University of Sussex, UK, September 21–22.

Smith M. P. and Guarnizo, L. E. (eds) (1998). *Transnationalism from Below*. New Brunswick, NJ: Transaction Publishers.

Smith, R. C. (1997). Reflections on migration, the state and the construction, durability and newness of transnational life, *Soziale Welt*, Sonderband 12: 197–217.

—— (1998). Politics of membership within the context of Mexico and U.S. migration, in: M. P. Smith and L. E. Guarnizo (eds) *Transnationalism from Below*. New Brunswick, NJ: Transaction Publishers, pp. 196–238.

—— (2001). Migrant membership as an instituted process: comparative insights from the Mexican and Italian cases. Working paper WPTC-01-23, Transnational Communities Programme. Online, available at: http://www.transcomm.ox.ac.uk/working_papers.htm.

Soysal, Y. (1994). *Limits of Citizenship: Migrants and Postnational Membership in Europe*. Chicago, IL: The University of Chigaco Press.

—— (2000). Citizenship and identity: living in diasporas in western Europe, *Ethnic and Racial Studies*, 23, 1: 1–15.

References

Spuler-Stegemann, U. (1998). *Muslime in Deutschland: Nebeneinander oder Miteinander.* Freiburg: Herder.
State Statistical Institute (T.C. Başbakanlık Devlet Istatistik Enstitüsü) (1996). *Milletvekili Genel Seçimi Sonuçları.* Ankara: Devlet Istatistik Enstitüsü.
—— (T.C. Başbakanlık Devlet Istatistik Enstitüsü) (1999). *Milletvekili Genel Seçimi Sonuçları.* Ankara: Devlet Istatistik Enstitüsü.
State Archive, Turkish Republic (T.C. Başbakanlık Devlet Arşiv Genel Müdürlügu) (1993). *Türkiye dışındaki türk vatandaşları bibliografyası.* Ankara.
Steinbach, U. (1996). *Die Türkei im 20. Jahrhundert: Schwieriger Partner Europas.* Köln: Gustav Lübbe Verlag.
Tarrow, S. (1998). *Power in Movement: Social Movements and Contentious Politics.* Cambridge: Cambridge University Press.
TBMM (The Turkish Grand National Assembly) (1986). *Sayılı siyasi partiler kanununun bazı maddelerinin değiştilmesine* (On changes in law on political parties), 17/26, 26 March, Ankara.
TBMM (The Turkish Grand National Assembly) (1989). *Yurtdışında çalışan işçilerimizin sorunlarına ilişkin* (Matters pertaining to our workers working abroad), 18/27, 23 May, Ankara.
—— (1990). *Federal Almanya'daki yabancıların* (On the new German laws on foreigners), 18/40, 8 February, Ankara.
—— (1992). *Almanya'nın Mölln kasabasında türklerin bulunduğu evlere yaptıkları saldırılara ilişkin* (Regarding the attacks on Turk's houses in the German town Mölln), 19/21, 24 November, Ankara.
—— (1993). *Almanya'da yaşayan Türk vatandaşlarına karşı yapılan insanlık dışı saldırılar ve ırkçı hareketler karşısında TBMM'nin görüş ve hissiyatına ilişkin, siyasi parti gruplari müşterek önergesi* (Proposal to form a joint group of political parties to look into the racist movements against Turks in Germany), 19/36, 15 June, Ankara.
—— (1995a). *Yurtdışında çalışan işçilerimizin, Meclis Araştırması Komisyonu Raporu* (Report on our workers working abroad), 19: 883, 28 July, Ankara.
—— (1995b). *Siyasi partiler kanunu ile milletvekili seçimi kanunun bazı madderlerinin değiltirilmesine* (On changes in law on political parties and election laws), 19/95, 26 October 1995, Ankara.
—— (1997a). *Yurtdışında açılan temsilcilikler, Meclis Araştırması Komisyonu Raporu* (Report on the diplomatic representations abroad), 20: 242, 27 February, Ankara.
—— (1997b). *Avrupa'daki vatandaşlarimiza yönelik irkçi saldirilarin nedenlerinin araştırılarak alinması gereken tedbirlerin belirlenmesi amacıyla* (On taking the necessary measures to investigate the reasons for racist attacks on our citizens in Europe), 20/25, 9 April, Ankara.
—— (1998). *Çifte vatandaşik uygulamasına Devlet Bakanından sorusu* (Question to the State Minster on the application of dual citizenship), 20/63, 23 January, Ankara.
TGT (Türkiye Göçmen Topluluğu) (1985). *Immigrantengemeinschaft der Türkel: Thesen zur Immigration*, Programm und Satzungsentwisnt.
The Turkish Constitution (Türkiye Cumuriyeti Anayasası ve Türkiye Büyük Millet Meclisi Içtüzügü) (1997). Ankara: TBMM Basimevi.
Tölöyan, K. (1991). The nation-state and others: in lieu of a preface, *Diaspora: A Journal of Transnational Relations*, 1, 1: 3–7.
Trautner, B. (2000). Türkische Muslime, islamische Organisationen und religiöse Institutionen als soziale Träger des transstaatlichen Raumes Deutschland–Türkei, in: T. Faist (ed.), *Traansstaatliche Räume: Politisk, Wirtschaft und Kultur in und zwischen Dutschland und der Türkei*. Bielefeld: Transcript.

UNHCR (1995). *The State of the World's Refugees 1995: In Search of Solutions*. Oxford: Oxford University Press.

van Hear, N. (2002). Sustaining societies under strain: remittances as a form of transnational exchange in Srilanka and Ghana, in: N. Al-Ali and K. Koser (eds), *New Approaches to Migration? Transnational Communities and the Transformation of Home*. London: Routledge, pp. 202–223.

Verfassungsschutz, Bundesamt für (1992) (Federal office for the protection of the constitution) *Aufgaben, Befugnisse, Grenzen*. Köln: Bundesamt für Verfassungsschutz.

—— (1981–2000). *Verfassungsschutzbericht*. Köln: Bundesamt für Verfassungsschutz.

Vertovec, S. (1996). Multiculturalism, culturalism and public incorporation, *Ethnic and Racial Studies*, 19, 1: 49–69.

Vertovec, S. and Cohen, R. (1999). Introduction, in: S. Vertovec and R. Cohen (eds), *Migration, Diasporas and Transnationalism*. Cheltenham: Edward Elgar Publishing.

Vorhoff, K. (1995). *Die Aleviten – eine Glaubensgeminschaft in Anatolien*. Unpublished paper. Istanbul: Orient-Institut Istanbul.

Vranken, J. (1990). Industrial rights, in: Z. Layton-Henry (ed.), *The Challenge of Political Rights*. London: Sage Publications, pp. 47–73.

Wahlbeck, Ö. (1999). *Kurdish Diasporas: A Comparative Study of Kurdish Refugee Communities*. London: Macmillan.

Wallraff, G. (1988). *Ganz Unten: mit einer Dokumentation der Folgen*. Köln: Kiepenheuer und Witsch.

Wapner, P. (1995). Politics beyond the state: environmental activism and world civic politics, *World Politics*, 47, 3: 311–340.

Weiner, M. (1986). Labor migration as incipient diasporas, in: G. Sheffer (ed.), *Modern Diasporas in International Politics*. Kent: Croom Helm, pp. 47–74.

YEK-KOM (1997). Informations mappe: Jahteshanpt versamm thug, 8–9 March. Dortmünd: YEK-KOM.

ZfT (Zentrum für Türkeistudien) (1997a). *Almanaya'daki Türkler 1960–1997* (Turks in Germany 1960–1997). Essen: Zft.

—— (1997b). *Kurzfassung der Studie zum Medienkonsum der Türkischen Bevölkerung in Deutchland und Deutchlandbild im Türkischen Fernsehen*. Essen: ZfT.

—— (1998a). *Das ethnische und religiöse Mosaik der Türkei und seine Reflexionen auf Deutschland*, Wissenschafliche Schriftenreihe. Münster: LIT Verlag.

—— (1998b). *Einstellung wahlberechtiger Personen türkischer Herkunft zum Wahlrecht, zur deutschen Staatsbürgerschaft und zur beabsichtigen Parteienwahl (Bundeswahl, 1998)*. ZfT Aktuell, Essen: Zft.

—— (2000a). *In Deutschland zu Hause und mit der Türkei verbunden Essen*, Pressemittelung. Online, available at: http://www.uni-essen.de/zft/ (14 November 2000).

—— (2000b). *Türkei-Jahrbuch des Zentrums für Türkeistudien 1999/2000*. Münster: LIT Verlag.

—— (2000c). *Zwei Drittel der Türken in Deutschland würden SPD wählen*, Pressemitteliung. Online, available at: http://www.uni-essen.de/zft/ (10 May 2000).

—— (2001). *Türkei-Jahrbuch des Zentrums für Türkeistudien 2000/2001*. Münster: LIT Verlag.

Zürcher, E. J. (1993). *Turkey: A Modern History*. London: I.B. Tauris.

Index

AABF 58–60, 126, 142; access to German policy-makers 104; cooperation with migrant organizations 68; information campaigns of 76–7; transnational networks of 81–3; *see also* Alevis
AADD 53, 64, 66, 81, 140, 152
Abadan-Unat, N. 20, 23, 33, 108
Adamson, F. 1, 148
Adler, S. 44
ADÜTDF *see Türk Federasyon*
advocacy networks *see* networks
Al-Ali, N. 19
Alawites 58
Alevi Kurds 60
Alevis 2, 3, 10, 11, 48, 49; cooperation with other migrant organizations 68–9; mobilization in Germany 59–60; number of Alevis 58; homeland political and immigrant political claims-making 64, 77–9, 124, 125, 126, 127; proposals for religious education 79; and German authorities 103–6, 130–2; and Sunni organizations 55, 66; support to Alevis in Turkey 120; transnational networks in Europe 80–2; Turkey's relationship with Alevis in Germany 118; *see also* AABF
ANAP 49, 54, 95, 110, 113–14, 145
Anderson, B. 15, 29, 61
Ankara 35, 54, 57, 120; perceptions and policies towards emigrants 109–18, 122, 125, 132; relations with Germany 37–42, 97, 119; 'tool of Ankara' 56, 65, 68, 97; *see also* Turkish government
Ankara Association Agreement 37, 40
Anti-racism Forum 68
anti-semitism 73
AP 54, 141
Arabs 17, 27, 30
Arbeiter Wohlfahrt 154
Arkacalı, B. 113
Armenian diaspora 2, 6, 73, 116, 157
Armruster, H. 20
arms embargo: in USA 54; calls for in Germany 43–4, 64, 88, 93

arms export from Germany 42–4, 98, 149
Armstrong, J. A. 148, 158
assimilation theory 16
asylum laws 39–40, 150, 151
asylum seekers 135; deportation of 36, 39–40, 42, 63, 64, 74; engagement in Turkish politics/Kurdish issue 7, 63, 126; German policies towards 86, 93, 99, 103, 133; number of Turkish and Kurdish asylum seekers in Germany 33, 39–40, 116, 135; reasons for departure 3; transnational mobilization of 19; Turkey's perceptions of 116–17, 99, 151; and Turkish migrant organizations 80, 96; *see also* refugees
asymmetrical interdependence 36
Atacanlı, S. 151
Atatürk, K. 53, 115, 118, 121
ATIAD 35, 144, 149, 152; lobbying of European Parliament 82–3, 153; lobbying of German–Turkish Parliamentarian group 86
ATIB 58, 142, 152
ATÖF 47
ATT 67–8, 77, 80, 106, 143
Ausländerbeirate 153
Ausländerextremismus 71, 73, 77, 105
Aussiedlers 150
Australia 7, 82, 107, 156
Autler, L. 19, 20
Ayata, S. 152
Azerbaycan 75

Bahçeli, D. 52
Baires, S. 19, 20
Balkans 121
Balkir, A. 41, 149, 151
Balladur 153
ban/closure: of arms delivery to Turkey 43; of deportation of asylum-seekers 40; different German positions on PKK ban 95–6; of extremist migrant organizations 17, 39, 61–2, 66, 70–3, 77, 89, 151
Barchard, D. 149
Barkey, H. J. 41, 58, 61, 62, 152

Index

Basch, L. 13
Baştürk, A. 89, 154
Bauböck, R. 17, 25, 130
BBP 146
Bell, J.B. 27
Berlin, 7, 8, 34, 52, 72, 74, 94, 95, 97, 100, 104, 149, 150, 151
Berlin wall 66
bilateral cooperation 30, 39, 44, 108; role of Turkish minority in 87, 99, 107, 131
Black, R. 19
Blanc-Szanton, C. 13
block voting 5, 133
Bonn 53, 75, 97, 119
Bonn Republic 150
Bosnian refugees 19, 126
BP 60, 146, 156
Braunthal, G. 150, 151
Brieden, T. 17
Brubaker, R. 150
Bruinessen, M. 60
Bundestag 8, 38, 42, 43, 54, 69; debates on extremist organizations 73–4, 77, 86, 101; debates on Kurdish issue 98–100; debates on passport harassment 119, 157; debates on Sunni Islam 102; members' relations with migrant organizations 78–9, 95; *see also* German federal government
Burkay, K. 62

Çaglar, A. 149
Canada 7, 121, 156
Caritas 154
Carlos, D.C. 15
Caucasus 121
CDU 144; Alevis 104, 116, 131, 151; dual citizenship 7–8; EU–Turkey relations 40–2, 115; human rights in Turkey 42; Islam 102–3; Kurdish asylum-seekers 40; the Kurdish issue 99; patronage of Hür-Türk 54; perceptions of extremist organizations 74–7; relations with migrant organizations 78; Turkish descent voters 86, 90, 95–8, 115–16, 131, 155
Cem evi 34, 58
C.E.M Vakfi 60, 142
Cem, I. 111
Central Asia 41, 64, 121
ceremonial calendar 76
chain migration 45
China 86
Chinese 25, 35, 87
CHP 145; Alevi issue 59, 92, 104; dual citizenship in Turkey 156; German election campaigns 115; migrant organizations in Germany 52–3, 92, 113, 140

Çiller, T. 153
Çinar, T. 149
citizenship: dual 3, 7–8, 91–3, 115–16, 132, 134, 149, 150, 156; German 3, 15, 34, 36, 38, 68, 150; naturalized Kurds 79, 136; naturalized Turks 3, 136; post-national 25, 130; and transnational political engagement 20–1, 23; turkish 38, 108, 127, 155
Civata li Kurd 143, 153
civil society 28, 31
Clifford, G. 14, 20
Cohen, R. 4, 14, 21, 123, 148, 158
cold war bi-polarity 26
Collinson, S. 44
Cologne, 34, 53, 57, 66, 71, 75, 77, 88, 94, 104, 117, 118, 154
communists 49, 50, 71
confrontational strategies, 12, 23–5, 70–1, 74–5, 77, 83, 128, 148
Conservative Liberals 53
Constas and Platias 4, 6, 19, 21, 157
consultative institutions *see Ausländerbeirate*
Consultation Commission for Turks abroad 110–11
cosmopolitan 16, 125
cross border voting 17, 47 111–13, 156
CSU: dual citizenship 7–8; EU-Turkish relations 41–2, 102; human rights in Turkey 42; Kurdish asylum seekers 40; perceptions of extremist organizations 77; Turkish descent voters 98
Cypriots 6, 151

Demetriou, M. 6, 29
Demirel, S. 54, 153
democracy 1, 27; German criticism of democracy in Turkey 41–2, 45, 88, 99, 102; as international norm 26, 30; migrant and refugees' contribution to 26–9, 131–2; migrant organizations advocacy of 50–1, 63–4, 83, 88, 99, 100–3, 131
demonstrations: as confrontational strategy 24–5, 128, 148; in Germany 49, 74–5, 77; transnational organization of 81–2; in Turkey 59, 71, 148; and violence 72–4
DEP 153
de-territorialized 31, 121, 132, 134
Deutsch, K. 44
Deutscher Bundestag see Bundestag
Devrimci Sol 39 50, 71, 72, 89
DGB 88–90, 144, 154, 157
DHKP-C 72
Diakon charity 154
diaspora: definition of 13–15
diaspora politics: definition of 21

Index   173

DIDF 50–1, 65, 66, 69, 140, 151
Die Grüne 144; Alevi organizations 104; arms deliveries to Turkey 43–4; dual citizenship 7–8; EU-Turkey relations 41–2, 99; extremist organizations 77; human rights in Turkey 42; Kurdish organizations 100; migrants' transnational engagement 69, 91; Turkish descent voters 93–4, 155
diplomacy 54, 114
Directorate of Religious Affairs, 56, 60, 108, 119, 141, 147, 156
discrimination: of Alevis 55–9, 104; German political measures against 93, 156; of migrants in Germany 3, 38, 149; mobilization against 6, 19, 21, 50–1; Turkey's critique of 38, 44–5, 109
DISK 89, 154
DITIB 56–8, 60, 65, 68, 117, 141
Diyanet *see* Directorate of Religious Affairs
DKHP-C 50
Doomenik, J. 5, 23
DPD 68
DSP 53, 110, 114, 117, 145, 156
DTF 95–8, 144
DTU 95–7, 126, 143, 155
dual citizenship *see* citizenship
DYP 49, 54–5, 95, 101, 110, 114, 145

Ecevit, B. 111
education: in own language 69, 125; religious 3, 8, 55, 60, 67, 125; Turkey's provisions for 108–10, 125, 155; of Turkish migrants 33–4, 55
EEC 40, 150; *see also* EU
elections: in German trade unions 88; in Germany 90–1, 102, 116, 132; in Turkey 47, 51, 56, 102, 111–13, 156; in the USA 5, 27
Ellis, P. 25, 126
EMEP 51
emigrant politics: definition of 21
Eralp, A. 151
Erbakan, M.S. 56
Erbakan, N. 56, 102
Eritrean refugees 19
ERNK 61–3, 65, 81
Esman, M.J. 6, 17, 19
ethnic minority 2, 3, 13, 87
ethnicity 60, 72
ethno-nationalism 16
EU: citizenship 64; lobbying of 82; migrant organizations' stance on 55, 64, 92, 96, 99–107, 125; relations with Turkey 3, 5, 36–7, 40–2, 44; Turkey's foreign policy on 113–15, 117, 123; *see also* Europe
Europe: cooperation with Turkey 40–5, 64, 86, 93, 96, 106, 149, 151; Islam in 41, 102, 104; kurdish homeland political mobilization in 7, 8, 72, 152; migrant transnationalism in 2, 3, 6, 20, 26, 28; migrants' political participation in 5–6, 20, 23, 70, 141, 151; transnational networks within 81–3, 130; Turkish media in 34; Turkish migration to 33, 47; *see also* EU
European Commission 40
European Council 25, 153
European migrant federations 48–9, 81
European Parliament 82, 83, 86, 153, 157
Euro-Turks 114, 122
Evren, K. 37

Faist, T. 2, 20, 26–7, 31, 34, 131, 152
family re-unification 33
fax-campaigns 115
FDP 42, 99, 131, 154
Federal Commissioner for Foreigners 3, 145, 150, 153
Federal Department of Statistics 35
Federal Ministry for Foreign Affairs 100
Federal Ministry for Labour and Social Security 46
Federal Ministry of Labour and Social Security 35
Federal Ministry of the Interior 73
Feindt-Riggers, N. 59, 152
Fennema, M. 27
Finns 151, 157
firebombing 7
Ford factory in Cologne 88
foreign policy 21, 22, 26, 30–1, 131; domestication of 27, 97, 133–4; Germany's 85–7, 98–9, 103–6, 129, 150; migrants' lobbying of 17, 26, 27, 87; Turkey's 2, 53, 97, 114
FP 8, 56, 59, 64, 84, 112, 141; *see also Refah Partisi*
France 6, 33, 44, 51, 56, 151, 156, 157
Frank, R. 5
free movement of migrants in the EU 36–7
Freeman, G. 2, 109
Friedrich Ebert Stiftung 80, 86, 92
Friedrich Wilhelm II 42
Frykman, M.P. 126
Fuller, G.E. 41, 58, 61, 62, 152

Garbaye, R. 5
Gastrecht 74, 105
GDF 50–1, 66, 67–8, 80, 140
Geddes, A. 149
gender 50
Genscher, H. 43
German federal government: attentiveness to homeland political lobbying 98–106, 119, 133; concern with extremist organizations 73–4, 98–103, 118, 131; dual citizenship 8, 38, 156; EU-Turkish relations 41–4, 92; immigration control 19, 37, 40; integration policies 38; *see also Bundestag*

174 Index

German–Turkish Parliamentarian Group 86
German–Turkish relations 6, 44–5, 55, 65, 80, 85, 149; and asylum-seekers 39–40; historical 36; and human rights issues 42; and migration 36–9; and military cooperation 42–4; and Turkey's EU candidacy 40–2
Gitmez, A. 10, 151
Glick Schiller, N. 13, 20, 27, 31
global: institutional structures 25; norms 26, 32; politics 29, 31–2; social movements 31
Goldring, L. 20, 27
Grand National Assembly 53, 101, 113, 147
grass-root transnationalism 5, 28
Greece 40, 41, 46, 72, 153, 157
Greeks: diaspora 2, 6, 13, 114; immigrants in Germany 35, 153, 154, 155; in the US 116
Greek embassy 7, 72
Greve, M. 149
Grey wolves 51, 52, 89
Guarnizo, L. 2, 4, 15, 16, 20, 22, 64, 123
guest worker 13, 34, 36, 37, 63
Gulf War 151, 153
Gür, M. 152
Gürbey, G. 62, 152

hac 57, 58, 151
Haci Bektaş Veli 120, 146
HADEP 62, 146
Haitians 27, 30
Hakk-TV 153
Halfmann, J. 150
Hammar, T. 5, 23
Hapel, D. 97
HDF 52–3, 65, 66–8, 77, 92–3, 111, 140, 143
head scarves 58–9, 101, 104
Heckmann, F. 150, 154
Heine, P. 152, 155
Heitmeyer, W. 20, 126, 152, 155
Helsinki summit 41, 92, 106
Hermes, A. 155
High Election Council 156
Hintze, P. 97
Holland *see* Netherlands, The
homeland: definition of 14
homeland politics: definition of 21
hometown associations 5, 15, 16
Hoyerswerda 150
human rights: and homeland political lobbying 25–6, 32, 51, 63, 80–1, 83–4, 115, 125, 130–1; and international relations 26–7, 30, 98–105, 149; and migrants' rights 25, 38; in Turkey 2, 36, 41–2, 44–5, 61; organizations 17, 62, 77, 115, 120–1, 126, 153
humanitarian intervention 26
hunger-strikes 71, 74
Huntington, S.P. 1, 27, 41
Hür-Türk 53–5, 64, 95, 96, 141

ICCB 57, 141; cooperation with German authorities 101; events of 76–7; extremism of 71–3; HAKK-TV 153; Turkish governments' perception of 117–18
identity: diasporic 13, 15; German national 7–8, 150; Kurdish 7, 48, 61–3; political 16, 69, 117, 126; reactive 20, 126; religious 41, 55; Turkey's national 2, 41, 48, 51, 61, 109–10, 121
IGMetall 46, 88–90, 119, 145, 154, 157
IGMG *see* Milli Görüş
IHD 62, 146
ILO (International Labour Organization) 37
Imam 8, 57, 108, 151
IMF 5, 35
immigrant politics: definition of 21
immigration control *see* German federal government
Imperial Naturalization Law 150
India 17, 25, 36, 86
Indians 27, 35
institutional channeling 11, 22–6, 32, 70–1, 83, 127–9, 130; *see also* multi-level institutional channeling
institutional participation 12, 70, 71, 83, 85–98, 105, 128–9; definition of 23
international institutions 25, 26, 130, 157
international organizations 25–6, 30, 37, 44, 71
Internet 1, 16, 25, 82
interviews 10, 137–9
investment schemes 21, 108
IP 146
Iran 40, 58, 60, 121, 157
Iraq 40, 43, 60
Irbec, Y. 33
Ireland, P. 5, 23, 30, 70, 128, 148, 149
Islam: Alevi 3; European fear of 41, 96; in German education system 8, 67, 79; and German government 101–6, 132; and organizations in Germany 51, 53, 55–60, 65, 79, 151, 152, 154, 155; and transnational identification 20; *see also* Alevis and Sunni Muslims
Islamic Federation 8
Islamrat 58
Ismet, E. 37, 156
Israeli consulate in Berlin 72
Italian migrants 35, 151, 157
Italy 17, 46, 148, 158
Itzigsohn, J. 15, 17, 21, 23

Jama'at Un-Nur 58, 141; *see also* Nurcular
Jelpke, U. 95
Jewish diaspora 1, 2, 6, 13, 17, 27, 30, 87, 114, 116
Joly, D. 151
Josselin, D. 31
jus sanguinis 38

Index 175

Kadioğlu, A. 149
Khan, Z. 25, 126
Kahramanmaraş 59
Kaiser, K. 31, 149
Kaplan, C. 57, 117, 142
Karahasan, Y. 88, 89
Karakaş, E. 52, 113
Karakaşoğlu, Y. 95, 152
Kashmiris 126
Kaya, A. 20, 104, 152
Keck, M.E. 25, 120, 149
Keesing 43
Kehl-Bodrogi, K. 152
Kemalism: and Alevi organizations 59, 66, 89, 125; and Kurdish organizations 61; and Sunni Muslim organizations 57, 66, 89; in Turkey 49, 52; organizations in Germany 52–3, 79; transnational organization of 81
Kenya 7, 72
Keohane, R.O. 31
Kılıç, M. 112, 156
Kilinç, K. 149
Kinkel, K. 43, 74, 102
Kirisci, K. 39
KKDK 153
Klusmeyer, D.B. 150
Koçak, B. 149
Kohl, H. 37, 97, 115
KOMKAR: activities of 76–9, 83; and German political institutions 86; organization in Germany 62–3, 143; relationship with other migrant organizations 66–9
Koopmans, R. 4, 6, 148, 158
koran lessons 8, 79
koran schools 57, 58, 101
Koser, K. 19, 126
Kossendey, T. 86, 97
Kramer, H. 36, 44, 149, 150, 151
Kundu, A. 17
Kurds: as asylum seekers 33, 39–40; identity of 10, 48, 62, 63; *see also* Kurdish organizations
Kurdish Exile Parliament 143, 152
Kurdish minority rights 61, 69, 79, 100–3
Kurdish organizations 7, 11, 48, 60–3, 124, 127, 142–3; cooperation with Turkish organizations 66–9; and democratization in Turkey 120; and German political parties 79, 95, 132; information campaigns in Germany 7, 70–80, 83, 100, 105; and trade-unions 90; transnational networks of 81; and Turkish government 116–19; *see also* KOMKAR and PKK
Kurdistan 51, 60–1, 75, 95, 153, 154

L.T.D. 154
labour diaspora 14
labour exchange agreements 33
laicism 48, 53, 55–6, 101–3, 106

Lamers, K. 97, 103
Landau, J.M. 151, 157
Landolt, P. 4, 15, 19, 123
Landstag 86, 95
Layton-Henry, Z. 5, 6, 23
Leopard-II tanks 44, 151
Levitt, P. 15, 16, 17, 21, 23
Libya 107
lobby: diasporas as 6, 25, 29, 157; Turkey's attempts to promote 107, 113–16, 121, 132; within German political parties 90–8; within trade unions 87–90
Louie, A. 17
Lozano-Ascencio, F. 5
Luxembourg summit 41, 115

McDowall, D. 60, 152
Mahler, S.J. 17, 22, 31, 44
Mahmut II 42
Mandel, R. 55, 149, 152
Maney, G.M. 29
Maoism 49–50, 71, 74, 80, 118
marginalization: of migrants 20; of migrant organizations 17, 28, 129; of Kurds in Turkey 121, 132
Marienstras, R. 13, 148, 158
Marshall, B. 40
Martins, P. 33
Marxism 59, 60, 72, 80
mass-meetings 25, 49, 71, 74–7, 83, 104, 112, 128, 148, 151
Medina, E.H. 15
MEDYA TV 7, 82, 142
Meier-Braun, K. 33, 36
Mertens, I. 2, 61
methodology 10, 137–9
Mexican migrants 2, 4, 5, 20, 133
Mexico 4, 5, 33
MHP 146, 156; and Türk Federasyon 51–2, 75–7, 84, 112, 140; supporters in German trade unions 88–90
Michalski, A. 151
Middle East 29, 41, 64, 107, 108
migrant organizations: cooperation among 28, 58, 67–9, 124, 132; representativity of 11, 28, 48–9, 52, 61, 68
migrant transnationalism *see* transnationalism
migrant's political participation: typology of 24
migration: from Turkey to Germany 33, 136
military co-operation *see* German–Turkish relations
military service 109, 119, 156
Miller, M.J. 6, 19, 23, 30, 148, 158
Milli Görüş: and CDU 97; cooperation with other migrant organizations 68–9; koran lessons of 8; organization of 56–8, 64–5, 142; German perceptions of 71, 73, 89; information campaigns of 80–1, 84; and

Index

Milli Görüş: (*Continued*)
  Turkish elections 112, 156; Turkish government's perception of 117
MIT 119
MLKP 50
Mölln 38, 51, 67, 150, 156
molotov cocktails 72, 129
mosques 34, 56–7, 80, 102, 104, 117–18
mother tongue teaching 3, 62, 66, 69, 79, 125, 129–30, 153; *see also* Kurdish minority rights
MSP 89, 142
Müftüler-Bac, M. 41, 156, 151
Müller, J. 20, 126, 152, 155
multicultural 20, 26, 27, 39, 96, 117, 131
multi-lateral relations 30, 44, 107, 108
multi-layered strategies 70, 83, 128
multi-level institutional channeling 11, 22, 26, 32, 71, 127–30
multinational corporations 31
Muslims *see* Alevis and Sunni Muslims

Naff, T. 151
NAFTA 5
national interest 30, 85, 98, 104, 131
national self-determination 26–7
national sovereignty 21
nationalism 20, 125, 155; long distance 15, 29, 61; Kurdish 61–3, 152; Turkish 51–3, 75, 112, 125, 127, 129, 152
NATO 40, 43, 92, 151; Cascade Programme 151
naturalization 7–8, 34, 134, 136, 149, 150
Netherlands, The 21, 51, 81, 117, 148, 151, 156, 158
networks: advocacy 5, 25, 149; between German and Turkish political parties 86; economic 33–4, 45; migrants' transnational political 1–2, 7–9, 22–32, 46, 71, 81–4, 124, 129–30, 134; social 16; Sunni 56
Neumann, I.B. 41
New Left 50, 63, 71–2, 77, 81–2, 118
New Zealand 107
NGOs 17, 23, 25, 31, 77–8, 82, 132, 149, 153
Nirumand, B. 152
Nonneman, C. 152
non-state actors 26, 31
NRW 49, 58, 62, 152
Nurcular 55, 56, 89, 141
Nye, J.S. 31

Öcalan, A. 7, 72, 74, 82, 95, 99
ÖDP 50, 146
Öker Tours 114
Olson, R. 61
Onur, L. 79, 86
OSCE 25
Østergaard-Nielsen, E. 4, 16, 27, 29, 30, 50, 80, 82, 151, 154
Ottoman Empire 36, 41, 42, 43, 151, 157

Ögelman, N. 2, 109
Özal, T. 43
Özcan, E. 47, 50, 151, 152
Özdemir, C. 38, 68–9, 91–4, 115, 150

Pakistani immigrants 27
Palestine 25
panel discussions 50, 77, 80, 132
Panossean, R. 29
pan-Turkism 51, 121, 122, 151, 157
Papandreou, G. 153
passport harassment 17, 38, 119, 157
PDS 42–3, 77, 94–5, 96, 100, 144
Pettifer, J. 149
pink card 155
Pir Sultan Abdal 59
PKK 2, 7, 39, 143; campaigns in Germany 71–2, 75–7, 82; organization in Germany 60–3, 65, 152, 153; relations with German political institutions 93–7, 99; Turkey's policies towards 117–18
PLO 25
Polish immigrants 150
political graffiti 74
political opportunity structure 11, 18, 20, 23–5, 32, 70–1, 84, 128, 130, 148
political rights 17, 20, 23, 62, 114
Pope, H. 37, 49, 59, 61, 149
Pope, N. 37, 49, 59, 61, 149
Popkin, E. 19
Portes, A. 4, 15, 16, 19, 20, 27, 28, 123
Portuguese migrants 151, 154
post-nationalist 130
Poulton, H. 58, 59, 121, 152
press-releases 24, 76, 82, 90, 110–11, 154
PSK 62, 143

racism 68, 111; racist attacks 98, 109
ramadan 58, 59, 104
Refah Partisi 2, 55, 59, 64, 101, 112, 142, 145; *see also* FP
refugees: and democratization in Turkey 131; differences from economic migrants 3–4, 10, 14; from Nazi Germany to Turkey 36; information campaigns of 24–6, 71–80, 84; Kurdish issue 7, 10; organization in Germany 46–8, 61–3; transnational engagement of 1–2, 6, 16–21, 27–9, 122, 123–5; *see also* asylum seekers
Regenspurger, O. 77
Reichs- and Staatbürgergesetz 150
religion *see* Islam
remittances: from Mexican migrants 5; from Turkish migrants 5, 34–5, 45; sending countries' policies on 17, 108, 113
Rex, J. 151
Risse-Kappen, T. 25, 30–1

Rivera-Salgado, G. 4, 5
Roberts, B.R. 5
Robins, P. 41, 65
Rogers, A. 4, 7, 82
Rosenau, J. 31
Rostock, 150
RTS 67–8, 77, 143
Ruggie, J.G. 27
Russia 7, 82

Safran, W. 14
Said, E. 151
şariat 56, 57, 101
satellite-tv 16
Saudi Arabia 107
Sayan, G. 100
Schäfer, H. 98
Scharping, R. 92–3
Schiffauer 16, 20, 126
Schily, O. 74
Schöneberg, U. 155
Schröder, G. 106
Schröder, H. 20, 126, 152, 155
Second World War 36, 43, 60, 108
secularism 8, 57, 67, 101–3, 108, 125
Seifert, W. 34
seminars 53, 77, 80, 83, 92, 132
Şen, F. 95, 149
sending countries 17–18, 22–3, 28–9, 31, 37, 44–5, 113; *see also* Turkey's government
Serdaroğlu, R. 111
Sezgin, S. 68
Shain, Y. 4, 6, 17, 26, 27, 30, 76, 148, 157, 158
Shankland, D. 152
Sheffer, G. 1, 4, 6, 19, 27
Shia Muslims 58
SIPRI 43, 151
Sikkink, K. 25, 120, 149
Sivas 59
Skrbis, Z. 20
Smith, M.P. 2, 4, 16, 31, 64
Smith, G. 26
Smith, R. 4, 5, 17, 23
social capital 17, 113, 132
social exclusion 3, 20
Solingen 38, 51, 67, 150, 156
South Asian migrants 17, 151
Soviet Union 17, 40, 43, 60, 121, 157; foreign policy of 26
Soysal, Y. 5, 15, 23, 25, 70, 80, 130
Spanish migrants 151
spatial diffusion of domestic politics 10, 106, 131, 133, 148, 158
SPD 144; asylum policies 40, 151; citizenship reforms 7–8, 38, 91; Commission for Foreign and Security Politics 93; consultations with migrant organizations 67, 78–9, 104, 119;

Index 177

EU–Turkish relations 41–2, 44, 99, 106, 157; perceptions of extremist organizations 74, 77; Turkish descent voters 86, 90–3, 106, 115, 154
Spuler-Stegemann, U. 152
Statham, P. 4, 6, 148, 158
Steinbach, U. 36–7, 42–4, 59, 61, 149, 150, 152, 153
Stercken, H. 54
Stoltenberg, G. 151
Sufi-tariquats 55, 152
Süleymancilar 55, 56, 58, 89, 141
Sunni Muslims 141–2, 152; and DSP 117; and education in Germany 8, 10, 79; and the CDU 97; cooperation with other migrant organizations 55, 66–9; European networks of 81; extremist organizations of 71, 73, 118; lobbying of 101–6, 125; mass-meetings of 76; organization in Germany 48, 55–8; relations with Alevis 3, 10, 53, 55, 59, 66
Sweden 151, 156
Switzerland 151, 156
Syria 40, 60

Tarrow, S. 148
terrorism 24, 129; Armenian 53; Turkey's policies on 99, 117, 129
TGT 67
third generation migrants 109
THKP/-C 72
Tibetans 25
TIDAF 144, 152
Tillie, J. 27
TIP 50
TKP 50, 88
TKP-ML 50
Tölöyan, K. 14
trade diaspora 14
trade unions: cooperation between German and Turkish trade unions 157; as gatekeepers 23, 87–90; the Kurdish issue 60, 90; in Turkey 47
trans-local politics 28; definition of 22
transnational communities 1, 2; types of 3; definitions of 13–15; applicability of concept 123
transnational networks *see* networks
transnational political practices: and democratization 26–9, 131–2; determinants of 16–21, 127; effectiveness of 29–32; German perceptions of 8, 85, 87; multi-level channeling of 22–6, 127–9; scope of 15–16, 123; types of 21–2, 128–30
transnational spaces: economic 35; political 20; social 20, 33–5
transnationalism: concept of 13–16, 123–4; determinants of 16–21, 125–7; as discipline in International Relations 25; impact of 26–32, 131–4; narrow and broad 30, 123–4

Trautner, B. 152
TRT 34, 109, 115
Truman Doctrine 43
TÜDAY 153
Turanism 121, 157
Turco-Islamic synthesis 59
Türk Federasyon 141; cooperation with other migrant organizations 66, 68; mass meetings of 76, 112; organization in Germany 51–2, 65, 151; protest against military coup in Turkey 75; relations with German political institutions 84, 152; suggested closure of 73, 77; transnational networks of 81
Türk Iş 120, 146, 154
Türkeş, A. 75, 76, 77, 152
Turkic people 121, 151, 157
Turkish army 43, 115
Turkish constitution 102, 108, 111
Turkish consulates 7, 38, 64, 109–10, 112, 118–19
Turkish elections 56, 60, 102, 111–13, 133, 156
Turkish government 3; contact with emigrant organizations 47, 110, 116, 127, 153; dual citizenship 7, 38; German–Turkish relations 37–45, 54; Kurdish transnational political practices 82, 101; long distance policing 118–19, 157; policies towards citizens abroad 68, 109–11, 127, 156; *see also* Ankara
Turkish media 8; availability in Germany 34, 45; role of 65, 92, 115–16, 126, 133
Turkish military coup 2, 33, 39–40, 42, 47, 49, 59, 75, 88, 116, 120, 153
Turkish Ministry of Education 108
Turkish Ministry of Foreign Affairs 108, 109, 114, 146
Turkish Ministry of Labour and Social Security 147
Turkish Ministry of State 110, 147
Turkish State Archive 157
Turkish State Statistical Institute 111
TÜSIAD 153

UN 25
unemployment 34, 109, 113
UNHCR 150

United Kingdom 17, 156
university students 20
United States: arms sale to Turkey 43; diasporas in 2, 6, 17, 26, 28, 114, 157; elections in 5, 27; Kurdish protests in 82; Mexicans in 4–5, 6, 20, 133; migrant transnationalism in 4, 9, 17, 20, 23, 133–4; Turks in 121, 156
USSR *see* Soviet Union
Uzun, E. 96

Vasquez, O. 15
Verfassungsschutz 39, 57, 71–3, 82, 150, 151
Vertovec, S. 4, 20
victim diaspora 14
VIKZ 55–6, 58, 141
Vorhoff, K. 59, 152
voting rights 21; for German Turks in Germany 64, 68, 84, 109; for German Turks in Turkey 21, 11–12, 127; for US-Mexicans in Mexico 5
Vranken, J. 154

Wahlbeck, Ö. 2
Wallace, H. 151
Wallace, W. 31
Wallraff, G. 149
Wapner, P. 31
weapon deliveries *see* arms export
Weiner, M. 6, 19
Welsh, J.M. 41
Williams, A.M. 41, 149, 151
Wilpert, C. 151
workers associations 46, 47, 62

xenophobia 38, 150

YEK-KOM 62–3, 79, 142
Yeşiller 93
Yilmaz, M. 37, 41, 115, 116
Yugoslavia 17, 35, 46, 121
Yumakoğulları, O. 112

Zentralrat der Muslime 58, 142
ZfT 3, 33, 34, 35, 58, 91, 113, 149, 156
Zürcher, E. 149